BRIGHT
UNDERGROUND
SPACES

BUFFET
ON
GROUND
FLOOR

MANSION HOUSE

UNDERGROUND

MANSION HOUSE

MANSION HOUSE

CANNON
STREET

David Lawrence

BRIGHT UNDERGROUND SPACES
the London tube station architecture of Charles Holden

Capital Transport

This book is for Leila

Illustration credits
All images are from the London Transport Museum Photographic
Collection (visit http://www.ltmcollection.org/photos/index.html)
unless otherwise stated below.
Jo Bossanyi: 160. Collection of David Lawrence: 11, 22, 23, 28, 34, 42,
46, 47, 49, 51, 52, 53, 57/8/9, 62, 65, 67/8/9, 91, 109, 117, 119,
124, 144, 151, 157/8/9, 162/3/4, 166/7/8, 170, 172/3/4/5, 177, 190.
Peter Heaps: 12. Hulton Getty 112. Royal Institute of British Architects British
Architectural Library: 62, 78, 174. Capital Transport: 45, 70, 175, 178.
Every effort has been made to give the appropriate picture credit
where one could be found. The author and publish welcome the
opportunity to correct any errors or omissions in future editions of
this book.

First published 2008. ISBN 978-1-85414-320-4 Published by Capital Transport Publishing, P.O. Box 250, Harrow Weald, Middlesex

Designed by David Lawrence. Cover design by Capital Transport. Printed by CT Printing, China. © David Lawrence, 2008

www.capitaltransport.com

Contents

Build plainly and good. Blank sheets if you like. A new style of architectural decoration will arise, compelled by need of satisfying the dissatisfied eye.[1]

With the opening of the terminal station at Cockfosters we are in full possession of the last-completed extension of London's railway system, and it is impossible for an architectural journal to resist the opportunity of congratulating the community that time, place and persons so far coincide as to put control now into the hands of Mr Pick, and furnish him with so able an executive agent as Mr C. H. Holden, to whose clear thinking, fertile imagination, and sound structural sense is owing work which it is no exaggeration to say has revolutionized our ideas of suburban stations.[2]

Turnpike Lane station transformed by the retouching artist, from a construction site to completed building. This sleight of hand was used for several publicity photographs promoting the Underground's new stations on the Piccadilly line extension to Southgate and Cockfosters of 1932–33, referred to in the quotations above.

Foreword BY EDWARD CULLINAN

David Lawrence's thoroughly researched and nicely written book is a timely addition to the spate of recent interest in Charles Holden. He takes Holden's collaboration with the great Frank Pick on the design of Underground stations as his particular study; and this must surely be the great period of Holden's journey from the Arts and Crafts to his own version of Modernism in architecture. Of course, this journey had already been made by Frank Lloyd Wright, Le Corbusier, Alvar Aalto, Willem Dudok and many others; but in England it came late, possibly due to a 'last days of Empire' attachment to the Edwardian Baroque and to 'Englishman's Castleism' as typified by rows of bypass semi-detached houses of the sub-Norman Shaw type. Modernism came in the thirties with Connell Ward and Lucas, Max Fry and Jane Drew, Owen Williams, F R S Yorke and others: but most importantly with the employment of architects by forward-thinking clients, such as Berthold Lubetkin for the London and Whipsnade Zoos, and for Remploy, and Charles Holden by the Underground, particularly by Frank Pick.

Charles Holden and Frank Pick met at the inaugural meeting of the Design and Industries Association in 1915 and that's where it all began. Today's architectural clients who are obliged to advertise their jobs Europe-wide, and today's architects, who must compete for jobs and are judged by committees and seldom meet real life clients, will both envy Pick and Holden deciding to work together after discovering their shared philosophy of design.

This book describes the general history of their working together on the Underground Railway, their employment of Edward Johnston for the graphics and their employment of many other designers and artists, including Jacob Epstein, Henry Moore and Eric Gill for sculpture. The general history is vivid and thorough and is followed by a detailed rundown on each and every station that they did together, and how they did them. Here it is very important that David Lawrence is good at the formal analysis of architecture; a skill which is quite rare among English critics, who sometimes tend to be rather better at gossip.

So, in the second 'Station by Station' section of the book we see Holden proceeding from the rather stodgy glazed block facades with neo-classical raised middle features at the Angel, the Oval and Clapham Common (1922–24), all of them openings in street facades; via the freestanding octagonal Portland stone foyer at Ealing Common (1929–31) to a rectangular brick foyer at Sudbury Town and a round one at the now famous Arnos Grove (1929–32) with fine centre poled modern interior: all of them leading forward towards Southgate (1930–33), which I think is the finest by far and a significant piece of modern architecture in its own right.

Rising up the finely lit and detailed escalators from platform level at Southgate you first perceive, and then flatten out into, the circular clerestory lit ticket hall. This foyer is an equally elegant introduction to the centre of Southgate itself, and a fine object in that centre as well. The shopping streets that make the centre of town sweep round this gem occupy three quarters of its circumference. The remaining quarter is reserved for a road having the same centre point as the foyer which is for more shops and for bus stops; and above the shops a single storeyed blank wall is terminated at both ends by fine bays of first floor office windows which spring forward from the façade as they escape from the shadow of the foyer building. A florist's shop was planned where the adjoining grass circle with huge stylish central lamp standard now stands, and I think that right now we should have a competition for its design and construction. Southgate is a truly lovely traffic interchange which works to this day; and it is very touching to go there and see the messages on the builders' hoarding which now hides part of it, messages which treat it with the same historic reverence as though it were some ancient monument.

Charles Holden refused a knighthood because he said he did not wish to distance himself from all the others who made architecture possible in the office and on the building site. He, himself, put different young people in his office in charge (with him) of each of the stations on the Piccadilly line, and for Southgate I've read the name Israel Schultz who worked in his office, Adams, Holden and Pearson. Any readers of this excellent book who can give me a short biography of Israel Schultz would be doing a great service to architecture; for clearly Holden moved from his early excellent Arts and Crafts self to the truly modern with his help. It is of course how we all progress.

Introduction

Much has been written about London's Underground stations, and a fair proportion of this material has featured the work of architect Charles Holden (1875–1960), whose collaboration with Frank Pick (1878–1941) as client acting on behalf of the railway company, has come to characterize the built environment of the tube for citizens of the metropolis. These icons of twentieth century modern design continue to serve travellers and tourists alike, and they have offered inspiration both in their own time for other world Metro systems, and for subsequent additions to the London network, in particular the 1999 Jubilee line extension which added eleven innovative stations to the network. This book explores the phenomenon of a modern architecture represented in a body of work produced steadily in the 1920s and 1930s, and spanning four decades between 1915 and 1959.[3] Focusing especially on design and architecture, and with detailed analysis of the buildings, it gives a comprehensive account in words and pictures of the factors contributing to the existence and appearance of London's Underground railway stations of the 1920s, 1930s, and beyond.

For the architectural and design historian, there are many '–isms' which arise in discussions of the theoretical and aesthetic aspects of Charles Holden's work: functionalism, modernism, stripped classicism, and rationalism. Here is shown how something of each was combined with an apparent economy of detail and simplicity of elements in pursuit of the ideal solution to a design problem, a process the architect summarized as to 'ruthlessly analyze your motives, eliminate everything which does not fulfil a definite and necessary function'.[4] Inspired by contemporary practice in European design and a thorough knowledge of enduring aspects of architecture in Britain, the products of Holden, his office team at Adams, Holden and Pearson and colleagues within the Underground/London Transport organization (including its own chief architect Stanley Heaps), are an early English example of total design. The stations, platform structures, signal cabins, electrical supply buildings, signs, poster panels, and items as small as door handles, all form part of what became a project of transforming the travelling environment and redefining the railway station. The work emerged from a special relationship between Charles Holden and Frank Pick,

one which was unusually free from mediation by others, and which as a consequence produced focused solutions to particular design problems, such as how to create a safe travelling environment, to protect the passenger, to make compact yet spacious buildings that would be immediately recognized as Underground railway stations, and how to present a complex array of travelling information and advertising in a coherent and visually interesting way.

This book is in two related parts. The first section discusses the architecture of stations and other buildings as a chronological and thematic account of developments in the design practice. Where an individual project relates to others in design terms but not in strict chronological or geographical sequence, it is included here to show how the architectural style developed. In the second part there follows a detailed description of each station arranged in broadly chronological order. As the station building and rebuilding programme was applied systematically, this arrangement also roughly coincides with a tube line by tube line sequence. This research has provided an opportunity for the accepted chronology of station developments to be scrutinized once more, and revised in the light of new findings. Also included here is the work designed by Holden and his team which was not built, because it shows how design experiments represent stages in the development process, and can help interpret the transition in thinking from sketch to building, and from Holden's early style to the projected late designs. The sketches and unrealized plans reveal how the London Underground station was to have developed had not war and economics intervened, a fascinating world of places that never were, rescued from archive material and discarded microfilms.

If thanks are any recompense for the forbearance and support offered by my friends and colleagues over more than a decade of research and travelling around the London Underground system, I am very pleased to record the unfailing generosity of the following individuals and organizations: Pauline Amendt, Jim Aston, Elizabeth Argent, Mike Ashworth, Peter Bancroft, Neil Bingham, David Bownes, Roger Brasier, Morven Brown, Barry Carpenter, Millie Chalke, Martine Chumbley, Ted Cullinan, Elizabeth

Darling, Lucy Day, S. K. N. East, W. P. N. Edwards, David Ellis, Eleanor Gawne, A. Stuart Gray, Oliver Green, Amanda Griffiths, Emilie Harrak, Martin Harrison-Putnam, Elain Harwood, English Heritage, Charles Hind, Jack and Jenny Howe, Justin Howes, Charles Hutton, Martin Johnson, Helen Kent, Knight's Park Library, London Transport Archives Beth Polak, the London Transport Museum, Elizabeth Moore, Simon Murphy, Sally North, Alan Powers, Sam Ratcliffe, RIBA Drawings and Archives, Hugh Robertson, Anna Rotondaro, Stone Firms Ltd [Portland]: Neil Fuller, P. R. E. Taylor, Sheila Taylor, Caroline Webster, West Barnes Library, James Whiting, Barry Wilkinson, Peter Woods.

Dr David Lawrence
London, March 2008

Two notes, firstly on measurement: for the purposes of giving dimensional descriptions throughout the text in both the original imperial units used by the architects, and the present metric measurements, one imperial inch has been taken as 2.54 centimetres, and one imperial foot as 30.48 centimetres, with figures rounded to the nearest centimetre. Secondly, certain stations have had their name changed one or more times within the timeframe that this book covers. To avoid confusion in listing and indexing, Post Office, which was renamed St Paul's on 1 February 1937, is identified by the latter name throughout this book. Highgate, 1907 terminus of the Charing Cross, Euston and Hampstead Railway (later Northern line) branch from Camden Town via Kentish Town, was superseded by a new Highgate station elsewhere in 1941, and is referred to here by the name it received in 1947: Archway.

Part One
Making the modern Underground station

The Underground Electric Railways Company of London Limited, created in April 1902 and referred to in this book as the Underground group, comprised parts of what are now the Bakerloo, Central, Circle, District, Northern and Piccadilly lines, and had a legacy of railway rivalry in the metropolis. From 1908 it used the collective fleet name 'Underground' in publicity. On 1 July 1933 the Underground group and many other transport operators in London became the London Passenger Transport Board (LPTB), a private organization with extensive public service responsibilities. At this time former private operators came into the Board's control, bringing in parts of what are now the East London, Hammersmith and City, and Metropolitan lines. It would remain in this form until 1948, when the then Labour government, as part of an extensive project to bring services into public ownership, created the London Transport Executive as a part of the British Transport Commission.

As the Underground group and then the London Passenger Transport Board gathered into its control several different surface, subsurface, and deep-level railway lines, so it also acquired a disparate selection of buildings erected to give accommodation to passengers and staff. These had been constructed to various budgets, from the generous to the barely sufficient, and in a range of styles including solid Victorian and Edwardian flamboyant classical design and the most perfunctory timber and corrugated iron sheds. Out of this tangle, which was compounded by the addition of an extensive network of bus services, the Underground group had to present to its passengers a single persona, a corporate identity of signs, publicity and buildings which would identify an assured standard of service across the city, wherever the traveller might be.

In the first half of the twentieth century, the Underground sought to improve and extend its services, through the central area and out into the suburbs of London and the fields beyond, aiding the creation of new suburbs in Middlesex, Buckinghamshire, Hertfordshire and Essex. Much of the extension work occurred in relatively short time frames. During 1922–26, the present Northern line routes were rebuilt and extended from Highgate to Edgware and Clapham Common to Morden. Stations in central London were rebuilt to receive escalators replacing the overcrowded and slower lifts. Between 1931 and 1933, routes now comprising the District and Piccadilly lines were driven north and west to ultimate termini at Cockfosters and Hounslow West. In the years 1935–38, another arm of the Piccadilly was taken north-west to Uxbridge, and during 1937–39 the Northern line was projected northwards in the direction of Watford and Alexandra Palace via Highgate and East Finchley. From 1937, design and construction of new portions of the Central line east from Stratford to serve new and expanding suburbs, and west from Acton (to relieve the previously extended Piccadilly line) began, to be halted in a few years by the second world war. It can be seen that there was one intense period of activity in the design of Underground stations and that most of the architectural ideas emanated from Charles Holden and his team in the office of Adams, Holden and Pearson. The result was that many of the projects have a family likeness, and most of them are located in the outer suburbs of London. The estates of semi-detached houses which followed the tube have gained their own notoriety in the ensuing years, and their buildings have been much disparaged by the architectural profession, but many of the stations which were developed to germinate and serve the suburbs have become exemplars of modest modern architecture.

Why good design?
We have come to accept Holden's work for the Underground as iconic, but why was this good design necessary at all? Frank Pick came from a background in the promotion of a main line railway company in the north east of England, and was joined at the American-backed Underground group by other colleagues from the north east including Walter Gott, who managed commercial advertising and the development of a strong publicity presence.[5] Gott's successors included Christian Barman, an architect, industrial designer, co-ordinator of design for both London Transport and the nationalized British Railways, and late in his life the biographer of Frank Pick.[6] Under the direction of Lord Ashfield,[6]

On 1 May 1912, Pick was appointed head of the Traffic Development and Advertising department of the group's constituent companies: the Metropolitan District Railway, London Electric Railway (which had been formed on 1 July 1910 by the merger of the Great Northern, Piccadilly and Brompton, Baker Street and Waterloo, and Charing Cross, Euston and Hampstead railways), London United Tramways and London General Omnibus Company. He was given responsibility for railway line extensions, bus route development and commercial advertising and publicity. This remit grew further with the addition of the Central London Railway to the group on 1 January 1913.

Pick took an interest beyond his remit and followed design developments in Britain and around the world. Whilst improving the environment of the Underground, and offering a model for how urban space might be made better, good design had one other attractive quality: it made money. This was later publicly stated by Evan Evans, one of Pick's railway operating managers, who observed that 'attractive and conveniently situated stations were profitable investments'.[7] Recognition of Pick's pioneering commercial strategy is given in the posthumous anecdote of how 'he broke away from the accepted tradition of Big Business and set a new standard for business men. As head of the LPTB he made it clear by the care he devoted to design, from buildings and rolling stock right down to individual advertisements, that his organization had been set up to serve the people of London'.[8]

Frank Pick observed that marketing of the organization depended upon communicating to the public the quality of service available, and an apparent ease of travel. Well-designed posters, signs, stations and trains conveyed to the staff and public a uniform image of high standard. Standardization, and repetition of elements as though they were mass-produced (even if they were actually hand crafted) was a pervading theme of modernity in architecture and design, bringing with it economy and consistency. He had been appointed operating manager of the Underground group, and became managing director in 1928. From 1933 until 1940 Pick was vice-chairman of the London Passenger Transport Board.

Charles Holden joined H. Percy Adams from the office of C. R. Ashbee, where he had been immersed in the world of Arts and Crafts design. He became a partner in the renamed practice of Adams and Holden. Lionel Pearson became the third partner in 1913, creating the architectural practice Adams, Holden and Pearson, to whose corporate authorship the Underground stations are attributed. The practice's chief other activity was in the design of hospitals and educational buildings. (During the first world war, Holden served as an officer in the Directorate of Graves Registration and Enquiries for the British Expeditionary Force in France, part of the team creating the graveyards of the Imperial War Graves Commission.)

Pick met Holden in 1915, through their founding membership of the newly inaugurated Design and Industries Association (DIA).[9] Formed in 1914 following a similar body in Germany,[10] the DIA provided a forum for those interested in promoting better design in manufacturing, and pursuing 'a common aim of trying to find a proper solution for the problems of everyday life'.[11] This was especially important as the rise in mass-production gave both opportunities for the proliferation of good design, and also the potential for poor but cheap objects to outpace those considered to be of acceptable contemporary design. With antecedents in the arts and crafts movement, and a passionate desire to improve the appearance of objects and the built environment, the DIA published texts by influential figures such as W. R. Lethaby and Frank Pick on topics of which it felt the wider public needed to be educated. Pick had a penchant for sentimentality, and a passion for the functional, as demonstrated by the juxtapositions of romantic, cloying, humanist, and ruthlessly progressive words and images delivered through his many speeches and lectures and in publications as mundane as the annual official desk diaries for which he selected the photographs.[12] At the best of times, these two seemingly conflicting urges combined to stimulate art and design that was complementary and modern, yet imbued with references to craftsmanship and Englishness. Like other members of the DIA, Holden demonstrated a rigour in his approach to design, working towards an architecture that was 'crystal clear in its purpose'.[13]

Frank Pick had the vision and the power to pursue and procure the best quality design in all aspects of the Underground's activities. Pick also had access to private and public funds with which to commission work. He was thus something of an autocrat, or as Charles Holden described him at a time when Europe was subject to the forces of two fascist leaders, 'a benevolent dictator'.[14] Pick was usually able to negotiate with his committees and departmental heads to secure the projects he considered important, and the consultants and freelance artists with whom he wanted to work; Holden was one such consultant. In dealing with seemingly complex or expansive projects, Pick 'would sum up the matter under discussion in clear, crisp sentences, and press forward to a conclusion, thus avoiding that immense waste of time and the somewhat inconsequent decisions so often made by [committees]'.[15] Holden conveyed his ideas to Pick directly through the medium of pencil sketches, and was later to comment that Pick 'was suspicious of large and impressive perspective [drawings], but a small freehand sketch on a half-sheet of notepaper to explain the plan would frequently set us going on an important scheme'.[16] Several such designs survive as evidence of the architectural shorthand upon which a number of schemes were agreed and priced. As Holden's former chief assistant Charles Hutton[17] recalled: 'if Pick approved then no further submissions were required and we were left to get on with the job until the stations were complete'.[18] This economical exchange of ideas saved time, ensured that the fundamentals of the scheme retained their integrity, and is a testament to the friendship and trust which existed between Pick and Holden. The practice only faltered in the late 1930s when Holden passed work to other architects because his own office was so busy. Whilst Holden still had his proposals approved by Pick before giving them to others to develop,[19] the resulting designs fell short of the standards Pick had come to expect and Holden had to reign in certain works or face dismissal. This difficulty was soon overcome, and Adams, Holden and Pearson continued to lead development of London's public transport architecture through and beyond the second world war and the 1940s.

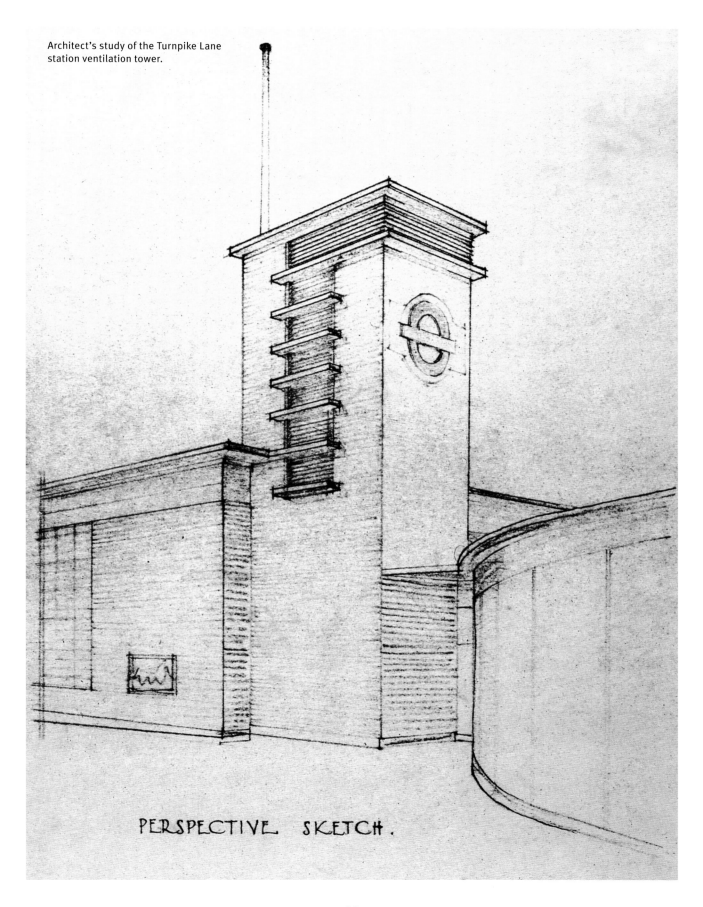

Architect's study of the Turnpike Lane
station ventilation tower.

PERSPECTIVE SKETCH.

Holden and Heaps

Stanley Heaps had worked for the Underground from the earliest days of tube railway construction in London, assisting Leslie Green on the design of the ruby red faience-clad buildings such as Covent Garden.[20] Green died young in 1908, and Heaps, who had operated the office for some time during Green's bouts of illness, was retained as the Underground's in-house architect to head the development of station design. Heaps was not a radical innovator but a pragmatic and thorough architect. He was a man of dependable ability, comfortable working within the prevailing architectural style and applying it to the particular needs of the Underground station. Some consistency of design was achieved with the extension of the Northern line to Edgware during 1922–24, for which neo-Georgian stations were designed by Stanley Heaps and his assistant Thomas Bilbow.

Stanley Heaps remained in post for the Underground and London Passenger Transport Board, working with the consultant architect Charles Holden and frequently acting to realize Holden's designs. Right through the great Underground expansion in the 1930s, when extensions were projected far east to Ongar (the Central line) and north-west

to Amersham (the Metropolitan line), it was Heaps who had the responsibility for redesigning the bulk of the stations and whose everyday work was concerned with the many and varied architectural needs of the entire Underground/London Transport system, including bus and coach garages, tram and trolleybus depots, staff quarters and ancillary buildings. His office was also, in the years 1930–1940, a virtual extension of Holden's own design practice, drawing up Holden's concept sketches for construction. This might mean that Heaps received little more than a basic plan and perspective view, from which he produced a working building by process of drawing and redrawing. Whilst this arrangement is not unusual in building, it is useful to understand the means by which the stations were produced.

Even recognizing architecture as a team effort, the arrangement between Holden and Heaps has given rise to a confusion over authorship of building designs. It is critical for this present book that the attributions are clear. A purportedly definitive list given in 1942[21] indicates that Adams, Holden and Pearson had sole responsibility for the design of St James's Park/55 Broadway, Piccadilly Circus, Sudbury Town, Chiswick Park, Green Park, Hyde Park Corner, Acton

Charles Holden

Stanley Heaps

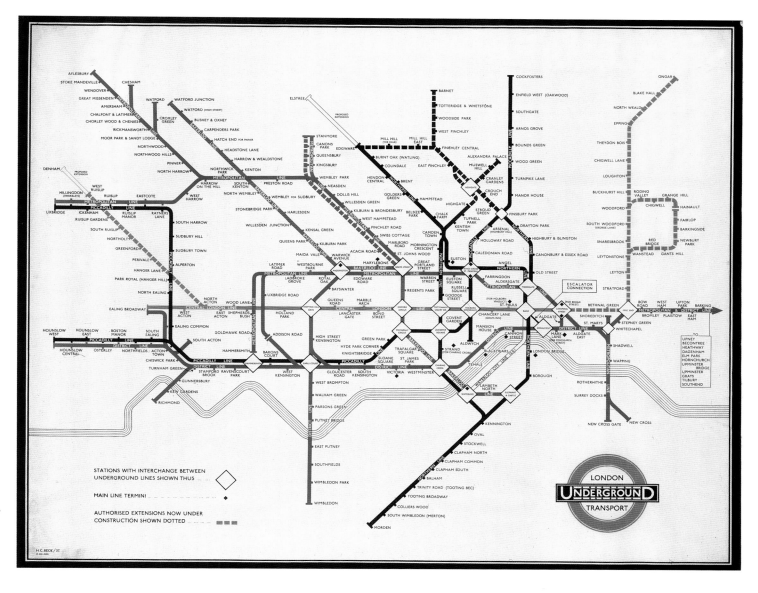

Town, Manor House, Turnpike Lane, Wood Green, Arnos Grove, Cockfosters, Boston Manor, Eastcote, Ruislip Manor, Highgate, Wanstead, Redbridge and Gants Hill. Adams, Holden and Pearson acting as consultants to Heaps as architect produced: Stockwell, Clapham Common, Clapham South, Balham, Tooting Bec, Tooting Broadway, Collier's Wood, South Wimbledon, Morden, Bond Street, St Paul's, Ealing Common, Hounslow West, Marble Arch, Sudbury Hill, Northfields, Alperton, Knightsbridge, Warren Street, Archway, Osterley, Leicester Square and South Harrow. Working with Charles James[22] of James & Bywaters, Adams, Holden and Pearson designed Bounds Green and Oakwood; working with Reginald Uren[23] the practice designed Rayners Lane, and with Leonard Bucknell[24] designed Uxbridge and East Finchley. Adams, Holden and Pearson were not the sole consultants to the London Passenger Transport Board; other practices, including Wallis, Gilbert and Partners, worked on the development of bus stations and garages for a number of years.

London Transport quad royal poster designed by Henry C. (Harry) Beck and issued in 1937. In this elaborate version of the Underground diagram are shown both the built, and the proposed, portions of the Central, Northern and Piccadilly lines which benefited from stations rebuilt under the direction of Charles Holden.

'What is a station? *An inviting doorway in an architectural setting that cannot be missed by the casual pedestrian'*[25]

Charles Holden's work for the Underground began in 1924 with a small project at Westminster on what is now the District line. A look at the pictures of Westminster before and after its redesign by Holden reveals several aspects of the way in which he used architecture and design to create a certain impression in the public mind. The transformation from old façade to new was assured yet measured, bold and definite.[26] The chief elements that would pervade station designs for the next thirty years are distilled here in a simple arrangement: flat surfaces with the slightest geometrical detailing, blue station name frieze panel over the entrance, the company's bar and circle identifying symbol (which had been devised some years previously[27]), carefully ordered publicity material and directional information including the system map. Christian Barman observed that the unobstructed opening in the façade was a 'forerunner of many hundreds of shops and supermarkets that were to invade our high streets a quarter of a century later.'[28] It was also a feature which had been used in Underground stations built since 1904–07. This simplicity and austerity had the potential to endow the Underground system with a uniform character. Visual communication through design is now termed corporate identity or branding; as we shall see, the Underground was an early exponent of the practice.

The uniform character of the new architectural proposition had a special and complex purpose: it was to convey to the travelling public that the services obtained beyond the station entrance were safe, of high quality, efficient and reliable. Through the architecture and art that the Underground commissioned as physical evidence of its often invisible system, the customers were also encouraged to believe that they benefited culturally from the environment in which they journeyed: they were in a small way educated and informed. Frank Pick saw the benefits of such social ordering extending beyond his organization into the wider civic society.

Holden was afterwards engaged for the design of rebuilt station exteriors and ticket halls for the City & South London Railway (C&SLR) line between Stockwell and Clapham Common, which opened in 1900 and now forms part of the Northern line.[29] These buildings of the early 1920s included traditional details, emphasized by the rendering in a contrasting colour glaze of mouldings, skirtings and friezes; they also had an overall streamlined appearance, with markedly rounded corners and edges in the spirit of the then contemporary *Bakelite* radio sets. The overall form of the buildings was not decided by Holden, but predetermined by the plan of the original structures on site, designed by Thomas Phillips Figgis.[30] Whilst this work was an innovation in the architectural style of the Underground, it was in the main a thin skin of modernity applied to the original

As the site which inaugurated Charles Holden's involvement with the Underground, this project of 1924 was the reconstruction of the side entrance to the ticket hall at Westminster District and Circle lines' station. First brought into use on 15 December 1906 and situated in St Stephens Parade, the entrance allowed direct communication with the Victoria Embankment, then an important thoroughfare for tramway routes. Holden's remodelling was accomplished by removing the fussy details, adding a small block in the centre of the parapet, and creating the stepped façade using smooth render: this was modernity literally overwriting classicism. Holden's work was short-lived: within a decade the façade was again refurbished, the central raised portion of the parapet was removed, and the appearance simplified by a facing of ceramic tiles. It had ceased to be used as a public entrance by the mid-1950s. To make way for the new parliamentary building *Portcullis House* over a completely redeveloped joint station serving District and Circle lines and the extension of the Jubilee line, all the existing surface structures at Westminster were demolished in the mid-1990s.

UNDERGROUND

WESTMINSTER STATION

TICKETS

ALL TICKETS
MUST BE SHOWN
AT THE BARRIER

THEATRE

go by
Underground

UNDERGROUND

FREQUENT
ELECTRIC
TRAINS TO
ALL PARTS
OF LONDON

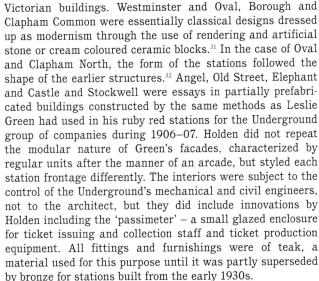

Victorian buildings. Westminster and Oval, Borough and Clapham Common were essentially classical designs dressed up as modernism through the use of rendering and artificial stone or cream coloured ceramic blocks.[31] In the case of Oval and Clapham North, the form of the stations followed the shape of the earlier structures.[32] Angel, Old Street, Elephant and Castle and Stockwell were essays in partially prefabricated buildings constructed by the same methods as Leslie Green had used in his ruby red stations for the Underground group of companies during 1906–07. Holden did not repeat the modular nature of Green's facades, characterized by regular units after the manner of an arcade, but styled each station frontage differently. The interiors were subject to the control of the Underground's mechanical and civil engineers, not to the architect, but they did include innovations by Holden including the 'passimeter' – a small glazed enclosure for ticket issuing and collection staff and ticket production equipment. All fittings and furnishings were of teak, a material used for this purpose until it was partly superseded by bronze for stations built from the early 1930s.

Holden's faience stations were fewer in number than Green's, and less successful in their attempt to embody a clear architectural style for the organization. What is interesting, however, is how Holden developed the basic principle of a screen wall into which was set an entrance (as at Westminster), and explored it in various ways: Oval and Clapham North in particular can be seen as prototypes for the stations which would soon follow on the extension of the Northern line to Morden. The design style, however, was soon to be abandoned in favour of something more radical.

There were three main patterns in the streamlined style of light brown faience blocks, with the parapet and skirtings picked out in moulded black faience blocks which Holden adopted. The first type used at Angel and Elephant and Castle consisted of a low rectangular building with a straight parapet finish to the façade. Above the ground floor windows and either side of the entrances, low relief panels were set out from the wall: a common Holden feature. The second version of this early Holden corporate design was evident at Old Street, Oval, and Clapham North. In this form, the parapet was built up either side of the main entrance by a series of steps to form a substantial plinth, emphasised by frames of dark coloured tiles set into the faience cladding. Onto the plinth was placed the word Underground in individual metal letters, a feature superseded within a few years by the company's newly-developed bar and circle device. The arrangement of plinth framed by stepped patterns echoes the appearance of Holden's first Underground work at Westminster. Walls were similar to those in the first type. The third pattern appears only at Borough and Stockwell: based on a low rectilinear building like that at Angel, but with a bold parapet superimposed over the entrance without any flanking steps in the roof line. The Stockwell plinth had a double frame of black tiles; that at Borough was entirely cream.

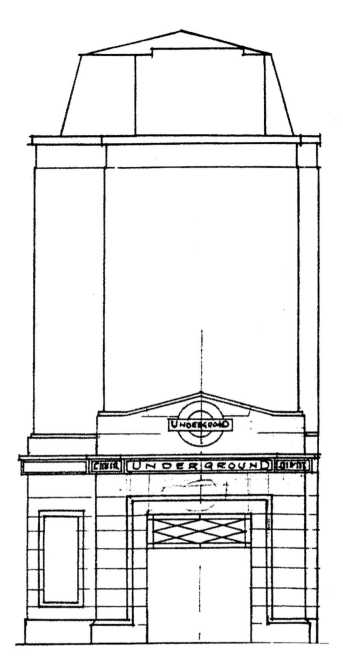

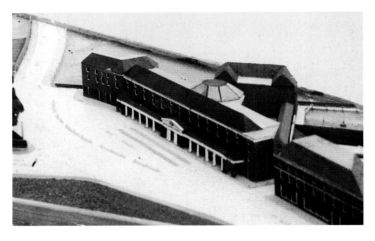

It is likely that this model, which was a successor to the neo-Georgian architecture of the Edgware branch completed by Stanley Heaps and his assistant Thomas Bilbow a year before, was one of a series of schemes drafted to provide a comparison with the work of Holden as consultant. This would show Pick demonstrating fairness and fostering competition by allowing his own staff to express their ideas. This addition to the Underground system required several stations to be built in existing suburban areas, and the terminal station at Morden to be developed on what would now be termed a 'green field' site: it was quite literally in countryside so that space for a large railway vehicle depot was available. There was sufficient space at each site for more than simply a flat frontage.

Holden's approach to station design at Westminster had been to create a form of plain screen around and above the entrance void. This screen was as much a publicity hoarding as an architectural feature: it formed a backdrop to the Underground's identifying signs and information panels, and it was itself like a billboard distinguishing the station from neighbouring buildings and attracting traffic to the system from the established and new suburbs of south London. An emerging philosophy of modernism in architecture and design was based on the consistent production of a standard image in three-dimensions. On the Morden extension the three-part screen used by Holden at Oval and Clapham North was extended to encompass the form of the building, permitting a consistent design to be applied to the several inconsistent sites and thereby promoting a clear corporate identity which could be generated more quickly than through different schemes.

Design of the Morden line stations coincided with the rise across Europe of the range of styles now often gathered under the heading of 'art-deco'. The term itself derives from

Morden extension: billboard architecture

The Underground Company, when extending the City and South London line to Morden in 1926, had the good sense to disregard both its own and other people's past exploits.[33]

When Adams, Holden and Pearson were asked to design stations for the southern extension of the City & South London Railway from Clapham Common to Morden which opened on 13 September 1926, the opportunity presented itself to begin making station architecture design in three dimensions.[34] A drawing for Balham of 1924 by the Underground's in-house architects had depicted a dull classical building, and even in June 1925 a model by the same office of Morden station included a colonnaded frontage[35].

the *Exposition International des Arts Décoratifs et Industriels Modernes*, held in Paris in 1925 and attended by representatives Underground group. Many of the temporary pavilions erected for the Paris exhibition, which gathered together some of the best architects, designers and artists in the world, displayed an emphasis on cubical forms, decorated by stepped, ribbed or ziggurat [36] patterns. These stylistic moves resonated with Charles Holden who had himself been interested in the potential for paring architectural forms down to their fundamental elements, with decoration made by emphasizing the geometry of the forms and sparing use of precise detailing. Throughout Holden's Underground work until the late 1930s there are traces of the art deco idiom, even though he was opposed to the application of superfluous detail which characterized the more excessive art deco buildings. This practice coincided with trends in modern European architecture prevalent in the late 1920s, and would be evident in Holden's work right through to the second world war and into the early 1950s. Holden's use of brick and stone, rather than layers of paint and plaster applied over other materials, has meant that his buildings have lasted better that many of those constructed to imitate directly the European white cubic style so evident in 1925.

A model was made of Holden's concept for the general style of stations on the Morden extension,[37] and in summer 1925 a full-size timber and paper facsimile *(see over)* built in an exhibition shed at Earls Court was used to evaluate the proposal before launching into construction. In the design, the central part of the screen was configured to face the principal corner of the road layout, with the two side portions folded back to suit the angle of the corner. The flexibility of the design can be gauged by comparing South Wimbledon and Tooting Bec: the shallow curve of the former and the near-ninety degree corners of the latter conveying the same aesthetic without awkward changes in arrangement of the key elements. After the faience-faced buildings at Clapham Common and elsewhere, these stations appeared as a startling change in the Underground architectural style: a sheer plane of white Portland stone two storeys high, dominated by three large windows over three entrance/exit voids. Strong and solid, the surface of the stone was barely detailed, except for a plain architrave at the perimeter of the façade, a similar recessed architrave to the windows, a fluted frieze band over the entrances, and the stepped plinth. In the brilliance of night-time floodlighting, the subtly modulated surfaces were framed and articulated by fine, strong shadows. Holden cited the churches of Sir Christopher Wren in the choice of Portland stone as the traditional building material of London;[38] he had also used a light stone on the buildings he designed for the Commonwealth War Graves Commission in the early 1920s. With its fine texture and good weathering qualities, the material was used in smooth blocks to give the station exteriors powerfully plain surfaces which were held to be effectively self-cleaning by the action of the rain.[39] (This theory is only partly correct, and stations thoroughly cleaned a decade ago are showing significant staining and marking by plant material.) The format of Portland stone façade which began with the Morden line would be taken forward for the reconstruction of stations in the central city area, and be used until the redevelopment of Holborn and Hammersmith in 1933–34.

Entrance voids – 'holes in the wall' – were inserted into the façades at ground level to suit the positioning of ticket hall, stairs, and escalators. Moving away from the traditional railway awnings which had been added to the entrances of many Leslie Green stations when the Underground extended its branding programme during 1908–10, the Morden line stations had only shallow canopies; in subsequent station designs of the early 1930s the canopy would disappear altogether, as for example at Arnos Grove. On the canopy fascia was the station name in Edward Johnston's Underground typeface.[40] Projecting from the canopy, further bar and circle devices bisected by masts served to identify the station from along the street. Some of these signs had glazed portions which were electrically lit to give a display at night, others were floodlit from lamps concealed in the upper part of the canopy.

Central to the upper elevation was a large window with two smaller side windows, and the distinctive feature of an Underground bull's-eye device which advertised the station by day, and by night when it was illuminated from behind by the interior lighting. Metal glazing bars were designed to hold tall, thin strips of glass, accentuating the apparent height of the windows. The top portions of glazing were omitted for ventilation purposes. These windows did much to remove the gloomy character of earlier Underground station vestibules illuminated only by artificial light. Between the three windows two square columns with slight entasis (tapering) rise up to inset plinths and capitals formed from three-dimensional plate and sphere abstractions of the Underground symbol. These columns were largely decorative; such confections would find little space in Holden's later functional modern station designs. Extensive glazing set into masonry walls was a characteristic of early modernism, and can be traced back to the engineering and architectural achievements of ecclesiastical and industrial buildings in earlier centuries. Kings Cross main-line railway terminus is one such example of this pattern.

Above the windows a cast-iron and blue enamelled fascia carried the station name. The lower walls had deep skirtings of three steps, which turned at right angles into narrow architraves around the entrances and then reverted to deep skirtings. The openings around the windows were similarly treated, and the extremities of the frontage received a single plain moulding. Each step was chamfered to weather better in the action of the rain as it swept across the façades. It

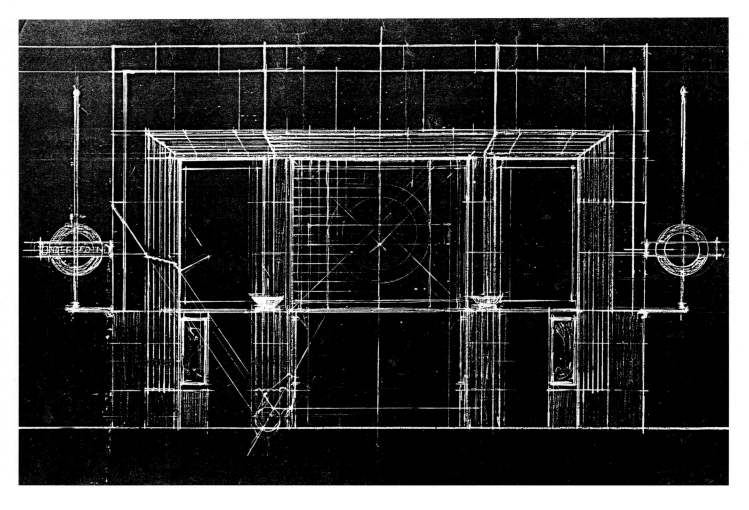

is a characteristic of Portland stone that it degenerates by powdering gently away over time, having the effect of helping to carry dark deposits off the building fronts and thus keeping them white. Where the rainwater did not hit the stone directly, pockets of dust and soot were left to create shadows, adding to the prominence of the mouldings. Low parapet walls stood above the level of the flat roofs and gave the buildings a sharply defined edge. The virtue of the flat roofs was that the stations could be built over, thereby giving the potential for revenue from development rights, now commonly called air rights.

Over the entrances a shallow canopy of concrete and iron repeated the horizontal theme, and lamps were placed on the upper side of the canopy to floodlight the façade. These structures were some of the first public buildings in London to be floodlit, and the availability of powerful equipment to produce strong raking lights across the façade was another influence on the choice of the boldest, simplest shapes in the stonework. Two decades earlier Leslie Green had introduced sodium lamps to make his oxblood red stations appear orange at night. Holden's floodlighting gave the stations a marked yellow glow, thereby using one of the more psychologically welcoming colours as a means of advertising. (On certain publicity photographs there appear to be searchlights mounted on the station roofs; it has since been discovered

that in most cases these rays of light were manipulated during the processing of the image and not a real feature of the buildings.)

To accommodate the varying street angles, Holden used a deep threshold so that there was a distinct vestibule circulation area between street and ticket hall. The protective function of the canopy was also assumed by the entrance vestibule which permitted passengers to wait for others, to unfurl or close their umbrellas, adjust their garments and gather themselves briefly before their journey continued. It is in the vestibule that the skilful use of site geometry to generate the architecture becomes evident: these double height spaces were planned as regular polygons, and their shape emphasized by the pattern of structural beams and the stepped ceiling decoration of four shallow bands. The polygonal form of the vestibules provided a controlled variety to the interiors, and where space permitted, such as at Morden, the polygonal theme was developed to give a distinctive character to what might otherwise have been plain rectangular spaces. (Interestingly, Holden would subsequently shift his design approach to use exactly such straightforward forms.)

Within the vestibules, which marked the limit of Holden's control over the design on these projects, he specified a wall covering of cream faience tiles. The fluted pattern of the door lintel was repeated in the tiled frieze. Harold Stabler[41]

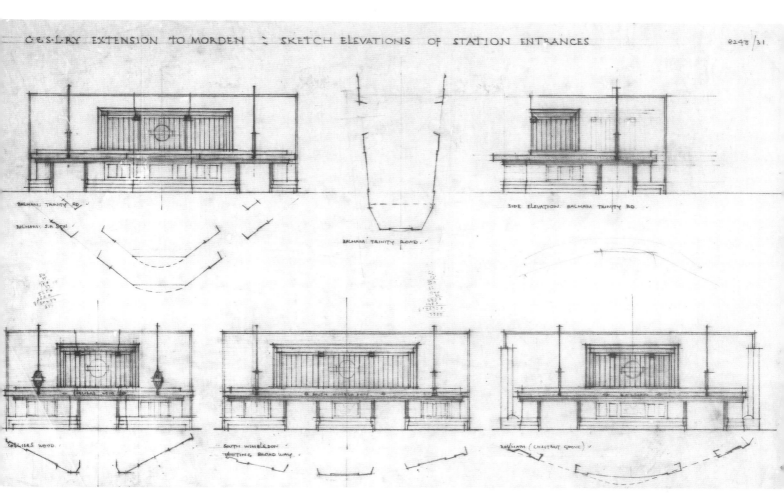

BALHAM: TRINITY RD.

BALHAM: S.R. STN.

BALHAM TRINITY ROAD.

SIDE ELEVATION BALHAM TRINITY RD.

COLLIERS WOOD.

SOUTH WIMBLEDON. TOOTING BROADWAY.

BALHAM (CHESTNUT GROVE).

also designed a decorative frieze in the art-deco 'jazz' style for one of the new stations. Here once again is the inclusion of the crafts into Holden's architecture. Photographic evidence of the mid-1930s suggests that in at least one station, the upper walls and ceiling were painted a dark colour such as green or blue. Tooting Broadway is a good example of the interior finishes, which were little changed from those specified for Leslie Green's Underground stations of 1906–07. Plaster enclosed the structural steel frame. Ticket hall, escalator shaft and platform wall surfaces were tiled following what was then the standard Underground practice of white bordered by green, grey and black. Fittings, and the ticket office booths otherwise called 'passimeters', were of dark timber. Morden's double-height tower was dual purpose. Set in a completely flat frontage (for this was the terminal station), it stepped forward from the general building line to announce the entrance, and formed a loggia and shelter for waiting passengers. This is the closest intimation we have of how Charles Holden's railway work would proceed: in Sudbury Town, the experimental station of 1930 which established an unambiguous new language for Underground architecture, there were the same features of extensively glazed tower vestibule associated with single-storey ticket hall on a logical axis, making the transit of passengers through the building as efficient as possible.

Part of Clapham South ticket hall.

23

An internal review of business activities by the Underground's operating manager J. P. Thomas highlighted 'the attractive and clear-cut appearance of the new stations, which have met with unanimous public approval',[42] and one architectural commentator described the work as the point at which 'a definite type of English railway station architecture came into being'.[43] The architectural press showed approval for the stations' progressive appearance as 'prophetic beacons of the new age'.[44] Alan A. Jackson has noted that in 1923 the Underground published a map of proposed south London lines showing routes to Wimbledon and Sutton as well as Morden. Had these lines been built it is possible that Charles Holden's Portland stone-clad stations would have been a distinctive characteristic of the southern suburbs alongside the Southern Railway's architecture of the period.[45]

Whilst extending new lines into the suburbs, certain locations on the Central London Railway (now Central line) had also to be rebuilt to handle increased traffic and to receive escalators in place of lifts. Bond Street (now demolished)

was completed by 1927, and St Paul's (now demolished) by 1929. From the Underground architects' office has emerged a photograph captioned 'Bond Street (a development of Morden) is the basis of present "In Town" design'.[46] In Bond Street, the features of the Morden line station façades were further rationalised and ordered so that the frontage was a plain stone surface bounded by a simple architrave, with three shallow steps at the base. Functional detail and decoration was reduced, with the removal of the columns and three-dimensional bar and circle capitals. A reference to classical design is evident in the fluted treatment of the piers either side and between the windows: Holden would use this motif in several subsequent schemes.

Above Post Office station entrance in Newgate Street. Renamed St Paul's in 1937, this building was badly damaged during the second world war and subsequently demolished.

Above Bond Street station in March 1929 when new. This design was demolished in the mid-1970s as part of the rebuilding of the station for the Jubilee line.

Left A late and modest manifestation of the Morden pattern was produced at West Kensington in the late 1920s, as a part reconstruction of the District Railway building which had originally opened in 1874. The stone façade was here reduced to a single storey devoid of windows, retaining the plain architrave and the stepped skirting characteristic of the earlier stations. As a new feature, the central portion of the façade was raised up in a semicircular plinth to carry the Underground bar and circle. One entrance has now been closed to make space for a ticket office.

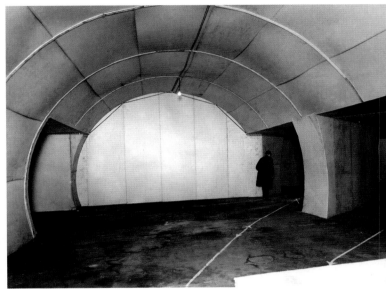

The layout of ticket hall, escalators and cross passages for Piccadilly Circus was first developed with a full-size mock-up.

Piccadilly Circus and 55 Broadway–St James's Park

... it is a pleasure to go down into the stations of the Underground, bright clean and orderly as they are. It is all carried out in the same sober style. The tunnels have no ornamentation or decorated mouldings. The walls are covered with glazed tiles as easy to clean as those of a bathroom. The stream of people passes through the smooth tubular channels and down the escalators. The trains themselves, with their long, red, cylindrical bodies, rush through the 'tubes' like a serpent shooting though the earth at great speed until they stop at one of the ... stations, which are also tubular. Here, there and everywhere, posters and signboards are the only decoration.[47]

Adams, Holden and Pearson produced two large projects for the Underground in the late 1920s which explored very different territories: one an entirely subterranean space, the other London's first skyscraper. Both schemes combined the functions of serving the railway and contributing new spaces for public use; both were notable for their use of many craftsmen to produce sumptuous finishes including travertine marble, imitation marble, plaster, and bronze for all the details which at previous stations had been made of wood.

Unique aspects of the projects are discussed here insofar as they relate to the development of the London Underground station, and the details are given in the second section of this book.

With Piccadilly Circus, Charles Holden secured his first full interior architecture project for the Underground group. The separate Piccadilly and Bakerloo stations built at this location in 1906–07 were very overcrowded by the mid-1920s. There was no space to build large ticket halls above ground, so between 1925 and 1928 Adams, Holden and Pearson recreated the 'circus' form below the streets, where an elegant elliptical space was formed to gently encourage the smooth flow of arriving and departing passengers. Under the several intersecting roads, the project also functioned as a public subway, to which were added a number of shop window displays to provide all-weather shopping. The design for this site was planned using full-size models of the ticket hall and escalator tunnels. Around the elliptical hall two rows of columns carried the roof, their regular spacing suggesting the loggia of a classical temple wrapped into a new form. In contrast to the timeless atmosphere of the hall, the completed station incorporated the latest technology in ticket issuing machines, mechanical information display and air conditioning.

The second large Adams, Holden and Pearson project for the Underground group was a headquarters building over St James's Park station on the District Railway (now District and Circle lines) and known by its street address: 55 Broadway. There was a philanthropic aspect to this work, in that Frank Pick unceasingly encouraged his team of administrators and engineers to believe that the Underground could be an agency for demonstrating how good, efficient design would improve the experience of living in the city. This idea of design pervading every facet of daily life was not new, but through mechanisation and modernity could be made accessible to many, rather than an elite, as had been the case in previous radical design movements. However, the Underground had another serious purpose in providing transport, and that was to make money. Generation of income required planning of projects, directing of operations, and counting houses to report the profit. More business required more administration, and in the late 1920s, without the benefit of electronics to secure mass storage space, all these factors demanded more space for people and paper. Operating staff needed to talk to the publicity team; the chairman and board must be seen to be part of the day to day life of the organization, and the public must have a place at which they could call upon the company. As the London-wide network of

Above Visualisation by Adams, Holden and Pearson of the ticket machines in the concourse of Piccadilly Circus station.

Right Construction in progress at Piccadilly Circus, showing the partial installation of the false ceiling.

Opposite The new Piccadilly Circus station opening ceremony of 10 December 1928, performed by Mayor of Westminster Major Vivian B. Rogers DSO MC JP, throwing a switch to start escalators and illuminating a marble and glass miniature tower called the *Verriers d'Art Light*.

tram, trolleybus, bus and train services grew, so did the need to accommodate the many functions necessary to administer a substantial business and its body of staff from a central location.

In contrast to Piccadilly Circus, this building of modern, American-style offices soared into the London sky, and gave Holden further opportunity to explore his interest in the expression of architecture through strong sculptural forms. It was a major reaction on the part of Frank Pick and his consultant architect to the many blocky, over decorated stone buildings which had begun to populate the West End and City of London in the Edwardian period. Holden worked through a series of less daring designs played out through hundreds of sketch drawings[48] before arriving at the solution of a central tower, flanked by lower blocks and descending into a cruciform structure, grounded in a two-storey street level building which efficiently exploited the full extent of a difficult site constrained by various streets. Below the pavement, cavernous basements filled space beside the railway platforms. As with previous schemes, 55 Broadway featured extensive use of Portland stone for the exterior, coupled with granite around the ground floor. The cross plan was common in hospital buildings, another of the practice's design activities, but had not previously been employed to any extent in British office buildings. Station entrances around the building followed the styling of Bond Street and St Paul's. Travertine marble lined the interior public, and major private, corridors, creating a sense of cool repose. Holden's subsequent Senate House in Montague Place for the University of London would share in common with 55 Broadway the laterally widened tower, and selection of Portland stone and travertine marble as building materials.

In 1929 the bulk of London's buildings were still designed in the bulky Edwardian classical style, generously garlanded with heavy cornices and swags: Regent Street or Kingsway show several good examples of the type. In 55 Broadway this fashion had been entirely erased, causing the architect, educator and critic C. H. Reilly to describe the Underground headquarters as 'steel-framed logic forcing itself upon our notice … and throwing out a challenge which only the dullest [architect] can avoid meeting'.[49] Holden brought together art and architecture at Piccadilly Circus by commissioning large painted murals depicting the activities of London and the Underground group, and at 55 Broadway by the employment of Jacob Epstein and others to produce sculptures for the building exterior. This desire to unite the arts in the very public realm of the mass-transit railway was a recurring feature of Holden's work for the Underground and its successors, and is in the European tradition of giving attention to the meaningful decoration of public spaces. In demonstration of the value which Holden gave to craft as an intrinsic part of realizing the design, he cited one feature in particular: 'I am very proud of a foundation stone in the Underground Building [55 Broadway]. It was laid by the foreman-mason and symbolizes a spirit of homage to all those men without whose skill our own labours would be in vain.'[50] Holden received the Royal Institute of British Architects London Architecture Medal for 55 Broadway in 1929.

Geometry in stone

With improvements to key stations complete, the Underground group turned its attention to the periphery of London, areas which it had identified as having rich potential for the generation of further traffic: if lines could be extended into London's countryside, then existing and new suburbs would provide passengers for the central area and increase company revenue. Started immediately after 55 Broadway, and identified by the Underground's own architects as being of the 'Morden type – adapted for "outlying" stations',[51] Ealing Common and Hounslow West together form an interesting transition between the double-height vestibule design established on the Morden line, and the brick tower buildings which were shortly to follow. (The succession was so short that the first design for Sudbury Town, the project signalling a seminal shift in Holden's Underground architecture, was essentially the Hounslow West building reworked in brick.) Without the hindrance of neighbouring buildings, the design of these schemes was focused on the use of geometry to generate polygonal ticket halls carried up into tower forms, effectively the Morden line façade in the round with glazing

on all sides. The stations were at once compact and conveyed an impression of space, whilst being distinctive landmarks. Charles Holden's railway architecture was moving into its mature style of 'a prominent building on a prominent site, wide entrances, direct access from the booking hall to the platforms, and orderly arrangement of accessories and equipment'.[52] Ealing Common and Hounslow West represent both Holden's last application of Portland stone for Underground stations, and the end of a particular decoration which referred back to the art-deco aesthetic, After these two buildings, new projects would be barely decorated brick boxes consisting almost entirely of right-angles.

Above Hounslow West, 1930.

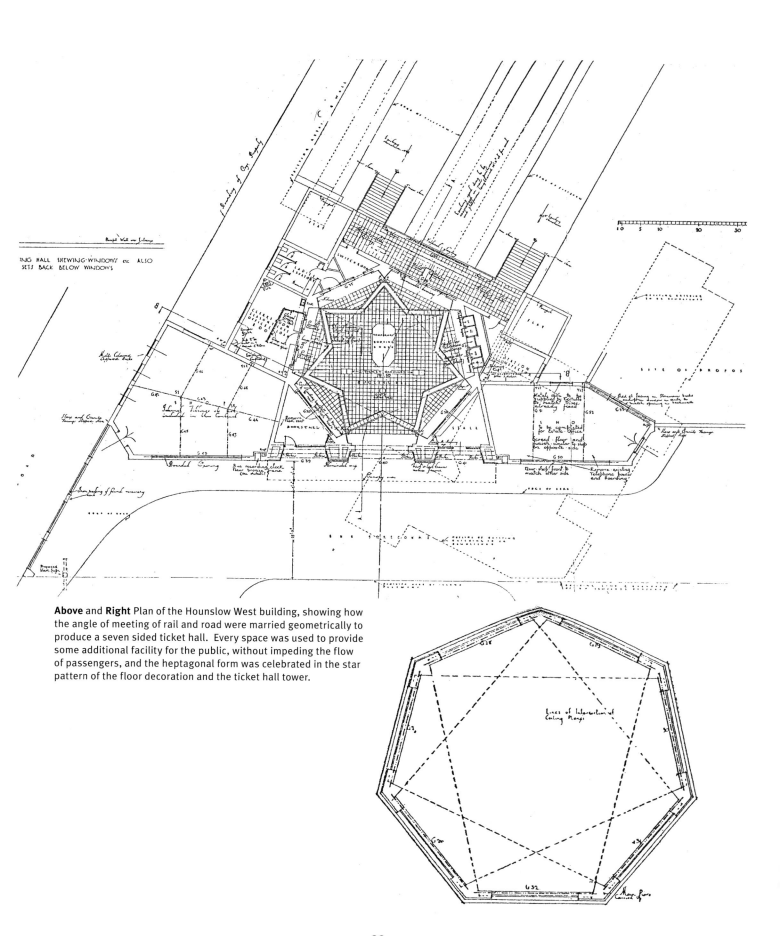

Above and **Right** Plan of the Hounslow West building, showing how the angle of meeting of rail and road were married geometrically to produce a seven sided ticket hall. Every space was used to provide some additional facility for the public, without impeding the flow of passengers, and the heptagonal form was celebrated in the star pattern of the floor decoration and the ticket hall tower.

Original street frontages at Archway (formerly Highgate) were designed by Leslie Green in ruby red glazed terracotta to a style of heavy Edwardian classicism; an additional entrance on Highgate Hill was operational from 1912. Building in an existing street, there was minimal space in which to work, so that Holden had to move away from the dogma of the three-dimensional box form. The dozen or so sketches which survive from this project show that a range of imaginative and fabulous modernistic sculptural forms was explored. They display many possibilities, the flutes, sweeps, setbacks, picture windows and canopies corresponding with cinema architecture of the day. In all the sketches the Underground bar and circle device featured prominently, even to the extent of generating a somewhat idiosyncratic circular canopy. Ultimately, the simplest design was chosen: a large window set into a surround of white render to imitate stone, with a shallow space behind to give the impression of a high-ceilinged ticket hall. This was a succinct solution to the problem of providing a pleasant modern frontage to what was an almost invisible service on a restricted site, and a reinterpretation of Frank Pick's notion of the station as doorway into the system. Work was completed circa 1930 (**facing page**). Escalators replaced lifts on 15 June 1931. Whilst the ticket hall interior was entirely rebuilt in October 1947, redevelopment of the station circa 1977 resulted in demolition of this façade. By this time it was in poor repair.

1930: THE GREAT PROJECT BEGINS

Lord Ashfield's one-time secretary W. P. N. Edwards has observed that 'both Lord Ashfield and Frank Pick attached great importance to building stations which were not only efficient from the point of view of passengers, meaning functional, but also would attract passengers by their architectural design'.[53] Across Europe, a distinct change in the perception of architecture, its forms and functions, had been emerging since the first decade of the twentieth century; evidence of these changes became much more marked with the 1925 International Exhibition of Decorative Arts in Paris. There are many useful histories of this development, and the full account will not be given here. There were also many different manifestations of the new ideas about building, to which were applied terms such as modernism, rationalism, and the International Style. Modernity in building was patronized by wealthy clients seeking to express their progressive sensibilities by commissioning houses from young practices; public and municipal authorities found that the principles of function and efficiency being advanced were well suited to the provision of mass housing and better public buildings: democracy sought through the social engineering of the built environment.

Early European modernism had its roots in the work of the Scot Charles Rennie Mackintosh, the American Frank Lloyd Wright, and the Dutchmen Hendrik Berlage and Willem Dudok, whose brick buildings with their arts and crafts details offered a gentle and expressive approach to modern architecture in contrast to the brightly painted forms appearing in France and Germany. These architects favoured an aesthetic of clearly expressed function and clean lines, which used bricks, concrete and steel, taking care also to embrace the craft traditions of stained glass, wood carving and metalworking. The Dutch in particular celebrated the great variety of bricks and brick bonding patterns in a revival of this material, as the building suppliers sought to defend themselves against the proliferation of concrete in architecture. Further refining the notion of machine-made building, Le Corbusier, Walter Gropius, Ludwig Mies van der Rohe and many others in Europe, the Americas and Britain, designed a number of schemes which were highly influential on an international scale. In all these schemes large areas of glazing ensured that the open-plan interiors were well-lit. Swede Erik Gunnar Asplund was responsible for the Stockholm Exhibition of 1930, where buildings offered models of design which architects reprised and evolved over more than a decade, with resonances right through to the Festival of Britain in 1951.

The modern spirit in architecture was diverse in its manifestation, but predicated on some key principles. Changing technology had much to do with the form of the buildings: increased speed of construction through prefabrication of structural frames, precast concrete panels to rapidly create roofs, and elements like factory-made steel windows encouraged designers to express the machine-made qualities of smooth lines and uninterrupted surfaces. Through the technique of reinforced concrete, buildings could be moulded into almost any form the architect desired with new freedom from traditionally accepted modes of structural support. In the first period of twentieth century modernism, building form was generally based on the most essential outlines: cube, cuboid, and cylinder, rather like a child's wood block building toy. The production of smooth surfaces, and an engagement with the forms effected by machine production, contributed to a taste for expression of the horizontal plane in buildings and this feature – so naturally suited to the linear nature of a railway line – would be evident in subsequent projects by Holden.

In Britain interesting examples of modern design produced by, among others, Maxwell Fry,[54] Welles Coates and Berthold Lubetkin (founder members of the Modern Architecture Research Group), the Tecton group, F. R. S. Yorke, Ernö Goldfinger and Connell, Ward and Lucas, were physical evidence of a burgeoning spectrum of discussions around modernity in architecture and planning. The architectural community in London was relatively small, facilitating rapid communication and discussion of ideas. Photographers like Frank Yerbury and Dell and Wainwright presented new work in formats which captured the imagination and portrayed ways in which architecture and technology were coming closer together. Charles Holden was an active member of the Royal Institute of British Architects and through this organization came into contact with many civic and private architects across Europe from the Netherlands to the

Balkans, and around the world. The British magazines *Architect and Building News*, *Architectural Review* and *Architects' Journal* were amongst those magazines that enthusiastically reported, illustrated and commented upon the new trends. Holden would already know certain overseas schemes which he had seen first hand or through publication in the British architectural press, and Frank Pick too had an awareness through his own travels and reading.[55]

The evolution of a new architecture for the London Underground railways coincided with a large programme of improvements to the tube network, announced in 1930, to expand the existing infrastructure and add new lines and facilities. The premise behind the work was twofold: to better serve London, and to create more London to serve through proliferation of housing development. Continuing an established Underground group custom of studying other transport systems, Frank Pick visited Berlin in January 1930, and came back with a bundle of photographs of new metro buildings, including two which had just been opened on 22 December 1929, at Onkel Tom's Hutte and Krumme Lanke, the penultimate and terminal stations of a Berlin *U-bahn* underground line. In a move that suggests Pick was excited by what he had seen and wished to imbue London's new stations with aspects of European modernity, he returned to Germany with Holden during June and July of 1930: just as work was in hand to design a new building for

Sudbury Town. The pair followed an itinerary which included Denmark, Sweden and the Netherlands, taking with them W. P. N. Edwards who made notes on the research, and subsequently compiled the report of the tour.[56] Their experience would feed directly into the design of the first fully experimental London Underground station at Sudbury Town on the District Railway.

Naturally Holden, Pick and Edwards inspected several transport installations. Among the municipal buildings and factories illustrated by the photographs are a series showing stations on the Hamburg (Stephansplatz, 1929) and Berlin *U-bahn* underground systems. From Pick's records, and from the report itself, it is evident that the trio were particularly impressed by the work of Alfred Grenander (1863–1931) as chief architect for the Berliner Verkehrs Aktiengesellschaft system. Grenander's Alexanderplatz station showed how a series of subsurface spaces could be designed with the utmost functionality and a minimum of carefully chosen features, including smooth bright green tiles on the walls and fully-enclosed lighting units.[57] The European stations used only the square, rectangle, and circle (or semi-circle): a more sparing approach to geometry than that which Holden had demonstrated up to this point. A characteristic of several projects was the absence of decoration: building components were assembled for their functional possibilities, not because they represented historical stylistic patterns or traditions. Features of the projects visited in Europe would recur in some of the London stations, as we shall see. One further point is of vital importance here: the Dutch buildings demonstrated that the architect could design all aspects of the built environment, interior spaces, signs, lighting, and all the paraphernalia of the railway station: this is the highly-ordered total design approach Pick and Holden would apply to the London system.

Charles Holden and Frank Pick made tours to northern Europe to study modern transport installations. German underground stations considered to be useful examples of new works, and whose influence can be seen in subsequent Adams, Holden and Pearson station design included a ticket hall with passimeters in Hamburg, a street entrance in the same city and the examples shown on the next two pages.

Krumme Lanke U-Bahn station and platform.

Above Stefansplatz on the Hamburg Hochbahn. **Below** Kellinghusenstrasse, Hamburg.

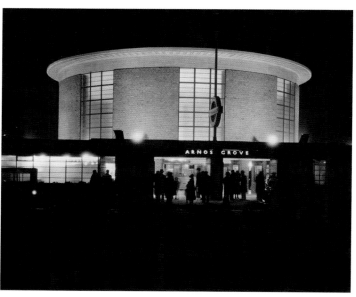

Advances in the technology of floodlighting of buildings achieved by the availability of reliable and cheap electrical power and equipment (developed for the advertising of buildings such as cinemas, and no doubt through military innovation), made it possible to design façades and forms where the effect of light and shadow took on another life after dark. The colour of the floodlighting could enhance the building material: Portland stone might be made to look more white, or more yellow, and brick appear more orange-red. The naturally inviting effect of this so-called night architecture was useful in restating the Underground's message that the system was safe, secure and comfortable. Compared to the typical gloomy and gas-lit railway station of the day, this was a significant improvement to passenger amenities.

Left Early proposal for Sudbury Town, a tall box form which began Charles Holden's exploration of the concourse ticket hall arrangement for London Underground stations. **Below (main picture)** Architects' drawing for the approved final form of Sudbury Town. **Below (detail)** The annotation to the drawing of the final form of Sudbury Town, below, indicating this significant change in the styling of Underground stations. **Opposite page** Sudbury Town under construction, 1930.

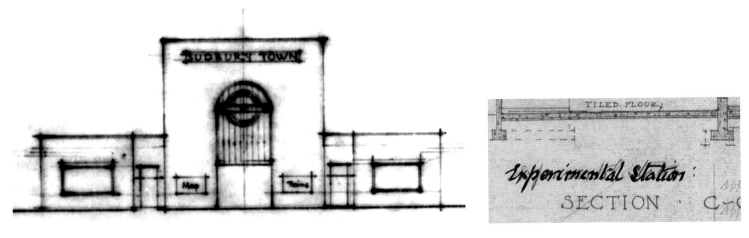

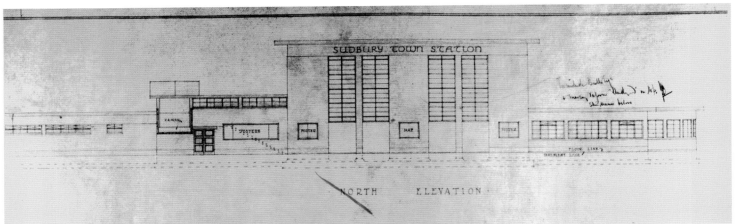

What happened on their return?

Neither Holden nor Pick prepared any notes, and after two or three months a report was drafted by W. P. N. Edwards and approved for circulation with minimal changes.[58] The report indicated a move away from the engineer-led method of producing a railway system, being one of the first Underground reports to focus on design rather than pragmatism and mechanical matters. Copies were also circulated to the architectural journals, increasing the public and professional awareness of changes that the Underground was seeking to make to its building estate. The report was less a blueprint than a manifesto, a framework of ideals. Charles Holden seems to have most admired those buildings which brought together tradition and modernity in modest, appropriate solutions to given problems, informed by a strict sense of service: 'we have no right to inflict upon our clients or upon the public a structure that offends the eye, or that ignores the desirable qualities of neighbourliness, of good form, of good material, of good execution'.[59]

Like other architects then as now, Holden and his staff were prepared to accept the aesthetic and stylistic details of other designers where useful, whilst proposing their own solutions to individual situations. When the stations produced subsequently by Adams, Holden and Pearson are studied, it becomes clear that a family of designs develops from a limited range of traditional and new materials and forms: well-proportioned, modest, English architecture skilfully reconceived and remade in light of modern needs. The stimulus of European design trends was perceptible throughout the period of intensive Underground station design: several features of Dutch and German railway architecture recur the London works and vice-versa: for example the Brest station by Urbain Cassan constructed 1936–37 resembles very closely in form and arrangement Holden's Chiswick Park of 1932.[60] Study of the photographs collected by Frank Pick indicates that features of the German stations were in part derived from earlier London Underground architecture as well as works in other parts of Europe and North America; similarly, Holden and his staff learned what they could from the overseas examples. Often developments were almost certainly contemporary. Architecture has always exhibited this interchange of ideas and formal and aesthetic

likenesses, and the modernists argued that that any similarities arose from common solutions to functional needs. With the superfluous decoration of architecture removed, this rationalization demanded all the more attention to the careful use of essential forms, structure and materials.

Fresh design: major moves and subtle shifts
Holden's stations on the Morden line were operating to capacity within a decade.[61] New schemes had to accommodate both present flows and traffic predictions. Holden described the ideal appearance of a station as one which would:

> put the passenger at ease and help him to pass along with the minimum of obstruction ... There is a very clear sign and the entrance somehow looks like a station and cannot be mistaken for a cinema. The first thing [the passenger] sees is a map ... The map faces both up and down the street ... Just inside the booking hall he sees a column marked 'Fares' in large letters ... He is next confronted with a set of upright columns [ticket machines] ... drops four pennies in the hopper [coin receptacle], duly receives

his ticket and passes on to the barrier ... and arrives at the head of the descending escalator. The regular passenger with a season ticket, takes a short cut to the barrier and the escalator ... Passengers arriving from the trains take a different path ... so there is no clashing of the incoming and out-going passengers. It all seems so simple if you think of architecture in terms of service instead of in terms of design by formula. There is no need to go out of one's way in the search for novelty: a proper sense of fitness for purpose will supply all the material for the adventure.[62]

Taking the American principle of a concourse space[63] through which all passengers circulated briefly to obtain their tickets and perform other necessities of travel, the new stations more or less grew upwards into real form from a diagram of these movements projected as flat planes in space.[64] Horizontal and vertical surfaces joined to create simple, bold blocks of building: 'form which is purposeful in all its parts arising from the play of the imagination on hard facts rather than from free and uncontrolled fantasy'.[65] F. R. S. Yorke, writing in *The Architects' Journal*, described succinctly the

Underground's approach: 'rather than be content to repeat the successful but transitional 1926 [Morden] type, the company, ever progressive, continued to encourage experiment, giving their architects an opportunity to review their earlier work in the light of present-day demands and resources, and so to evolve a plan and elevation that might be in accord with modern conditions'.[66]

The model building for this new phase of work was located in the unassuming settlement of Sudbury, west of Wembley. When striking into Middlesex in 1903, the Ealing and South Harrow Railway had economized in serving this lightly populated area by building corrugated iron sheds for all staff and passenger facilities. Quaint as this shack was, it was no advertisement for a modern metropolitan railway system, and therefore provided the site for testing new ideas away from crowded city streets. The site was large too, with room enough for a bus waiting area to be included in the overall design: a precursor to the type of urban planning which would characterize ensuing stations of the 1930s. The project was speedy, with the station constructed in seven months between December 1930 and July 1931.[67] In the evolution of its design, Sudbury Town began as a brick version of Hounslow West, and was then modified first to a narrow tower with flanking wings, and finally into an elegant, and wider box constructed of brick with a flat concrete roof and minimal decoration. Walls were punctuated by large units of prefabricated windows.[68] The adoption of a cuboid form was in line with contemporary European practice embodying the concept of an all-enclosing container for the various functions and activities of the railway station. Schemes on this principle were produced in rapid succession: Sudbury Town was started in 1930, followed by Arnos Grove and Chiswick Park (both started 1931) and a number of stations in north and west Middlesex and Hertfordshire on the extensions of the Piccadilly line.

The great inspiration for Holden at Sudbury Town was in the simplicity of his approach to the design task, and the economy of means by which it was realized. The station comprised two platforms, one with the main building placed on the side for commuters into London, and the other with a canopied passenger waiting area serving the Harrow direction. Holden saw the architecture as two things: shelter for the passenger movements, and physical expression of the Underground's aspirations to an enlightened and efficient transport operator. The first factor was achieved by analysis of routes to and from trains through the necessary railway facilities, and the result of this was a plan which was essentially one concourse, merging the British concept of a railway booking hall with the American practice of using a concourse or circulating area. In this way nearly every facility could be reached under cover. The second factor Holden addressed by using research into architectural design developments was to convey a contemporary image which might be applied to a variety of sites with some consistency. The skill was in combining function with aesthetics in a way which compromised neither and drew upon new design concepts and established traditions.

To speed new works, in-house architect Stanley Heaps was required to pass several station building projects to Adams, Holden and Pearson, and to design other elements – platforms, signal boxes, substations – in keeping with the functional and aesthetic principles established by the consultants. Later, Holden designs were passed back to Heaps' office for execution. All the while, Heaps's office was submitting sketch designs for the new stations (see for example his design for Arnos Grove), and also having to bring to completion the ideas produced by Holden by procuring the builders and overseeing much of the construction. Construction of several stations was supervised directly by Adams, Holden and Pearson. Through this procedure, the resulting schemes were a combined effort on the part of a team of architects, engineers, contractors, building tradesmen and administrators.

There is some doubt over whether Chiswick Park or Arnos Grove was started after Sudbury Town: Stanley Heaps produced the detail drawings for Chiswick Park, whereas Arnos Grove was managed directly by Charles Hutton at Adams, Holden and Pearson. Chiswick Park was an existing operational station and therefore came gradually into use from mid-1932; Arnos Grove did not open until September 1932. It must be remembered that several stations were designed within Holden's office simultaneously, by a team of assistants including Frederick Curtis,[69] A. Stuart Gray, Charles Hutton and Felix Lander,[70] working up the sketch designs produced by Holden. A little work was shared with outside architectural practices (more would be farmed out as the decade progressed), so that Bounds Green and Enfield West (both 1932) were brought to design resolution by C. H. James.

Variations on the theme

After the box and drum of Sudbury Town and Arnos Grove, the tower form began to develop in a number of interesting ways. Thus while a development of the architecture over a number of years can be identified, the variation of station forms along a line such as the Piccadilly was partly the result of local circumstances and opportunities, and partly stemmed from the flair and taste of individual designers. Evidence of this is given by the 'plans at Turnpike Lane, Wood Green, Bounds Green and Arnos Grove [being] rectangular, elliptical, octagonal and circular respectively',[71] by the station arcade adjoining the tower at Acton Town, and the internal colonnades (now partially obscured) at Northfields. Until 1935, Holden rarely used the cylindrical form for Underground stations, preferring instead the cube. The Sudbury Town type was developed to suit varying conditions, so that the rectangle changed size according to the space available, and occasionally changed shape altogether, becoming a tall drum at Arnos Grove, a low drum at Southgate, a chamfered box with small tower at Bounds Green, and a uniquely curved box set into the existing façade at Wood Green. (Interestingly, an early drawing for Wood Green shows a box-type façade simply superimposed onto the frontage wall, complete with short section of overhanging roof cornice: a direct application of a rectilinear style onto a curved surface.)

Holden designed Sudbury Town to be constructed by traditional methods: the walls were built, a layer of concrete cast in place to form the canopy and supports, more brick walls added for the ticket hall tower, and finally a concrete roof cast on top of the box. Difficulty with achieving a satis-

Below Stockholm City Library, by Erik Gunnar Asplund, built 1920-28, and an inspiration for the cylindrical form of Arnos Grove station.

factory finish to the roof forced a rapid redesign of the next station on the drawing board: Arnos Grove, on the northern extension of the Piccadilly line opened in 1932–33. The proportions of the station building and associated footbridge had to be changed part way through the design process so that a separate structural frame of concrete columns and roof could be cast without marking the brick, and could then be used to protect the builders. Where it was appropriate, prefabricated roof sections were inserted into the frame to save time. All stations after Arnos Grove were made by this method.

In several of the projects windows were set into all tower sides, creating interiors filled with light. There was generally a lower range of buildings around the tower wider than the tower itself. At Acton Town, the station was approached from the side through a corridor behind a range of shop units, and at Northfields the ticket hall box was set back from the road to create a small plaza. Where the site was confined or circumstances dictated odd arrangements, the ticket hall might be below ground. Alongside certain experiments in station design, this box pattern persisted through the 1930s – varied in plan dimensions, height and window arrangement – and was still being specified for small stations at the beginning of the second world war in 1939. Proposals for Redbridge and Wanstead, carried over from the mid-1930s to the late 1940s, retained the basic features of brick drum or box, and sketches for future stations including Hillingdon and Hounslow East also employed the box form. Some variation in design detail occurred as the architects tried out different ways of displaying the station name or incorporating signs, towers and other elements. The scale of these structures also changed from site to site, but even the smaller developments often had basements for staff offices and escalator machinery rooms, so that they were in fact three-storey buildings.

Materials
England's London and South Western Railway Company had begun to use reinforced concrete products in 1913, and its successor the Southern Railway extended application of this material to a wide variety of uses on its system after 1923.[72] Engineers and architects in Europe had been exploring the possibilities of the material since the latter part of the nineteenth century.[73] To achieve the flat roofs and seemingly unsupported canopies which characterize the Underground stations of the 1930s, concrete was employed, made richer by the incorporation of Portland stone chips and other aggregates in the concrete mix. This recipe was first used by Holden at Morden on the Northern line during 1924–26. Concrete provided a monolithic form shaped exactly to the architect's requirements; when it emerged from the moulding process, the marks of the timber shuttering moulds could be left exposed to celebrate the craft of the process, or the concrete could be ground smooth to expose the aggregate and produce a clean, shaped form such as the fluted mouldings over station entrances or the stepped undersides of roof projections.

In moving towards a modern aesthetic, Holden retained in his architecture proven building methods. Besides concrete, he also experimented with brickwork techniques to add subtle interest to otherwise plain wall surfaces. Brick weathered well, and suited the suburban surroundings. Its warm colour formed an effective counterpoint to the bright white concrete and coloured advertising signs. He chose hand-made multicoloured bricks[74] produced not far from the stations of which they were built, arranging the bricks, and the mortar joints between them differently at every site. There were also brown bricks from the Welsh valleys, and dark red, brown-grey and blue bricks from other parts of Britain. Bands of bright blue or green tile set into concrete friezes contrasted with brick, and the horizontality of the buildings was emphasized by the use of thin horizontal bands of Portland stone or cement-based artificial stone.

Innovations in factory production of plate glass gave rise to increased sizes of windows, both as individual panes, and in the scale of multiple units fitted in steel frames. Window frames were not white (this was a later deviation now redressed at most stations) but painted in shades of dark blue-grey, sand-grey and green to complement the brickwork or to match the colour of the glass as it reflected the sky. In this way Holden had followed the practice of builders in the Georgian period, in making windows seem bigger by diminishing the impact of the glazing bars.

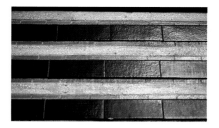

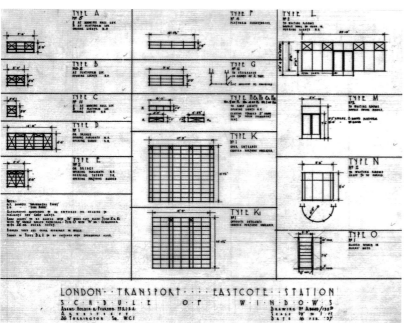

Opposite page left and centre Different brick types and patterns of brick bonding from Underground stations on the Piccadilly line extensions of the early 1930s. **Opposite page right** Coloured tile exterior frieze at Oakwood; tile interior frieze at Acton Town. **Above** The structural steel frame at Turnpike Lane prior to its being encased in concrete to form a frame which would then be infilled with bricks and window panels. **Left** A schedule of all the windows at Eastcote station, drawn as a series of standardized units for ease of manufacture and installation.

Interior architecture

Frank Pick criticized the Sudbury Town station project because the engineers and tradesmen were allowed to place equipment in the station after the building was finished, creating a cluttered and disorganized appearance. After this, much effort was expended by the architects to apply the total design approach, designing the staircases, bridges and crossings with the same level of quality as the primary buildings, and incorporating all the small operational necessities in the main design: fire extinguishers, telephone directories and litter bins, timetables, signal lamps, water taps and sand buckets. Within the ticket halls, walls were usually of exposed brick, sometimes of a different type or laid in a different bond pattern to that of the exterior. Around the concrete beam which carried the upper walls, some minimal decoration might be applied in the form of a row or more or coloured tiles. To increase the durability of lower walls and reflect more light, glazed bricks were introduced in some schemes such as Chiswick Park, Northfields and Oakwood. Floors were surfaced with polished off-white cement tiles. Holden developed a range of glass light shades which were used extensively alongside mass-produced examples through-

out the station projects until the advent of fluorescent lighting in 1945. The aim with this apparently complex system of equipment was to provide either focused or diffuse, local or general lighting as might be most suitable for specific situations in both ground level and subsurface ticket halls, escalator shafts and tunnels.

To speed traffic, ticket sales were made from free-standing booths of glass, wood and metal construction called 'passimeters' after their original function in Europe and North America of having integral turnstile devices which counted the persons passing through. Staff in passimeters were intended to both issue and collect day and season tickets, but were seen as secondary to the banks of automatic ticket machines installed in ticket halls. In practice the passimeter was a relatively confined space for more than one clerk to operate, and by the 1970s considerations of staff and financial security and standards of working conditions made the passimeter increasingly unsatisfactory. When London Underground introduced its new ticketing system in the late 1980s all but a few passimeters were removed. Those retained for preservation may be found in certain of the Holden stations described in this book.

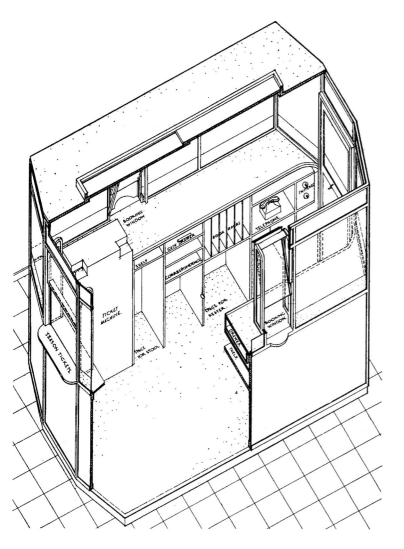

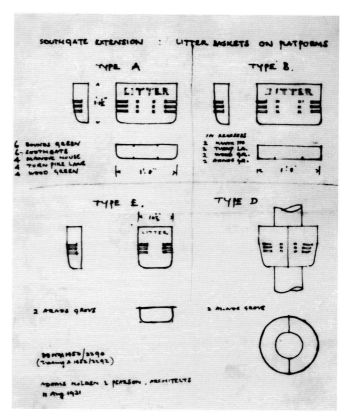

At platform level, clear and easy-to-read direction and travel information signs were developed by experiment from the Underground line diagram of Harry Beck,[75] and using the Underground typeface. Special enclosures were made for signalling equipment, and the platform walls had niches where banks of machines in repeated units delivered penny chocolate bars of every description. Holden worked with the Poole Pottery of Carter, Stabler and Adams to develop 6 inch (15cm) square tiles in an eggshell glaze coloured off-white with tiny brown speckles called colloquially 'biscuit-cream', to reflect light without glare and wear well in the dusty environment of the Underground.[76] A similar treatment had been seen by the Underground touring party on the trip to Northern Europe in 1930, and was akin to simple glazes used in traditional pottery. These tiles were used extensively in projects over more than three decades until the introduction of 'off-the-shelf' (and inferior) tile products in the late 1950s. Tube tunnel platforms were lined throughout in the biscuit-cream tiles, with bright colour borders.

Holden believed that advertising could form the main means of decoration in passageways and platform tunnels, drawing on the Underground's programme of commissioning leading and innovative artists of the day to produce publicity posters. In tandem with the unadorned brick walls above ground, the tiles affirmed the choice of restrained interiors as a backdrop for the business of the railway: 'the posters and their lighting remained almost the sole means of colour decoration, the architectural treatment of the stations being carried out in subdued or neutral colours in order to give the poster its value, a fact which incidentally added to the commercial value of the poster display'.[77]

Opposite page, main picture The typically rigorous selection of wall finishes at Turnpike Lane: exposed concrete roof, brick tower walls; lower walls lined with unglazed ceramic tiles; a floor of polished terrazzo tiles.

Opposite page, detail A litter bin and a wall recess to display directories of telephone numbers, adjacent to phone kiosks.

Above left Axonometric view of a typical London Underground passimeter booking booth used circa 1932–1987. Everything needed for the rapid sale and collection of tickets in a compact space.

Above right A unified range of litter bins designed for the extension of the Piccadilly line, 1932–33 and a direction sign planned as part of the decoration at Rayners Lane.

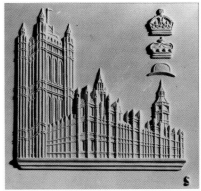

Top Platform tunnel at Bounds Green. **Left and above** Platform wall tiles designed by Harold Stabler. **Opposite above** The lower escalator concourse at Southgate, with bronze and plaster uplighter columns. **Opposite below left** Architect's drawing of a platform tunnel 'headwall', with all the signalling and safety equipment designed as a unified whole. **Opposite below right** A similar headwall and the platform tunnel design of the 1932 Piccadilly line extension at Wood Green.

55 BROADWAY

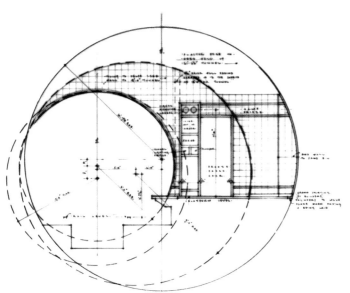

Throughout the Underground works supervised by Charles Holden, encompassing the District and Piccadilly line extensions of the 1930s, the station environments were considered as total design projects. Here are a selection of Adams, Holden and Pearson drawings which convey the work of the architect in all its precise, hand drawn detail.

This page, clockwise from right To make further use of a circular column bearing the subterranean roof of Manor House, a circular seat was designed. Ceiling-mounted illuminated sign boxes provided neat, visible and un-obstructive directional information. The underside of the ticket hall tower roof at Arnos Grove was treated with a simple and strong pattern of steps moulded into the concrete. Bronze uplighter columns were produced for the escalator balustrades, to give even and glare free illumination to the ceilings.

Facing page An essay in the potential of reinforced concrete to provide fencing, lighting standards, poster panels and station name board units in various combinations, in a typical example for Eastcote station.

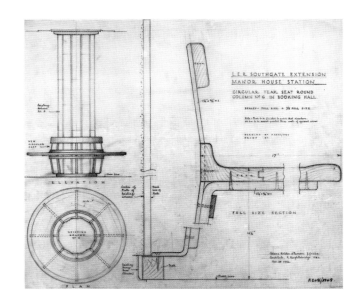

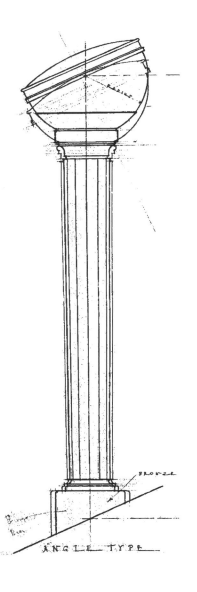

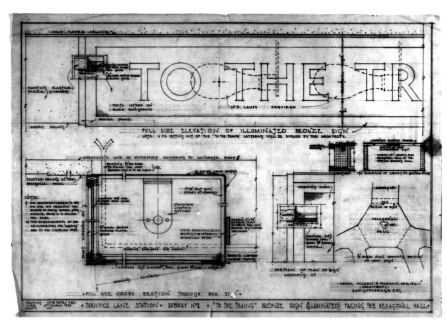

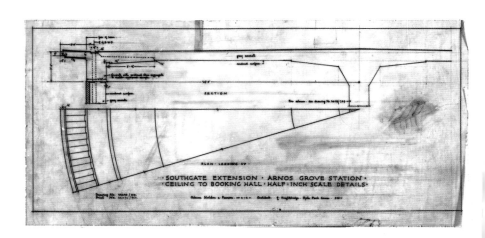

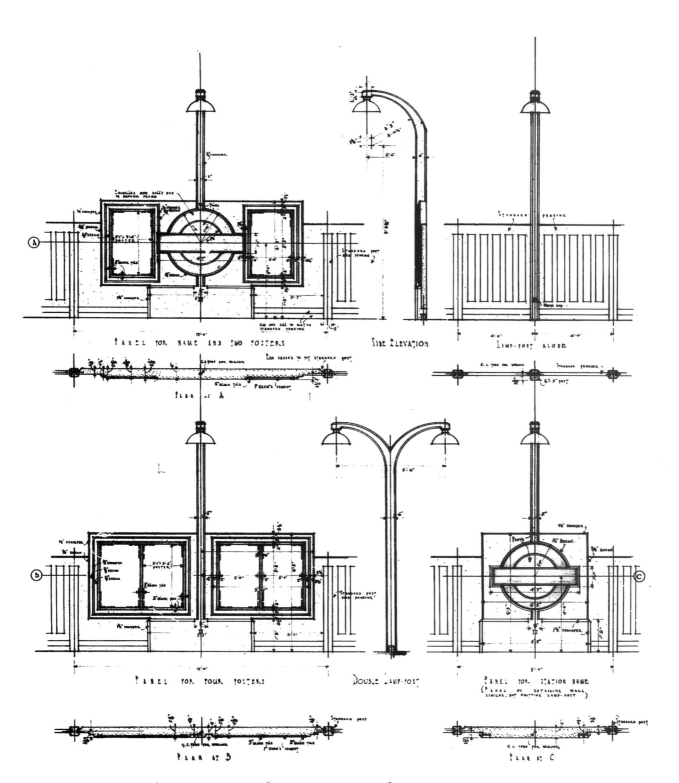

PANEL FOR NAME AND TWO POSTERS   SIDE ELEVATION   LAMP-POST ALONE

PLAN AT A

PANEL FOR FOUR POSTERS   DOUBLE LAMP-POST   PANEL FOR STATION NAME
(PANEL ON RETAINING WALL
SIMILAR, BUT OMITTING LAMP-POST)

PLAN AT B   PLAN AT C

·LONDON·TRANSPORT·EASTCOTE·STATION·
·NAME·AND·POSTER·PANELS·COMBINED·WITH·LAMP·POSTS·

ADAMS, HOLDEN & PEARSON FRRIBA
ARCHITECTS
26. TORRINGTON SQ. WC1
DRAWING N° A 9140/272
SCALE: ½ IN. TO 1 FOOT
DATE: 19 NOV. 1937

53

A civic focus

With a few exceptions, railway companies in Britain had historically given scant thought to the relationship between their buildings and the town or city. For railway station planners in the twentieth century a function of prime importance was the interchange of passengers between different services, and between street and train. Frank Pick considered that the Underground group had a role in serving the public directly by providing transport, and also in educating the public through the provision of better public buildings and spaces. With an eye on European examples and his own sense of townscape, Holden brought Pick's interests together by considering the activities which took place at and around stations, and embodying this in the urban design of the station environs. Those projects on the extension of the Piccadilly line north to Cockfosters are good examples of how Holden addressed public spaces; they were planned in the advantageous circumstances of being part of redevelopment programmes or on open land. Most exemplary is Southgate, where the site was sufficiently large to permit a bus lay-by around the station, which was itself situated on an island. Arriving and departing travellers could thus make a quick transition between modes of transport, and the station became a focal point in the town. Of further benefit to passengers and the Underground group was the provision of shop units, providing a retail income as a return on the investment in developing the facilities. Several sites on the northern part of the Piccadilly line included bus shelters and public subways in their designs, and Manor House and Turnpike Lane had special waiting shelters for tram passengers, the latter location being augmented further by a bus station, public conveniences, shops and a cinema. A yet more ambitious exercise in town-planning was to have been the terminus of the extended Northern line at Bushey Heath in Hertfordshire, where Holden proposed a complex of railhead, shops, café, public house and bus station; this scheme was abandoned as a result of the second world war.[78]

Critical acclaim and official censure

By 1933 Underground works were receiving much positive attention in the architectural and general press. Southgate, Oakwood and Chiswick Park stations were applauded by

The Architect and Building News as being distinctive amongst contemporary architectural designs:

> Rarely can there be so striking an example of not merely progress, but rapid progress in architecture as that afforded by the new stations erected by the London Underground Railways ... it hardly seems possible that Mr Holden could have improved upon improvement, which, in fact, is what he continues to do in his quest for the architecturally and functionally perfect station.[79]

A royal visit by the Prince of Wales (later Edward VIII) on 14 February 1933, when he travelled on the Piccadilly line between Wood Green and Hyde Park Corner, brought the new stations on the northern extension of the Piccadilly line into the broader public realm. The Design and Industries Association, the body which had brought Pick and Holden together at the beginning of this work made an inspection 20 June, and on 9 October the same year Charles Holden and fellow consultant architect Charles James, who had developed the designs for Bounds Green and Enfield West stations, took a party of officials from the Royal Institute of British Architects to visit the Piccadilly line. The event was recorded in the Institute's journal with glowing praise,[80] and the projects received favourable press attention in architectural journals across Europe. A representation of Sudbury Town by A. Bryett was exhibited at the Royal Academy in 1932,[81] and a similar image of Arnos Grove shown there in 1933, situating Holden's work both in contemporary discussions about architecture and modernity and at an art establishment of international standing.

The Underground group was merged with other transport operators in London to become the London Passenger Transport Board (LPTB) in July 1933. By 1934 several Adams, Holden and Pearson-designed stations were in use

Above This photograph of the Prince of Wales's visit to the Piccadilly Line new works in February 1933 shows him leaving Wood Green station. In the picture the Prince is greeting the waiting crowd, but it also nicely shows the entrance details such as the *art deco* lampshades and gently stepped entrance canopy.

on the northern and western arms of the Piccadilly line and the District line. Each was to some extent experimental as the architects and operator gained experience in what was required. Not everything had worked as well as had been expected, and in an internal report J. P. Thomas, LPTB operating manager, offered some criticism and recommendations for future projects.[82] Thomas made comments about detail, and some more fundamental observations. Considering particulars, he called Sudbury Town 'too shabby' (we have already seen that Pick was dissatisfied with this venture), arguing that light-coloured concrete and plaster used in the walls of the Underground stations which had recently been built were susceptible to severe marking from passengers and dogs: he proposed the use of granite or bronze for public areas up to shoulder or head height.[83] Continuing the theme of materials, reinforced concrete with its 'line of symmetry and neatness'[84] was also praised when used as a construction material in Holden's designs (in contrast to the exposed steel platform canopy frameworks evident on the Northern line to Edgware), although Thomas was not sure how concrete would weather in comparison to more proven materials such as brick and stone. Holden's open-plan ticket halls, with their generous entrances permitting free-flow of passengers, were found to be 'too open and draughty. Passengers whilst taking tickets and staff in control of ticket examination are very badly exposed to weather in the seven winter months'.[85] Thomas referred to amendments which had been recently made at Oakwood by the addition of doors to the entrances, and suggested that this feature, or a screening partition, be introduced on new projects. (Stations already completed such as Southgate and Arnos Grove were not altered.)

As a preamble to the most radical aspect of the report, Thomas questioned the need for the longevity which Holden built into his designs: a brick or stone station might last a century or more, yet from changing traffic patterns and travel habits, stations could require a number of changes and adaptations. With cost-savings also in mind (he felt that the cost of new stations might be halved) Thomas proposed that the internal walls of stations be made of lightweight materials, creating brick and concrete shells with a working life of three decades, and more flexible internal spaces.[86] At this time, Adams, Holden and Pearson were working on the further rationalization of the Underground station. Design development reflected cost-savings, and the desire to capture the essential features of the station with the minimum of additional building is evident in a series of studies for small projects along the Metropolitan/Piccadilly branch from Harrow-on-the-Hill to Uxbridge – Eastcote, Ruislip Manor, Ickenham and Hillingdon – planned concurrently during early 1936. With this sequence we have an opportunity to compare and evaluate the efforts to simplify and cheapen London Transport station design. Adams, Holden and Pearson produced generic plans for single-storey stations constructed using steel frames infilled with glass: it is possible that the basic building units would have been prefabricated to the architect's specifications by Crittall or another industrial window manufacturer using technologies developing rapidly in the 1930s. Concrete was to be used only for building bases, and brick was barely in evidence.

Certain elements recur in the sketches. At first, all addi-tional facilities were removed, so that the station offices could be placed in three or four small rectangular spaces set behind or around a ticket booth under a canopy roof and entirely open to the street. The canopy was cantilevered to project over the pavement. For the most extreme example (Ickenham) the booth was removed altogether and replaced by a combined staff room/ticket office. This station could be staffed by one or two persons operating the booth and ticket barrier. In the most elaborate designs, all four stations are shown as having ticket halls with roofs elevated above a strip of clerestory glazing, and set within parades of shops. The configuration was to be used in the whole range of station situations from platforms on embankment to platforms in cutting.

The lightweight station was not realized on the London Underground system despite Holden's designs for bus shelters showing how painted or vitreous enamelled steel could be combined with glass to make attractive and functional structures. Thomas's rationale for moves towards a more transient architecture seems confused given his earlier comments about the use of granite and bronze as building materials, and his concern over draughty stations. Contradictions aside, the debate does reveal the efforts expended in developing a flexible, functional, and pleasant railway architecture. This modular approach to station building design was innovative for its time, and predated other similar initiatives such as the development undertaken by Leslie (later Sir Leslie) Martin[87] and Richard Llewelyn-Davies.[88] for the London, Midland & Scottish Railway in the late 1940s,[89] which took further the exploration of prefabrication in station buildings as developed lightweight enamelled metal structures which made up into a kit, and which could be rapidly assembled on site. Whilst this work was largely abandoned after the private LMSR was absorbed into the nationally-owned British Railways in 1948, the notion of modernizing railway station premises was reprised by British Rail to replace many Victorian railway stations with the CLASP[90] system of building in the late 1960s, and this concept of prefabricated modular buildings was significantly influential in architecture generally.

The wooden hut inherited by London Transport from the Metropolitan Railway at Ickenham.

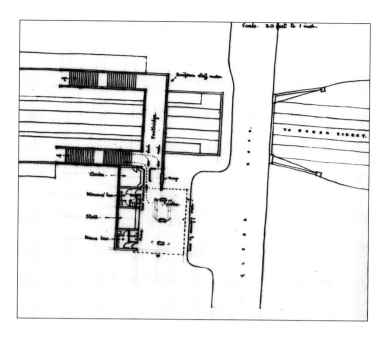

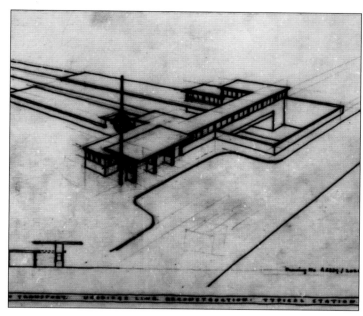

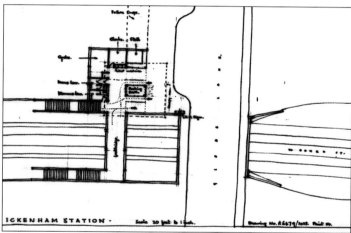

ICKENHAM STATION ·

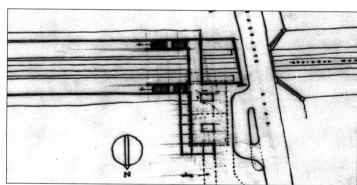

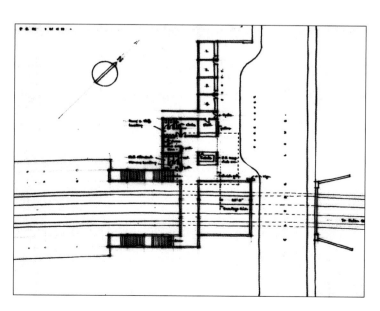

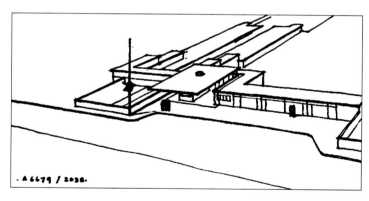

- A 6679 / 2038.

Left to right and **top to bottom** The development of an experimental lightweight station design for Ickenham on the Uxbridge extension of the Piccadilly line, planned in 1936. The first pattern comprises a semi-open entrance much like a bus shelter, with a ticket office at the rear and a few essential facilities as satellites to the footbridge. Following on from this a single free standing passimeter booking booth was proposed – truly a shop window to the system - and then two such booths for busier stations. A further modification featured a series of shops to increase revenue from the station.

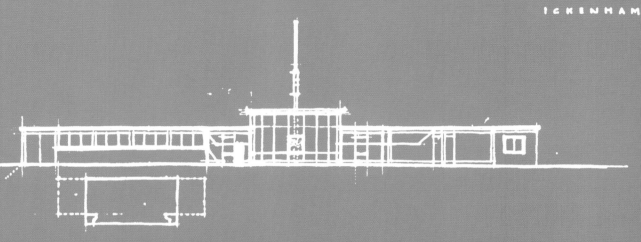

Above and right The final version of the lightweight station structure proposed for Ickenham, and a similar example to be built at Eastcote. Both indicate that the Spartan provisions of the initial designs were considered too basic, and here they have been superseded by substantial steel and glass bay-fronted ticket halls. Below The first and second prototypes as they would have appeared at Ruislip Manor. None of these schemes was realised.

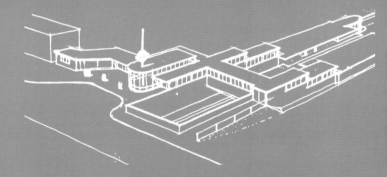

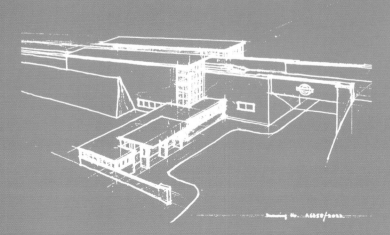

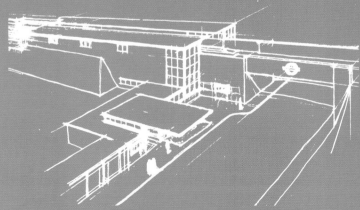

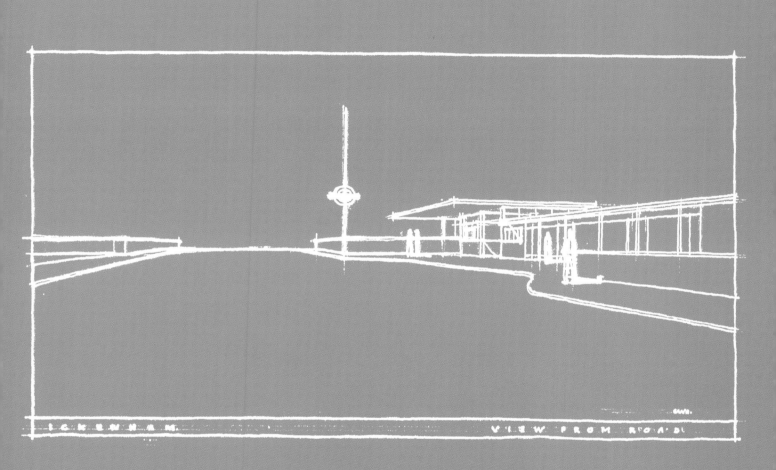

ICKENHAM   VIEW FROM ROAD

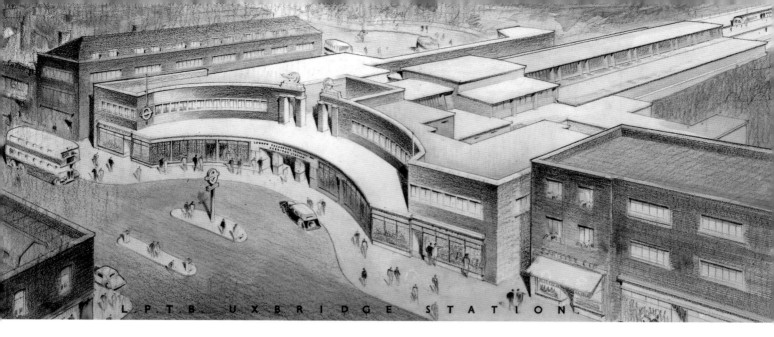

L.P.T.B. UXBRIDGE STATION.

THE NEW WORKS PROGRAMME 1935–40

A second five year plan for the Underground system was published in June 1935.[91] In this document was outlined extensions to the Bakerloo, Central, Metropolitan, and Northern lines, taking the Underground network further into Middlesex and out to Essex and Hertfordshire in new tubes and over routes that were to be shared with other railway companies (the London & North Eastern, and Great Western railways), and electrified for use by London Transport services. Many new station designs would be needed for the New Works programme, their design being allocated to architects working for the various railway operators. Charles Holden gained the bulk of the work, although chiefly in a consultancy capacity,[92] whilst the London and North Eastern Railway retained two design practices,[93] and the Great Western Railway used its own architectural department.[94] Stanley Heaps too was responsible for several station reconstructions, including stations on the Bakerloo line link between Baker Street and Wembley Park, and the rebuilt Aldgate East (1938), Sloane Square (1940) and King's Cross Metropolitan line (1941).

A fundamental change affected Underground station design from around 1933: Charles Holden began to be occupied in the major task of producing new buildings for the University of London, taking up the time of staff who had been focusing on Underground work. In consequence of this situation, Holden retained some station schemes (for Redbridge, Wanstead, Gants Hill), and passed others to office assistants and additional consultants. He also recognized that further development of the Underground station could be valuable and suggested to Pick that new architects might 'break fresh ground'.[95] In the main, Pick resisted this departure from established practice, thereby ensuring that an interesting but ultimately conservative set of stations ensued. Whilst the first Piccadilly stations were being built, and in light of the comments in J. P. Thomas's 1934 report, Adams, Holden and Pearson shifted its interest to encompass other building forms. As the decade progressed more complex combinations of box, drum and tower were evident in projects. Low ranging buildings at Boston Manor and Osterley (both 1934) were provided with vertical features as

a counterpoint: the box remained only in plan and as a band of clerestory windows above the cornice/canopy level.

An account of the development of Charles Holden's Underground station architecture can usefully be said to fall into three parts: the exciting new buildings up to Cockfosters in first half of the 1930s; secondly the expansion in scale of designs for stations to Uxbridge and East Finchley, and lastly those Central line works which were shelved during world war two and then completed to reduced budgets. South Harrow (1935), with Boston Manor and Osterley, comes at the juncture between the first two phases because it represented a transfer of focus from the standard Holden idiom of box ticket hall with overhanging concrete cornice, to more flexible forms determined by the site. As such South Harrow is another essay in the problem of designing a station having a street level building and platforms elevated on an embankment; it would soon be followed by yet another version at Ruislip Manor (1938) where bridge and building came together elegantly. Stanley Heaps carried to completion the Adams, Holden and Pearson design. Reginald Uren proved very capable of accomplishing a variation on the Sudbury 'box' at Rayners Lane. Evident in these late schemes, and those for Redbridge (design begun 1935) and Wanstead (first sketch designs date from 1936) on the extended Central line, was the presence of extensive glazed portions built as curtain walls – weatherproof enclosures which did not contribute substantial structural support to the building. Had Redbridge and Wanstead not been rationalized in the post-war rush to rebuild and open new lines (Wanstead as built was a crude and lightweight structure adapted from a non-specific building), the stations would have shown evidence of Holden moving away from standardized brick box designs. Likewise sketch schemes for Finchley Central, also by Reginald Uren, and Elstree (both unbuilt) embodied new features and materials.

Other factors indicate that attitudes towards a unified architecture were changing subtly. Stained glass at Uxbridge and the archer figure installed at East Finchley, are among the few built examples of the Underground's projected but uncompleted 1935–40 New Works programme. However, they were to have been accompanied by a number of similar sculptures, figures and emblems at the several stations on the Northern and Central line extensions. *Passenger Transport Journal* announced the following in 1938:

We understand that further designs have been selected by the London Passenger Transport Board in furtherance of its scheme for designating new stations by distinctive symbols. Denham [the proposed western terminus of the Central line], famous for its trout stream, will be distinguished by an angler, and Elstree, site of Sullonicae, a post on the Roman Watling Street, will be indicated by a Roman soldier. The new station at Red Bridge [afterwards Redbridge], ... will have the Britannia window from the British Pavilion at the recent [1937] Paris Exhibition. The Fairlop station, near the city's airport, will be embellished with an aeroplane. At Woodford, which is associated with a ford over the river Roding, there will be an heraldic tree and river. At High Barnet, the site of the battle of Barnet in 1471, red and white roses will be employed in the mural decorations. Mill Hill East will have the crest of the Middlesex Regiment, and Mill Hill (The Hale), which is named from an old mill, will be surmounted by a windmill. At Perivale, which apparently was derived from pear tree valley, there will be a pear. South Ruislip and Ruislip Gardens or West Ruislip, names meaning places with rushes, will have bullrushes in the decorations.[96]

With almost every location identified as having some local or historical feature worthy of being integrated with the architecture, there is a concerted effort here, no doubt driven by Pick who traversed London by day and night and immersed himself in its local peculiarities, into a phase where the stations would be knitted further into the civic fabric as they were in European railway buildings. But the projects were not built, and this art-into-architecture project did not progress beyond Uxbridge and East Finchley. To relieve the workload, Holden had asked Leonard Bucknell to work on these two stations. Bucknell's considerable efforts did not please Frank Pick

in either their appearance or cost when the designs were submitted in early 1937. Reportedly unimpressed by the Uxbridge, East Finchley, Rayners Lane (by Reginald Uren) or Eastcote (by Adams, Holden and Pearson) designs, Pick was also upset by what he saw as an abuse of the trust in his working relationship with Charles Holden, who was required to immediately revise the designs or receive no new projects from the LPTB, and forgo his post as consultant.[97] Holden recovered control of the work and remained engaged with it whilst working on the University of London.[98] In place of Bucknell's suggestion that a lightweight timber structure be employed at Uxbridge, the train shed was an adaptation of the reinforced concrete design used for Cockfosters five years earlier. It is likely that the episode with Pick was meant to bring Holden into line than an actual threat, and it also reflects Pick's sometimes abrupt manner when dealing with people. The consultancy work continued, and the pair remained friends, Pick writing to Holden in 1940:

I get even now far too large a share of the credit for the work in which we have been associated, for without your patient and careful collaboration I could never have got my elementary and sketchy notions realized. If we have not always agreed, that to me has been a good sign that we still could hold and develop ideas of our own and still strive, even competitively as nature does, to achieve something better than what we had ... so can I wish you joy as soon as this war is over in another attempt to catch up with requirements and add to the monuments of London suited to this industrial age.[99]

Their dispute over design works was overtaken by other events. Construction was attenuated by shortages of both building materials and workers. Traffic did not increase as quickly as London Transport had forecast. Projects began to fall behind, some being postponed until 1941; suspension of the extended programme for tube extensions then came about as a result of the second world war which began in 1939.[100]

Left Detail of the Archer figure at East Finchley, identifying the station with local historical references. A similar landmark on the skyline was proposed for Highgate station. **Right** The etched and carved glass screen of Britannia, made by Gertrude Hermes for the British Pavilion at the *Exposition Internationale de Paris 1937*, and intended for re-use in the tower of Redbridge station. **Opposite page** Entrance stairwell at Gants Hill, Central line. The brick building (less its proposed clock tower) forming the roof of the ticket hall can be seen in the middle of the road intersection.

Terminus

In architectural design and passenger amenity, much was accomplished in the production of London Underground stations during the 1930s. The projects were ambitious, some unrealized, and exhibited a peculiar mix of dynamism and reserve on the part of both Frank Pick and Charles Holden. Reviewing his work with Holden in 1936 when the architect was presented with the Royal Gold Medal of the Royal Institute of British Architects, Frank Pick had observed:

I think it may be fairly said that he has given to the Underground railways and to the London Passenger Transport Board a group of buildings which have distinction of their own, which have emphasis of their own, which have value of their own as punctuating the suburbs of London, and yet which are not buildings into which advertisement has entered at all. There was no attempt to arrive at a self-sought result such as is the basis of advertisement.[101]

Bearing Pick's comments in mind, the positive reputation which this team achieved through their railway work was bolstered by interest from the press in the early years of the programme. Pick was after all a publicity man,

marketing his organization by every means, and he was also in touch with the architectural and general media through the Underground's public relations office and his own professional memberships and tireless lecturing activities. The attention drawn to new Underground stations by respected architectural writers such as F. R. S. Yorke could only enhance the public perception of what were inherently good buildings, spreading awareness internationally in the early 1930s. Later in the decade new Underground stations were reported less often, and after the second world war they rarely featured in the architectural press.

The war brought building developments to a halt. Frank Pick began to lose staff, including his secretary Anthony Bull, to the war effort from September 1939. Some correspondence survives from the period which documents the end of Pick's career and offers a self-penned appraisal of Holden and himself. Pick retired from the London Passenger Transport Board to join the Ministry of Transport on 17 May 1940,[102] telling Holden 'what the future holds is blank. For once I am without aim or purpose and feel quite lost'.[103] His explanation for leaving London Transport was that he disagreed with the Board 'over government control and its consequences'.[104] Pick had requested that no leaving celebration be arranged by his staff, afterwards remarking 'it was maybe scarcely kind of me to go as I have … It is a grievous affair suddenly to sever ties of long-standing and to leave a flock that you know and trust and find yourself alone. I realize acutely how much I have relied all these years on the company, the help, the encouragement which the officers of the Board have given me'.[105] Pick in turn left the Ministry of Transport, and 55 Broadway, for the last time, in autumn 1940,[106] moving to the Ministry of Information, where he occupied an office in another Charles Holden building: the University of London Senate House. Pick died in November 1941 after a brief and troubled time at this second ministry.[107] Holden wrote of him in 1942:

It was an inspiration to work with Frank Pick. Always ready with helpful suggestions he needed only the ready response in others to bring his own seed to fruition. He was always ready to start out on some new adventure and the opportunities for adventure were many and various … Behind the austere exterior this man of affairs was moved by a clear ideal of service and this ideal of service was applied to every detail, large or small – there was nothing too small, nothing too remote.[108]

Adams, Holden and Pearson continued to produce work for London Transport during the war, although the consultancy was formally ended in February 1942 when the fees were diverted to more immediate necessities. In March of the same year, writing to his friend Hope Bagenal, Holden made reference to his interest in combining the arts, crafts and design: 'I was born in an industrial age … I was urged by a passion for building and for service … I have an invincible belief in the power of the human soul, the God in man, to rise above, and master, ugliness … I must exercise this passion even in the industrial age in which I was born'.[109] The efforts of the managing director and the architect were evaluated by *The Architectural Review* in 1944 as 'the conscience of the Puritan and the Quaker, who provide "good stuff", regardless, on the principle that the only reason why people don't recognize good design is because they are never given a chance to get conditioned to it'.[110] In a later commentary, the architectural historian Nikolaus (later Sir Nikolaus) Pevsner described the Piccadilly line stations as 'among the first designs in England to be modern in the novel Continental way, and they were at the same time modest, accommodating, not out of sympathy with essential English traditions and sensitively adapted to their surroundings. Moreover they were part of a house style more sweeping and successful than any before or after'.[111] This praise of innovation, consistency and national style was reinforced by Norbert Dutton, a member of the practice Design Research Unit[112] which would effectively succeed Adams, Holden and Pearson as consultants to London Transport, when he described the organization's pursuit of:

conscious and continuous recognition of good design as a worthwhile objective. It is effort, not accident, which has developed the idiom; subtle but unmistakable, orderly yet never austere, infinitely flexible, contemporary yet never ephemeral, urbane, impersonal, intrinsically English: an idiom so pervasive as to weld into a recognizable unity the independent efforts of many architects, designers and engineers working in a multiplicity of different media.[113]

Holden had been working on the University of London for a number of years before the war, and towards the end of his career was engaged on master plans for London's South Bank. Of London the metropolis, he was acclaimed for 'doing much to initiate the process of its modernization'.[114] There was little money for Underground works, and in any case Holden was by this time seventy years old. His practice was re-employed for completion of individual projects in the late 1940s. Stations on the Central line east of Stratford were revised and rationalised, so that Redbridge, Wanstead and Gants Hill were completed to reduced budgets and with less inventive use of forms and materials than had been envisaged. This was due in part to the reduced availability of building materials for some years after the war, and also suggests a loss of direction as Pick's autonomy was replaced by boards, committees and political control. A number of other Holden projects were not built in any form, but their features suggest increasingly sophisticated arrangements of forms. Drawings dated 1943 for stations on the projected, but never built, Elstree extension of the Northern line to Aldenham/Bushey Heath reveal an ambitious array of schemes combined with augmented road routes and urban development. The unrealized projects are discussed in part two of this book.

The London Passenger Transport Board was brought into state ownership from 1st January 1948 as the London Transport Executive of the British Transport Commission. Holden declined the offer of a Knighthood in the New Year's Honours List for that year.[115] The Underground had been a model for the development of the subterranean railway system in Moscow,[116] and the cavernous concourses which the Russians produced were coveted by Pick and Holden. There were not the resources to try out the same scale of works in London, but some success was achieved at St John's Wood, the first sketches for the underground concourse there having been drafted by Holden (to whom the work was originally allocated) when the project was called 'Acacia Road'. Gants Hill, a wholly subterranean space was the last great innovation in Underground station design by Adams, Holden and Pearson. Working with engineering methods not previously attempted in London, and not repeated until the Jubilee Line Extension was built some half a century later, Holden created a concourse which was the below ground equivalent of his station ticket halls: a bright, empty space. Final work by the practice for London Transport involved alterations at Mansion House station in 1959. At this time Holden was described as a consultant to the architectural practice of Adams, Holden and Pearson. Holden lived to eighty five, dying in 1960.[117] Soon after this, planning commenced on the Victoria line, and Design Research Unit, a diverse multidisciplinary practice, was recruited by London Transport to consult on the works with in-house architect K. J. H. Seymour. Design Research Unit's Misha Black sat on the London Transport design panel formed by Sir Alec Valentine in 1963. Adams, Holden and Pearson continued as an architectural practice based in London and Sheffield, later becoming AHP Partnership, and ceasing business in 1994.

The wall tiling at Gants Hill Station

was made and fixed by

CARTER

Park Royal, Felix Lander of Welch and Lander, 1936

Earl's Court (Warwick Road), Stanley Heaps, 1937

St John's Wood, Stanley Heaps, 1939

Loughton, Easton and Robertson, 1940

The precedent established by Holden for cuboid brick stations was perpetuated by other architects designing for London Transport. His former assistant Felix Lander produced Park Royal in 1936.[118] Earl's Court (Warwick Road) and St John's Wood by Stanley Heaps opened in 1937 and 1939 respectively. Loughton, commissioned in late 1937 and operational from 1940 on what would become an extension of the Central line, took its styling from Holden stations, contemporary Dutch railway buildings and the Kings Cross main line terminus of the London and North Eastern Railway.[119]

Also on the Central line extension eastward, Liverpool Street, Bethnal Green, Mile End, Leyton, Leytonstone, Snaresbrook, South Woodford, Fairlop, Hainault, Grange Hill, Chigwell, Buckhurst Hill, Debden and Theydon Bois, designed under Stanley Heaps and his successor Thomas Bilbow after the war, all demonstrate some trace of the Holden archetype.[120] In the west of London, Bilbow and K. J. H. Seymour designed White City during 1947–50. This building displayed larger areas of uninterrupted glass than had

been evident in Holden stations, and its form is the result of a different programme arising from the needs of the site and a route to the nearby sports stadium.

Brian B. Lewis had already taken the concept of the glass-fronted brick box to one extreme with his West Acton of 1940. Beyond White City, Hanger Lane, Greenford and the Ruislip stations (South, Gardens, and West) continued the general theme of brick box buildings, accomplished with varying degrees of quality. Designed by Lewis for the Great Western Railway, the first two of these stations (Hanger Lane and Greenford[121]) were completed after the second world war by Frederick Curtis, another former assistant to Holden. In the 1930s, the Southern Railway operating across the south part of England from Kent to Cornwall, built a number of brick stations under the direction of John Robb Scott which, whilst exploring the potential for a more streamlined modernity close to the style of cinemas, are true to the railway station as a type and have a distinct likeness to Holden's work for the Underground.[122] As an interesting aside, Frederick Curtis had also been Assistant Architect

Leytonstone, Thomas Bilbow, 1946-8

Perivale, Brian Lewis, Great Western Railway, 1939-48

Stratford, H. H. Powell, London & North Eastern Railway, 1946

Bishopstone on Sea, John Robb Scott, Southern Railway, 1938

to John Robb Scott before he joined Holden's office. Until the Jubilee Line Extension of the late 1990s, achievements in British railway architecture were confined to a limited number of projects on the main-line system, under the direction of designers including Paul Hamilton, John Bicknell, and John Ward.

The team assembled for the Victoria line project did not want to repeat the design idioms of Holden and his contemporaries, but aimed 'to create a machine for getting on and off trains, not a display of architectural virtuosity'.[123] Drafted by staff who had worked in the time of Holden, the project was constrained by budgetary restrictions and the fact that most of the stations on this route were subterranean additions to existing facilities. The quality of the design took Holden's minimalism a little further, but like much architecture of the period, it was realized with poor materials.

Looking back on the first half of the twentieth century in his book *Modern Architecture*, J. M. Richards, editor of the influential British journal the *Architectural Review*, wrote in 1962:

There were at this time a few exceptions to official architecture's general conservatism . . . But there was one semi-public body that had a far more profound influence. In the eighteenth century, as we have seen, a high standard of design was set by the cultivated taste of an aristocracy. Though our modern bureaucracy, which acts in the same capacity, has not yet succeeded in acquiring enough standards of its own to exert a similar influence, we have the benefit of some equivalent: namely that of certain big public and industrial corporations, notably the London Transport Board, whose good influence on design in the between-war period was incalculable. Not only were its Underground stations – often placed in instructive contrast in the middle of the worst bogus Tudor housing estates – the most satisfactory series of modern buildings in England, but all the details of their equipment – signs, lettering, staircases and litter baskets . . . – were well thought out and in a consistent modern taste.[124]

The collaboration between Pick as client and Holden as consultant, free from the intervention of others, was unique in British transport architecture, and indeed in architecture generally.[125] Holden's partnership with the Underground's own architectural department under Stanley Heaps functioned creatively and effectively to produce the many other buildings required to complete the system. Co-operation with certain other architects was successful too, notably C. H. James and Reginald Uren. Holden and his colleagues transformed the image of the British railway station from adapted house or shed to a carefully crafted structure created especially for its purpose. Whilst it is true to say that Holden saw no need to produce a new design where a proven and satisfactory solution was already available, the difficulties with other practices and with Pick over Uxbridge and East Finchley did preclude further experimentation in the use of materials and aesthetics. The selection of a brick box type building for Eastcote after a number of more flexible buildings had been proposed, is further evidence of a late conservatism in application of the idiom. Holden was busy, Pick was distracted with other matters, and both were growing older and changing their attitudes towards the way in which architecture and design could be arts or industrial processes in service to society: the conflict of making or mechanization which had given rise to the arts and crafts movement, and which had inspired much of the two men's philosophy, had returned.

Given that much of the Underground architecture occurred in the suburbs around London, the occasional traveller might not detect the presence of a common theme in the appearance of the stations on many lines. It could be surmised from this that Holden's impact on the environment of the tube system was patchy. One must remember nevertheless that the system was somewhat smaller when this work was carried out, and the city itself of a different scale. Pick and Holden made the Underground station into a shop window, and then developed it as a three-dimensional expression of a set of principles and a palette of materials, which strove to suffuse its actual complexity with an order, simplicity and harmony. Each scheme was slightly different, and every project nevertheless managed to retain the essential characteristics of a railway station. The modernity and clear efficiency of appearance was achieved through the repeated sifting and testing of ideas in the design process: elimination rather than omission.

The important legacy, besides a number of interesting and high quality modern buildings, is the distinctive functional style that developed into an archetype which was pleasant, durable and adaptable both by other architects and for future needs, as part of the Underground's own image, and as part of the image of the metropolis itself.

What the Underground architecture of Adams, Holden and Pearson might have become: their design for a new Mansion House station of 1956, evolved into the plainest of forms, but using the same choice of granite and Portland stone that characterised their stations some four decades earlier. Alterations to Mansion House, completed in 1959, were the last works completed under Holden's supervision before his death in 1960.

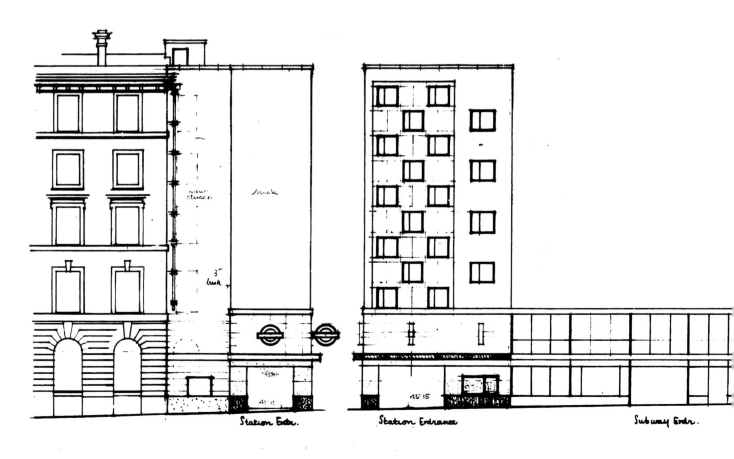

Station Entr.   Station Entrance   Subway Entr.

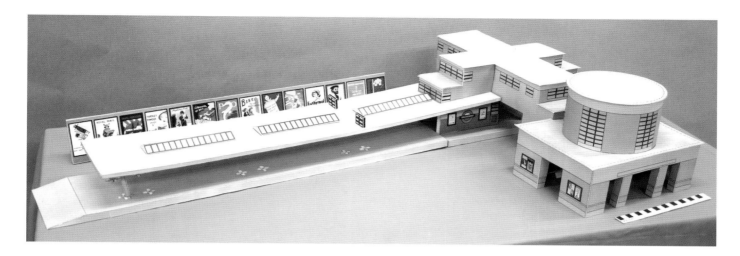

The iconography of the modern Underground architecture was re-presented in other contexts.

Above A model of the fictional 'Broadway' station, based on Arnos Grove and sold by the Underground as a poster kit for children to assemble.

Right The children's *Picture History of Britain* written and illustrated by Clarke Hutton featured this building inspired by St. John's Wood.

Below left The *Building of London*, written and drawn by Margaret and Alexander Potter, celebrated Underground stations as part of the modern architecture in the capital, whilst proposing to a surprisingly young audience the progressive reconstruction of London after the second world war.

Below right The city of the future as imagined by satirical cartoon artist and author Osbert Lancaster in his study of modernisation, *Drayneflete Revealed*.

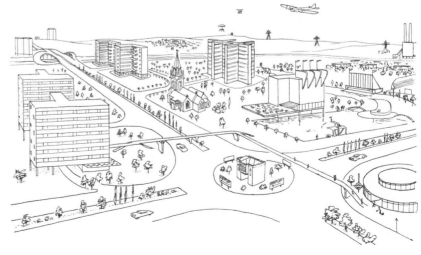

Part Two
The stations in detail

In this part, each station is described in its original and present forms, with notes on its particular design elements. Unbuilt schemes are also reviewed. The stations are arranged primarily in the chronological order of their design. Hence, Arnos Grove appears after Sudbury Town in the sequence it emerged from Holden's office, and not as it is geographically positioned between Bounds Green and Southgate. The dates that the sites first officially operated as railway stations are given, and also the details of when they were reconstructed to designs supervised by Holden; in several cases this can only be approximated by making reference to the opening of the route on which they are located.

Above Angel station in original form as designed by Charles Holden, 1924. The City and South London Railway building is seen behind it.

Opposite page Angel with the parapet reconstructed to incorporate a plinth bearing the Underground's bar and circle sign, which had by the late 1920s become a standard identifying symbol of the network.

The City and South London Railway: Angel to Clapham Common

To carry increased traffic and improve the network, the City and South London (or Bank) branch of the Northern line was rebuilt during 1922–24, and connected with the Charing Cross branch of the Northern line at Camden Town and Kennington, the latter link coming into use on 13 September 1926 when the Northern line first ran through to Morden. With the bulk of the architectural work undertaken between 1924 and 1926, this hectic period of major subterranean works, ticket hall alteration and the substitution of escalators for lifts, brought the first large-scale station projects into the Adams, Holden and Pearson office.

Angel

Angel station on Upper Street is a creation of the 1990s. But walk around to Torrens Street and City Road, and there are the remains of the streamlined *moderne* entrance building built between August 1922 and April 1924 to supersede the 1901 station. Clad in cream glazed blocks, the building abutted the older edifice. A canopy over the entrance continued as a line of framed panels displaying the station name and Underground signs on a frieze of blue glass. In July 1924 it was photographed with a plain parapet emphasising the horizontality of the frontage, much like a *Bakelite* wireless radio set. Either side of the 'UNDERGROUND' logotype were raised panels, a feature used by Holden right through the period of

his Underground station work. Everything in the façade is restrained and in repose. A year later, in September 1925, the frontage had been substantially altered using the same materials, with the central portion of the parapet raised to accommodate an Underground bar and circle device. This had recently been devised by Edward Johnston, and the Underground management led by Frank Pick was keen to see it displayed at all points across the system. By the 1980s the ticket hall interior was a dark and often crowded lift lobby in poor condition, making arrival at the station on a rainy day, at a time when it was still a convenient shelter for smokers, a somewhat gritty experience. Holden's structure was closed in 1989, and the lifts superseded by two banks of escalators.

Oval

At Oval, as at its near-relation Clapham North, we see the precursor to Holden's classic three-sided Underground station façade, applied to the shell of the 1890 building. The origin of Oval's design, closed for works between November 1923 and November 1924, is a pragmatic solution to the problem of building on a street corner, and demonstrates that Charles Holden worked with proven design solutions as well as new ideas. The two side wings rise in the centre to present the vestiges of a pediment: all decoration stripped away save for the moulded ceramic blocks and black edge detail. The parapet was formed with a ziggurat pattern, steeper than Old Street and without the traces of console brackets. Escalators replaced the original lifts from May 1925, and the original dome was removed. Over the years Oval deteriorated to become quite shabby, presenting a very poor image of the organisation. In 1996 it was decided that this station, with nine others on the Northern line, should be refurbished to improve amenities and enhance security

through the installation of help points, information booths and security cameras. Holden's exterior was replaced by a simplified version. Polished concrete tiles replaced Holden's glazed block walls. A steel and glass canopy provides extensive shelter around the building, a feature much-improved on the earlier facility. At this time the ticket hall was refurbished and incorporated a mural in white, off white and green by design practice Minale Tattersfield.[126] Work was completed in 1998. On the platforms the tiled walls are a combination of original and replacement material. Station name boards are replicas.

Clapham North

The new façade at Clapham North (opened 3 June 1900, formerly Clapham Road) was built during closure of the station over a year from November 1923. Escalators commenced operation in May 1926. On a corner site, the building contained one narrow entrance and short side wings finished in plain brickwork. The double stepped parapet was highlighted

by black edging; further black lining identified poster and map panels. Floodlighting units were fixed to the upper side of the entrance canopy to advertise the Underground sign by night. In the early 1990s the exterior was completely rebuilt, the pediment removed, and walls clad in unpolished concrete tiles up to canopy level, and white, black and grey tiles above. The style can best be described as sub-post-modern-Egyptian. There is an island platform here which retains decorations dating from the 1920s reconstruction.

Clapham Common

When the City and South London Railway reached Clapham Common, a station was provided by Thomas Phillips Figgis on the north corner of Clapham High Street and Clapham Park Road. The street building was abandoned after the station was rebuilt and escalators installed to connect with the existing island platform, the work mostly taking place between November 1923 and November 1924, and completed in the first months of 1925. Situated at the northern tip of a traffic island, the bulk of the new station facilities were built below ground. The street level building, a round structure surmounted by a dome (glazed to light the stairwell below), was styled after a classical temple. Around the upper part of the drum a continuous frieze of blue enamelled iron carried the Underground name. A further entrance on the west pavement of Clapham Common South Side connected via a subway with the ticket hall. The surface building was listed as being of architectural and historic interest on 27 March 1983, and the ticket hall was rebuilt first in the late 1980s to accommodate the Underground Ticketing System machines and booking office, and secondly in the 1990s with a new station control room. There is replica tiling throughout the station. During 1999–2000 a new stairwell entrance by Auketts Associates was built on South Side.[127]

Overleaf The street entrance rotunda to Clapham Common station in 1934.

On to Morden, and a new-old architecture

Construction of the City and South London line extension to Morden started on 31 December 1923 and the line opened to passengers on 13 September 1926. Work co-incided with other additions linking this line in the south to the former Charing Cross, Euston and Hampstead Railway under the River Thames between Kennington, Waterloo and Embankment, and on the north side to the same railway at Camden Town. In the first few decades of the twentieth century, it was common for banks, offices, civic and ecclesiastical buildings in London to be built using Portland stone as the main exterior material. This continued a tradition of city building established over several hundred years. For the Morden line too the buildings would have façades of Portland stone, with main structures of brick, steel and concrete, but now all the Imperialist ornament and leaden detailing of the shops and offices would be swept away. Holden determined that this series of stations would have double-height tower entrances. In South Wimbledon and Morden is seen the formal arrangement presaged in Holden's earlier Northern line stations: a central space accompanied by lower wings. This would be reprised at Ealing Common and Hounslow West. Here too, especially at Morden, is the form which more than any other defined Holden's Underground work: a rectangular box-tower. Ticket halls were placed at street level where space permitted, and below the roadway elsewhere. All stations had escalators except Morden, where access from the street was by stairs.

A scheme began in 1972 for the overhaul of facilities on the southern end of the Northern line. Clapham Common and Tooting Broadway received new lighting, and other stations gained improvements, but the process was patchy. In 1976, the Morden line stations were the test-bed for new architectural treatments intended for the first section of the Jubilee line which opened in 1979. Testing ways in which passengers might be better directed around stations by the use of bright colours, the areas around platform entrances-exits were painted yellow; the ends of the platform tunnels were likewise redecorated in bright green. This work by Design Research Unit was approved for adoption on the Jubilee line; it did not enhance the station style of 1926. All the buildings were refurbished externally in the early 1990s, with new signs replicating the originals, and a host of technology introduced in the form of specially designed lighting, closed circuit television and public address equipment, and control rooms in station ticket halls. Critically, the replacement signs were in some cases inserted into units which had not been present at the time the stations were built, and the workmanship suggests that the installations will not be as long-lasting as the equipment they replaced. Some are also now rusting. Another major security programme has seen many television cameras installed in all areas of the stations, as a further overlay to the architectural design.

Clapham South

A walk towards Balham along Clapham Common South Side will give the reader an easy and useful contrast between Charles Holden's first style of Underground architecture (Clapham Common), and his first fully-developed station style (Clapham South). The vestibule was of compressed and elon-gated hexagonal plan. Its location on the corner of Balham Hill and Nightingale Lane, and its three entrances, enabled station users to access it from all directions and travellers to wait under shelter. As the prototype, Clapham South possessed unique details: the vertical elements within the vestibule were expressed as columns, with ceramic tiles applied with fluted faces in the classical style. These tiles, in black and a beige colour known as biscuit-cream, are the only feature to be realised of a modernistic scheme prepared by Harold Stabler. At other stations on the line standard white, green, silver-grey, dark green and mauve tiles were installed. Above door height there was a ceramic tile frieze formed with another moulding, echoed outside the building in a strip of Portland stone over the entrances. Five shallow steps – a recurring theme in Holden's work – decorated the vestibule ceiling. Beyond the vestibule there was a spacious ticket hall of rectangular plan, lit by two octagonal skylights and a series of clerestory windows with wrought iron grilles. Further wrought iron decoration was present in the balustrade around the top of the escalators. Unlike certain of the original City and South London stations, platforms on this extension were provided in separate tunnels for additional space and capacity. Platforms featured the standard pre-Holden finish, a series of framed panels of white tile bordered by green, grey, dark green and silver-grey over a skirting of dark maroon tiles. A brick residential building was added over the station in 1934. The escalator shaft was refurbished in the early 1990s with stainless steel fittings and new uplighters. Walls have been carefully repaired with new tiles, but the exterior has been partially and roughly patched with cement render which contrasts with the stonework. Platform name boards are replicas.

Opposite page The design by Harold Stabler for a ceramic wall decoration shows, in its colours and forms, the influence of Iberian and Asian art. Whilst this proposal was not realised, Stabler and his Poole-based company Carter and Co. did produce many thousands of ceramic tiles for the London Underground.

Above Clapham South soon after opening.

Right To experiment with ways in which the arched escalator shaft might be illuminated effectively, the ceiling at Clapham South was modelled with a prominent stepped pattern. This was removed after a short period and not repeated at other stations.

Balham

Opening on 6 December 1926, construction at Balham had been delayed by striking workers. Two entrances served opposite sides of Balham High Road, with a single ticket hall below the road. In the east building a narrow central portion enclosed the stairwell, with entrances in the relatively broad wings; the rear of this space was curved, minimising the cost of land. Proportions of the west building, which abutted the Victorian railway station, more closely resembled Clapham South. Like its counterpart across the road, the entrances were set away from the windows either side of the stairwell. Here, the middle window was narrow in relation to those that flanked it. Piers of the adjacent main line railway bridge were reclad in Portland stone to match the Underground buildings. At the base of the escalators a small concourse gave circulation space between the platforms. The platform tunnels are not far below ground at Balham; when a bomb penetrated the station and breached water mains, sewers and gas pipes within the sealed platform tunnel on 14 October 1940 sixty four civilians and four staff were killed. After a three month closure to repair the damage, the north end of the platform remained untiled for many years, and the trackside wall at the Clapham South end of the south-bound tunnel is still in this condition. Both entrance building interiors and the ticket hall have entirely new wall finishes. Original 'UNDERGROUND' bar and circle signs over the stair-wells have been removed. Platforms retain original tile finishes with the addition of red granite and white enamelled steel portal surrounds, and the name boards are almost all reproductions.

Tooting Bec

Originally Trinity Road and renamed on 1 October 1950, this station has two diagonally opposed entrances on the north-west and south-east sides of Tooting Road-Balham High Road. The north-west building has three faces, enclosing a stairwell of octagonal plan. Across the main road the other enclosure has the most markedly angular plan of any on the line, a result of the site and the need to set the entrances well back from the road to achieve the necessary depth and headroom. For this reason, the double-height space of the tower occupies only part of the site, whilst the ground floor reaches forward to enclose the stairs. The exaggerated angles display effectively the three faceted frontage of Holden's design and emphasise the bold vestiges of classical orders in the skirting [entablature] and moulding over entrances [architrave]. Tiling throughout has been matched with modern replacements. Station name boards are replicas.

Above and opposite page upper Subtle variations on the Morden line station design, on either side of the road at Balham.

Opposite page lower A more marked contrast at Trinity Road (now Tooting Bec), between the acute, and rather severe entrance adjoining Stapleton Road, and that at the junction of Trinity Road and Upper Tooting Road.

81

Tooting Broadway

Facing a busy intersection, the single building at this site has a broad, curved frontage behind which is a shallow vestibule of half hexagon, part curved plan, sufficient to permit lighting behind the windows and create a useful waiting space. Towards the rear of the hall were two skylights and clerestory windows decorated with wrought-iron grilles. Escalators descended over one of the platform tunnels and at right-angles to the railway lines, landing in a concourse with passages to the platforms. In the 1990s the escalators were replaced and new stainless steel uplighter units installed in the shaft as a modern interpretation of the Holden idiom. A lighting and communications system is present as a suspended duct throughout the station. The platforms retain original and recent tiles, stone and metal portal surrounds, and reproduction signs.

Colliers Wood

This station had a similar façade to those at Balham, except that here the side windows were narrower. Behind the angled façade and single entrance, the ticket hall is an elongated rectangle aligned with High Street. As with other stations on the line, the escalators were rebuilt in the early 1990s with predominantly stainless steel finishes. Platforms retain original tiling and direction signs. Colliers Wood and its neighbour station at South Wimbledon had their renovation completed in mid-2001 at a total cost of some £18 million at contemporary prices.

South Wimbledon

Sympathetically-designed stone clad shop units flanked the broad, curved sweep of frontage at South Wimbledon. Wooden kiosks inside the entrance ran back towards the ticket hall, so that there was a shallow vestibule to give light after dark. Here the three openings were aligned with the glazing above. Escalators descend at right angles to the hall. In the early 1990s the platforms were rebuilt with granite and enamelled steel entrance-exit portals and new tiles carefully inserted to repair the walls. At least one original station name board carries the original title 'South Wimbledon (Merton)'. The ticket hall received lighting and communications ducts, and a control room. One of the kiosks is now closed.

Opposite page Tooting Broadway ticket hall. The Arts and Crafts 'electrolier' is visible top right, hanging in the station's front vestibule.

This page Variations on a theme. Colliers Wood and South Wimbledon, completed in 1926. The street-level building at Tooting Broadway was almost identical to that at South Wimbledon.

Morden

After the feeling of permanent night on the Northern line passing under south London, the terminus at Morden[128] is all daylight. Arriving passengers step onto platforms sheltered by a standard trainshed carried on steel trusses. Two foot-bridges, clad entirely in the green, grey and white tiles used throughout the Underground during the early 1920s, separate arriving and departing passengers. Both routes converge at the rear of what appears to be an undistinguished industrial structure, but passing through this wall one enters a ticket hall planned to Holden's designs. Derived from the geometries of track and street, the space is octagonal, its plan reflected in the skylight above and the shallow, sensuously bulging concentric steps of the ceiling. From the ticket hall, there are doors to prevent through draughts, and then a square vestibule occupying the tower form.

Below the tower windows the moulded frieze was like those at other stations on the Morden extension except that it showed the introduction of a cheaper substitute for Portland stone, using chips of the material mixed with concrete and then polished mechanically to a smooth finish. This artificial stone would be used extensively in Holden stations throughout the 1930s. On either side of the tower were lower buildings, their windows and clerestories formed from voids cut crisply into the stone. At the wing ends two final units without clerestories were set slightly forward in the classical pattern of pavilions terminating an arcade. The station plan was asymmetrical, there being a further extension to the west with two retail units.

A bus station occupied the land in front of the terminus. Between 1927 and 1930 hexagonal timetable columns were added in the forecourt on either side of the loggia, bearing an alternative form of bar and circle symbol with the bus fleet name 'General'. The architects had proposed a pair of loading islands for bus passengers beneath a reinforced concrete canopy projecting from the entrance: this was not built. However the bus station grew in use as the new Morden rose in a frenzy of mock-Tudor, semi-detached villas, so that between summer 1932 and early 1936 additional covering was provided for travellers by the construction of a canopy along both wings, made the same width as the projection of the tower from the main building, and with glass block pavement lights set into the roof to create a bright space below.[129] At their outer ends these canopies were pierced by masts carrying Underground bar and circle symbols.

Alan Jackson has observed that substantial traffic volumes in the mid-1930s gave rise to a call for duplicating the line.[130] This did not occur, but certain of the stations had two additional platform tunnels built when large air raid shelters were constructed in 1942.[131] An unremarkable commercial office block was added over the Morden station building in 1962. Alterations to the ticket hall for installation of ticket issuing machines in the late 1980s have not detracted from its appearance. There remain some original enamel signs on the platforms, and the stairways too retain the curious bronze and white glass lighting standards. Having undergone restoration and cleaning, the exterior of the building has been subject to the addition of incongruous shop fronts, and is showing wear from many years of use.[132]

Classical-modern hybrids –
Piccadilly Circus

At Piccadilly Circus there is an excellent illustration of what the Underground has done for modern civilisation … There down below lies the Underground Railway Station … This subterranean station is a thoroughfare with splendid show-windows along the sides of it and is always filled with people. In the morning it is like a turbine grinding out human beings on all sides. In the evening it sucks them in again, through the circle and down the escalators to the rushing stream of trains.[133]

… that up-to-date subterranean rendezvous is certainly a marvellous place, with its brilliant lights, wonderful shops, fine frescoes, and fast-moving escalators, whose perpetual rumble gives the final cachet to a scene that always reminds me of that remarkable German film "Metropolis".[134]

Leslie Green's 1905–06 station at the crossing of the Bakerloo and Piccadilly tube lines, with a surface building and passenger lifts on the south side of the Circus, was overcrowded and needed enlargement by the mid-1920s. But this whole area of the city was crowded too, giving rise to the problem of creating increased access, more circulation space, serving points north and south of the Circus. The street pattern, part of John Nash's town planning project in the early nineteenth century, formed an open space where routes converged from all directions. Working with a team of engineers and other staff fresh from the rebuilding of the subterranean installation at Bank (Central, Northern and Waterloo and City lines), Charles Holden copied the Circus itself, proposing an elliptical ticket hall built as large as the foundations of neighbouring buildings and the proximity of pipes and cables would allow. This solution was innovative in Britain at the time, and, whilst the excavations began a full-size timber model was made in October 1924 to test the arrangement of passages and escalator shafts – a valuable way of assessing what would be, in reality, an entirely hidden space. The concourse, only 9 feet (2.74m) below people and vehicles, was carved out by hand with great care from a number of individual tunnels springing off one central hole where the statue of Eros and the fountain (officially the Shaftesbury Memorial) had stood until 1924, when it was placed temporarily in Victoria Embankment Gardens.[135] There were six points of access to the station, and an underground subway into the basement of the Swan and Edgar[136] department store at the foot of Regent Street. To carry the weight of roads and traffic the steel reinforced concrete roof gained support from seven columns in the centre of the ellipse, and a further fifty columns arranged as a colonnade around the concourse and its perimeter.

In addition to specifying the latest ventilation and lighting equipment, the architects had the bare engineering surfaces of the space richly appointed, masked by traditional materials used in modern forms. The ceiling was made using modern techniques of construction, with the fibrous plaster panels secured to a separate frame: what would now be called a suspended ceiling. The columns, which in a more functional interior would have been left as simple steel tubes, were encased in cast bronze inlaid with dark red scagliola, a

polished plaster material from a recipe of some antiquity crafted to imitate marble. In the permanent yellow electric glow of the cylindrical lampshades mounted on rectangular bronze capitals (treated with Holden's signature fluted pattern), the scagliola took on a rich lustre at the column tops. Near the dead centre of the hall the main column was embellished with a flared uplighter unit, showing a form which would recur in Holden's work at Sudbury Town and Turnpike Lane in the early 1930s. To smooth the flow of travellers, the walls were lined with travertine marble, a material with links back to ancient Rome. Travertine has a warm cream colour and a figured patterning which wears well and hides dust. Features of the station were celebrated by *The Architect and Building News* who commented: 'not only does the company derive full advantage from commercial exploitation of the site, but secures for the boundary walls of the station a highly attractive type of adornment, for there can be no question that the brightly-lit shop windows will give the approaches to the station and the circular ambulatory itself the qualities of a very pleasant arcade'.[137]

Five escalators connect with the platforms. The 'headwall' beneath which they descended presented an opportunity for promotion on a grand scale. The Underground commissioned a fantastical mural to act as a unifying element spanning the separate Piccadilly and Bakerloo line escalator shafts. Artist Stephen Bone took the stylised illustration techniques of the time to create a tableau of the Underground Empire and the British Empire. Central to the five canvas panels, Bone placed Frank Pick and Lord Ashfield in an operations room at Underground headquarters, and through this composition affirmed that the company was at the heart of a London then having dominion over England and many far off lands.[138] The piece of propaganda was perhaps too subtle for the passengers to unravel as they glided briefly beneath it, and within a decade self promotion had given way to commercial advertising, initially for a malted drink product.[139] White, green, grey and black tiles lined the lower concourses and, intriguingly, the platform walls retained their original 1906 tiles.

Construction work took four years, the station opening with some ceremony on 10 December 1928. The former surface buildings closed on 21 July 1929 except to act as a stairwell enclosure. This was demolished with the redevelopment of the block on the Criterion site in 1990. The platform tunnels were the first on the Underground to be lit with fluorescent tube lamps as part of an experiment on 2 October 1945. The booking hall was made a Grade II listed building on 7 February 1983 and restored in 1989; features including the scagliola on columns are not original. The platform, lower concourse and escalator areas were modernised during 1984–86 with decorations intended to represent the neon lights of Piccadilly Circus. One subway has now been extended into the basement of the Trocadero entertainment complex. Sir William Holford, who had worked on the replanning of London's South Bank with Holden after the second world war, recalled the station with admiration: 'every time I pass through Piccadilly Circus I am reminded of [Holden's] quiet discipline and his patience and his sense of orderly design, which helped to transform the confusion of passages into a piece of subterranean architecture'.[140]

Right Floor plan of the elliptical ticket hall at Piccadilly Circus, with shop showcases and telephone booths around the perimeter, and ticket machines, escalators and retail stalls contained within the central zone. The wide subway seen top left presently connects with the large music store at the corner of Piccadilly and Regent Street.

Below This view looks from left to right across the plan above, between the automatic ticket machines and the money change boxes. In the background is the indicator 'See How They Run', with six dials recording train movements on the Underground. The columns, with their paired lamp shades, are based on a design in Berlin. The coffered plaster panels overhead give interest to what would otherwise appear an oppressively low ceiling.

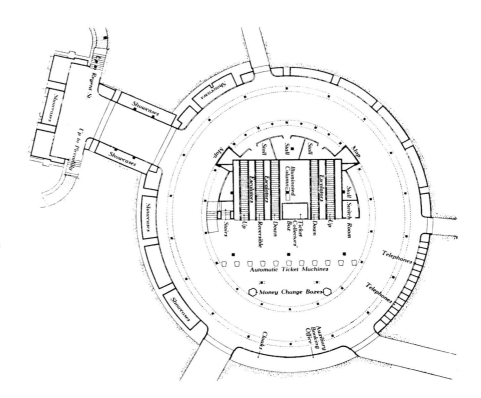

Soon after Piccadilly Circus opened, three London Underground staff demonstrated different aspects of the installation. Their snappy contemporary dress and hairstyles provide an interesting contrast with the stately modernity of the architecture.

Above Under the slogan 'See how they run' (an intriguing reminder through nursery rhyme of Frank Pick's attraction to things English), an inner wall of the ticket hall presented this train interval recorder. This enigmatic mechanism had an ingenious and simple purpose: electrical impulses generated by trains passing certain points on the system, caused needles to strike paper discs as they revolved around at clock speed. By reversing the process of a normal timepiece, this equipment marked the frequency of trains over the twenty-four hour period to create a perpetual graph of activities.

Opposite upper A further view of the retail displays present around the ticket hall, giving light and colour to this subsurface space. Swan & Edgar was the landmark department store on the west side of the Circus between Regent Street and Piccadilly.

Opposite lower Several ungainly ticket issuing machines were provided to sell tickets of single fares. Cased in wood and enamelled steel, the bulk of these automatons suggests a crowded atmosphere in the central portion of the ticket hall. Displaced by the machines, staff occupied two change giving booths. There were also telephones, a cloakroom, and public lavatories.

St James's Park–55 Broadway

London's most majestic skyscraper. Even American architects have expressed surprise that such a vast building could be erected in London.[141]

In the quiet back streets of Victoria, the Underground group operated from a number of small and undistinguished office buildings adjoining the District Railway's St James's Park station.[142] It had acquired in the first two decades of the twentieth century a number of rail, omnibus and tramway operations stretching out to the fringes of what was then defined as London, and was growing ever more ambitious for its transport empire. With the ongoing acquisition of transport interests, employees from across the massive network needed to be united by an identifiable centre: the Underground must have a completely new headquarters.

Charles Holden and a number of assistants worked on its

design, and site works commenced in December 1927. The Underground wanted their new building to be next to their offices at the junction of Petty France, Broadway, and Tothill Street, and also over the station exploiting what are now termed 'air rights'. The site was awkward: a kite or diamond shape having the station at its centre, and a location right on a route between the busy streets of Victoria, St James's Park itself, and Westminster. Holden's difficulty was to craft a building containing offices, circulation passages, storerooms, directors' suites, lavatories and canteens all layered over the station, and to provide each with daylight and efficient connection to the ground and each other. In Britain, the typical office block followed a long-established practice of rising straight up from the perimeter of the site around light wells. The more senior staff had views to the street, and the lesser workers looked onto the light wells and service areas. It is evident from his own writings that Holden scorned this

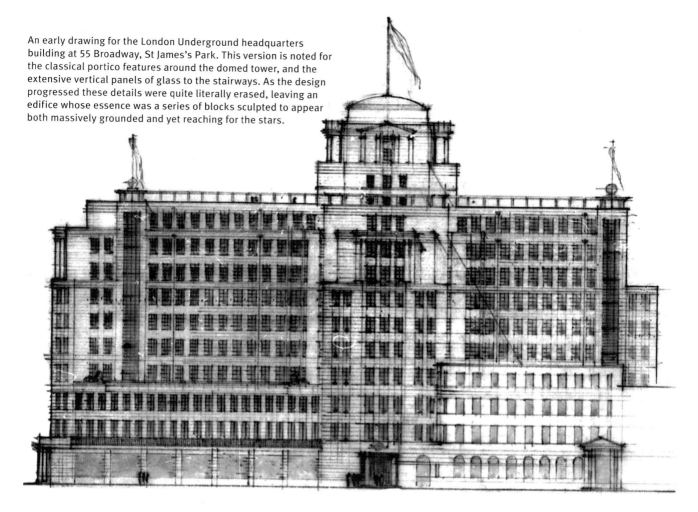

An early drawing for the London Underground headquarters building at 55 Broadway, St James's Park. This version is noted for the classical portico features around the domed tower, and the extensive vertical panels of glass to the stairways. As the design progressed these details were quite literally erased, leaving an edifice whose essence was a series of blocks sculpted to appear both massively grounded and yet reaching for the stars.

approach as undemocratic, and he argued that employing it for the Underground building created more problems than it solved by blocking views across the junction, and making a physical obstacle to pedestrians traversing the area. The Americans were building another way in their cities, where towers ascended out of the central cores of lower blocks, their height and slimness made possible by the innovation of the passenger-carrying lift. This was part of the answer to Holden's problem, and to deal with movement at street level he identified two clear cross routes which were used to generate the building's base plan. Holden described the progress of the planning thus:

the site for this building was most unpromising: after trying many plans it occurred to me that it would be great convenience to an office worker in Victoria Street if he could be allowed to cut across the site to St James's Park station instead of going round the blind corner. A line was drawn along the desirable route of this imaginary passenger. This line produced an outline shape which was, roughly, an isosceles triangle which, bisected, established the central axis of the future plan. I don't think I was ever more excited in my life than when I realised the full possibilities of this cross-shaped plan: good light, no interference with neighbour rights, short corridors, compact centre containing all services complete with lifts and staircase communicating directly with all four wings.[143]

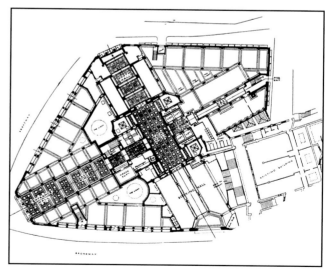

The stepped profile of the building owed much to Holden's taste for such forms in tandem with a sensitive response to the site and the need to comply with the London Building Act, which was intended to prevent tall buildings from dominating the street line with sheer and unbroken façades. Site works started in July 1927. Clad in Portland stone, the ground floor followed the line of the streets, the two

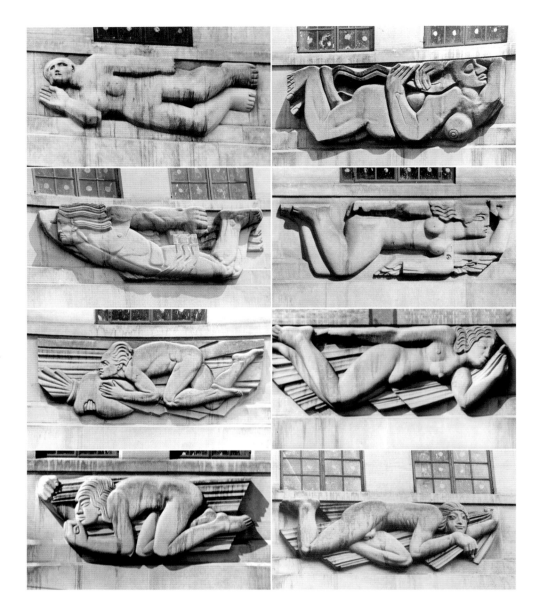

The eight 'Winds' carved as bas reliefs around the seventh floor of the 55 Broadway office building. **From top left to bottom right:** Henry Moore: West Wind; A. H. Gerrard: North Wind; Eric Aumonier: South Wind; Samuel Rabinovitch (incorrectly reported as F. Rabinovitch): West Wind; Allan Wyon: East Wind; Eric Gill: East Wind, South Wind, North Wind.

Opposite page top Artist Jacob Epstein with the sculpture group 'Night'. This photograph was taken inside the timber shelter constructed alongside the building so that Epstein could work on the sculpture in situ, and therefore meet his aim of working as directly as possible with the subject and its material.

Opposite page lower Jacob Epstein's sculpture 'Day', facing towards the rising sun. The photograph shows the sculpture in its amended state after Epstein's work had been criticized for its apparent immodesty.

main frontages on the north and east sides converging at a splayed corner which contained the east entrance to the station. From north to south a second passage made a crossing of the long axis, and gave two further points of access to the station. The ground floor appeared higher than that immediately above it, an impression created by the blue-grey granite columns[144] giving vertical emphasis and the small first floor windows below a banded cornice and parapet. At first floor level, a thick band of stone bore the fluted pattern so favoured by Holden.

At the second floor the cruciform plan became evident in the four wings aligned almost to the compass points. This arrangement gave nearly every office a view to the exterior and sunlight at some point in the day. Above the fifth floor, the wings were set back some distance, to rise two further storeys before being set back once more. Each parapet had the traditional detail of balustrading. There then followed three more floors. Floor ten straddled the building from north to south, having only a slight projection in the other two directions. Above this, the tower continued another three levels, its ascent marked by a series of horizontal bands and setbacks. This piled-up form was used by Adams, Holden & Pearson for St Luke's Hospital, Malta, a project developed in the office concurrently with 55 Broadway. It recurred in Holden's Senate House for the University of London (1931–37), and featured in the speculative designs by Holden for the urban design of London's South Bank.

The massive array of windows were Georgian in character, with small panes in metal frames painted a dark yellow-grey. The north entrance on Petty France was not remarkable. It resembled the style of the Morden stations, rationalised to a single window containing the bullseye motif in coloured glass, and a series of horizontal mouldings in stone to match the rest of the street façade. Bays projected either side of the window, reducing the emphasis of the stone and glass screen.

This skyscraper, which for a time was the most modern and tallest office building in London, carried an ancient reference too. Holden styled it as a modern 'Temple of the Winds' after the water clock in the Roman Forum in Athens, an octagonal building with eight figures carved in its upper walls representing the four winds. In the spirit of Frank Pick's ambition to enrich public space with art, he commissioned a number of sculptors to produce figures for the sides of the wings. Completed with varying degrees of success, the carvings were made partially in studios, and partially by the artists suspended in cradles surrounded by the air currents to which they paid tribute. These bas-reliefs can be seen above the seventh floor.

The sculptures on each wing are:
East wing aligned towards Tothill Street
north face: west wind by Henry Moore,[145]
south face: west wind by Sam Rabinovitch,[146]
West wing aligned towards Palmer Street:
north face: east wind by Eric Gill,[147]
south face: east wind by Allan Wyon.[148]
North wing towards Petty France:
east face: south wind by Eric Gill,
west face: south wind by Eric Aumonier.[149]
South wing towards Broadway:
east face: north wind by Eric Gill,
west face: north wind by A. H. Gerrard.[150]

Holden also wanted art at a level visible to the passer by, and to provide this he chose Jacob Epstein, with whom he had worked some twenty three years previously.[151] Observing that the south-east face of the building was brightly illuminated in the morning, and the north was out of direct sunlight, Epstein made two figure groups called 'Day' and 'Night'. He worked through the winter of 1928–29 on scaffolding behind timber hoardings, cutting the figures out of the stone façades and thereby truly integrating art and architecture. The sculptures offended some viewers and reportedly aroused 'the anger of the Underground Directors',[152] but in doing so attracted press criticism which served to publicise Holden's work.[153] Debate over Epstein's controversial work rumbled on for many years, so that even after world war two Holden was asked to explain the rumour that Epstein had been required to 'perform a small operation on the anatomy of "Day" and that, in fact, he removed 1½ inches (3.8cm) of the offending portion'.[154] Holden's reply was to say that Epstein may have returned to make changes to "Day" as part of his usual working practice, but that he doubted the accuracy of the rumour.[155] The architect noted that "Night" was more successful as a three-dimensional figure than "Day" because it had been carved after Epstein had gained more awareness of the site and situation. Holden's own taste for celebration was more understated. With his early exposure to Arts and Crafts design, he had a deep belief in the role of the workers who realised his designs, and undertook the necessary, but prosaic daily tasks of service. To honour this principle Holden had Pick select the foreman stonemason and the new building's Housekeeper to ceremonially lay foundation stones. Holden declined a Knighthood in the New Year Honours' list of 1948, saying 'I did not want to widen the gap between myself as designer and the workmen who are the partners in my endeavours'.[156]

To the east, entering under the enigmatic yet logical name for the building: 55 Broadway, the access was via a series of doors treated much like the other ground floor bays, but passing into a sumptuous hall described as 'surely the most delightful approach to any station in Great Britain'. In the first two storeys of the building were located the station, public circulation routes from four points on the block, the main hall and lift lobbies for the Underground offices above, and a number of facilities including a shop and enquiry counters. Passages were lined throughout in the rich, if austere, travertine marble which had been used extensively by the Romans. Also lined throughout in travertine, the ticket hall of St James's Park station had faceted columns very like those at Piccadilly Circus, but here clad in marble. For a time, there was an experimental ticket office booth also fabricated from travertine set into a bronze frame structure. The flat columns, or pilasters, which divided the east corridor into bays were completed by the plainest of capitals

flared outwards at their upper ends (this flaring would recur in light units for Sudbury Town and other Holden stations of the early 1930s). Ceilings were of plaster, those in the south and east wings being coffered with square recesses. In the east corridor the ceiling was swept up above the general height to halfway up the first floor, and the walls were punctuated by bronze ventilation grilles. Special glass lamp shades were a further part of the sumptuous styling. To improve the lot of the building's cleaning staff, the junctions between walls and floors were treated like those in a hospital (of which Adams, Holden and Pearson had much design experience), creating curved transitions instead of dust-harbouring corners.

Four lifts lined with bronze panelling and mirrors served the Underground's own offices on floors one, two, three and seven, and tenanted offices on floors four, five, six and eight. Prevailing regulations prevented the ninth floor and the tower being occupied by people. All staff had the benefit of a

roof garden above the ninth floor provided with tubs of plants and deckchairs.[157]

55 Broadway was officially opened on 1 December 1929. The design was awarded the London Architecture Medal in the same year. When the London Passenger Transport Board was created out of the Underground group and many other undertakings on 1 July 1933, 55 Broadway became the centre of bus, long-distance coach, Underground rail, tram and trolleybus operations covering 2000 square miles (5180 square kilometres) across London and the Home Counties. With the start of the second world war it housed part of the Ministry of War Transport, and from 1948 it was part of the British Transport Commission. 55 Broadway remains the headquarters of the Underground.

The west wing was bombed on 14 October 1940 and rebuilt in brick for expediency during January-February 1941. Holden designed a war memorial which was installed in February 1953. The present public areas are also now different, as a result of replanning undertaken by architects Manser Associates in the late 1980s to create a shopping mall on the ground floor and close the central crossing so that a secure reception area could replace the rather restricted concierge post. The east entrance hall, which had been closed early in the building's life and converted to a staff library, was revived from its dormant state as a store-room to become a main access route. A small display was mounted adjacent to the central core of the mall, describing the history of the building. First installed in 1950, a tablet and sculpture memorialising Lord Ashfield was moved from the exterior of the building to the east side of the reception area.[158] To inaugurate the new facilities this was the subject of a ceremony on 5 December 1988 performed by one of Lord Ashfield's successors, the then Chairman of London Regional Transport, Sir Neil Shields.

Ealing Common and Hounslow West

All but one of the Morden line stations had been developed on existing sites, and consequently were designed with the façade as the dominant feature. In outlying districts, such constraints did not apply. After Morden, Underground line extensions took in just such open country on the northern and western fringes of London. Holden could develop his Portland stone station into three dimensions. With this move the double-height vestibule became a true tower form, interpreted variously as a cube, cylinder or prism, and emerged as the new characteristic feature of Underground stations. Extension of the Piccadilly line to Hounslow and South Harrow gave rise to the first two tower stations, on which work began in 1929: Ealing Common (first opened 1 July 1879, rebuilding completed 1 March 1931) and Hounslow West (opened as Hounslow Barracks on 21 July 1874, renamed 1 December 1925, rebuilding completed 5 July 1931). With St Paul's on the Central line, these stations were the first Holden designs to incorporate a ground floor faced in granite to prevent marking and wear. The towers had seven sides, with all but the front windows displaying the Underground symbol in clear and coloured glass. In the Morden line stations a blue enamelled iron frieze had pro-

vided an upper margin to the windows: it was now wrapped right around the tower hiding the edge of the concrete roof slab. These two buildings were the final Holden station designs to have parapet walls concealing their roofs. There was another innovation at Ealing Common, in the introduction of coloured glass for the canopy edge so that it could be illuminated by night, creating a strong blue band of light to emphasise the station name. Shops and advertising panels animated the front.

More evidence of the structural design was visible inside the ticket halls, where the roof beams formed a star pattern with a recessed central portion, modelled at Hounslow West with the familiar shallow steps: another link with the Morden line stations. A second star motif was set into the ticket hall floors of polished cement tiles. The Ealing Common hall contained an enlarged version of the passimeter booking booth, augmented with passenger-operated ticket machines in one side. This cannot have been overly comfortable for the booking clerk. Hounslow West ticket hall had a conventional rectangular passimeter, which can still be seen there although it is now out of use.

Having come from the 55 Broadway project with a mood for visible decoration, Holden engaged the noted designer

Basil Ionides.[159] Ionides had only the dado and frieze of the ticket hall walls to work with, but he succeeded in bringing an atmosphere of gaiety to what would otherwise have been a busy assemblage of walls and structural piers. The dados he finished in terrazzo inset with bands of tile: green with grey at Ealing Common, yellow with pink at Hounslow West. The frieze patterns of square and rectangular tiles were geometric, Art Deco interpretations of the ziggurat in flame red, yellow and pink (at Hounslow West) and the classical key pattern in dove grey, mid grey, charcoal grey, cream and green (at Ealing Common).

There are some original enamelled signs at Ealing Common, and the original finishes largely remain although they have been affected by the installation of electrical equipment. The blue band around the tower at this location was removed some years ago and replaced by some poorly placed blue ceramic tiles. Hounslow West was rebuilt for the opening of the line to Hatton Cross on 19 July 1975, with the old platforms abandoned and tracks realigned through new platform tunnels. The covered way between the station building and the platforms remains of a temporary nature. In the ticket hall, the passimeter was preserved.

Opposite Ealing Common was constrained by its position on a road bridge over the railway. Either end of the building stood forward to create a narrow loggia, and the canopy was correspondingly projected further from the building. Other, separate, shops were added on either side of the station by others at a later date.

Above With space to spare, the Hounslow West building was elongated to include two shop units, behind a forecourt for buses and cars on the north side of the strategically important and busy Bath Road. A proposed motor garage next to the station was not built. Charles Holden's approach to Underground station architecture was increasingly to strip designs of extraneous detail (although he saw functional decoration as valid embellishment). Banded with grey granite to head height, and Portland stone above, the Hounslow West front had a plain and blocky moulding to the parapet and shallow steps in the skirting and around the windows. As first designed, the shops were entered by doors set into short angled walls at either end of the station.

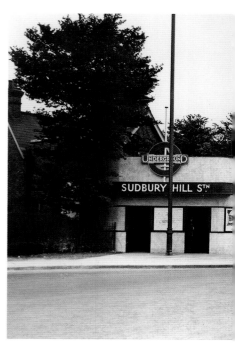

Temporary stations

Whilst stations underwent reconstruction, old buildings had to be wholly or partially demolished. So that passengers might not be deterred from travel, temporary structures made in timber, steel and plaster were provided to house booking offices and limited facilities. Intended to be used only for a matter of six months or a year, the interim installations are an intriguing representation of Holden's earlier stations at Oval and Clapham North, with a parapet wall stepped up in the centre. An example at Boston Manor was even a modernist façade applied to the partially demolished Victorian ticket hall. The exteriors had a light coloured surface and prominent dado panels. One of these constructions outlasted the others by many years. With Northfields being served by a second entrance one overbridge east of the station, South Ealing was in turn to have been moved just under half a mile east to Ascott Avenue. Its old buildings were succeeded by a provisional shelter, but then plans were changed and no move was made. Until 1988 this remained in use, looking increasingly scruffy. It was then

replaced by a more permanent building in pastiche Holden style. At platform level eastbound passengers benefited from a new streamlined canopy and matching waiting room.

Overleaf In January 1932 *The Architect & Building News* commented: 'it is sufficient to say that the architects seem to have attained a truly functional architecture. It is, indeed, a tribute to the Underground Group that it encourages this experimental spirit, as valuable to architecture as it is necessary to efficiency. Finally, it is too modest of the architects to suggest that this station was designed to harmonise with typical suburban houses; surely it is an example which the "Little Palaces of Sudbury" might well follow'.[160]

The Sudbury box

Sudbury Town had opened on 28 June 1903 as a corrugated iron shed station on the Ealing and South Harrow Railway. Preliminary schemes for its redevelopment began with the adaptation by Underground architect Stanley Heaps of the Hounslow West polygonal tower pattern into a brick version. A natural move, given that the design for Hounslow West was just then being realised, but one which showed Heaps following innovation, not initiating it. He was to repeat this approach for his design of Arnos Grove station which followed soon after Sudbury Town.[161] After this Holden's team produced a three storey, box-like design with single central window (continuing the Morden theme of a stained glass bullseye, this time in an arched apex) and entrance, in the style of certain contemporary Dutch station buildings. Inside there would have been a square ticket hall with no fewer than four kiosks and a shop-buffet. Over-massive, and with private accommodation stacked above the station, the proposal was rejected.

Ultimately, a rectangular box was produced, exaggerated in height so that the wings seemed secondary. All the bulk of the earlier schemes had been designed away. Windows were placed in the two long sides of the box only. The street elevation (in this modern idiom 'façade' was considered an inappropriate term for one side of a three-dimensional whole) was a study in the art of proportion and subdivision. Three panels of plain brick bordered two pairs of windows divided by much narrower piers. Above the four openings, the glazing was ordered into thirty-two near-squares which served to unify the arrangement of elements, and these panels were further divided into thirds horizontally.

The one feature which more than any other distinguished this station as a new move in railway architecture was the flat, overhanging roof described by Holden as a concrete lid to the brick box. Cast in place directly onto the brickwork, leaking cement prompted subsequent projects to be built around a concrete frame, but the overall appearance of deep cornice and gently stepped eaves gave a bold clarity of the walls and became a signature of Underground stations throughout the 1930s. Observing the work of European architects such as Le Corbusier,[162] Holden played with the surface treatment of the concrete. It is not true to claim that he merely respected the concept of truth to materials by leaving the concrete with the marks of the timber boards in which it was cast, for he also took pains to have much of the material, here and at other stations, ground and polished to a smooth surface which resembled an artificial stone. Harmonious as this design now seems, it was starkly plain in comparison to the monotonous semi-detached villas huddled around it and from which its passengers came. A drawing by A. Bryett was shown in the architectural exhibition at London's Royal Academy in 1931. Reviewing the works, Baird Dennison wrote for the *Architects' Journal* that 'Sudbury Town projects itself ... by virtue of its actuality, from the potpourri of lavender-scented memories from all our yesterdays ... Here [English station design] is suddenly revitalised ... its functionalism is of an un-provocative and genially inviting nature'.[163]

Regarding the station from the street on the north side, the left wing enclosed a staircase up to the footbridge, which itself extended as gentle ramps terminating in simple concrete portals on either side into the road approaches, for the convenience of a easy crossing the railway. Opposite the ramp, a wing wall helped to create a sense of civic order in the forecourt for cars and terminating buses. On the right of the ticket hall, a lower building enclosed the station buffet, accessible from street and train and generously glazed. A cycle store to the left and waiting room alongside the buffet were open-plan extensions of the ticket hall. For the secondary entrance from Orchard Gate, a small brick and glass kiosk gave shelter for the ticket collecting staff. A walk to the Harrow end of the platforms, and a glance back past the rounded end of the main waiting room reveals the way in which the footbridge was integrated with the overall design. Concrete was used extensively here to form the roofs of the waiting areas and the fully cantilevered canopies on both platforms. Given the short development and construction period, the project was very successful, and established the template for many Underground stations built in London throughout the 1930s. On the cornices to both street and platform, a neon sign proclaimed the station name in red with a blue frame by night, hovering above the welcoming glow of the windows.[164]

The neon signs were removed before 1958, and the frontage has undergone a series of alterations and restorations over the years with a variety of signs fixed to the exterior. The present bar and circle symbol with replica Underground motif is a fanciful but incorrect fixture. Sudbury Town was listed as being of special architectural and historical interest on 19 February 1971, one of the first four Underground stations to be afforded this statutory protection. For many years the buffet and newsagent's kiosk have been out of use. The ticket hall was rebuilt in 1986–7 to incorporate a new ticket office and ticket machines, partly in the former cycle store, and the timber passimeter booking booth has been preserved with an original ticket issuing machine. Much of it is now painted. Lamp posts are replicas of the originals. Many years ago the interior floodlights were removed, and the austerity of the hall has become crowded by the introduction of contemporary light fittings and their attendant wiring ducts.

Bricks were supplied from a works some miles north in Buckinghamshire, where they were hand made. Laid in a traditional English bond pattern, they were chosen for their old English appearance and capacity to weather well. Yet the windows were the result of the latest processes in manufacturing. Through their stippled glass grid streamed the constant north light, giving an even brightness to the interior, and their steel frames were painted dark blue to match the sky reflected on the glass.

Above right Sudbury Town ticket hall and platform buildings below the cantilevered concrete canopy. The neon tube station name sign is seen below the cornice.

Right The first ticket hall lighting, built into poster stands, was criticized by Frank Pick as 'two illuminated tombstones[165]. They were replaced by these flared columns resembling machine-made flowers, with their shafts painted in yellow graduated to white, Ticket hall colours complemented the red-grey-mauve bricks: the ceiling was grey and saxe blue, and the direction signs, with their Johnston lettering[166], were blue and cream.

Arnos Grove came into public use on 19 September 1932, and served as the temporary terminus of the Piccadilly line extension from Finsbury Park until 13 March 1933. Charles Hutton, who handled the scheme within the Adams, Holden and Pearson office, explained that Arnos Grove was designed during the completion of Sudbury Town, and his work was considerably disrupted by construction difficulties at the latter station. Hutton had quickly to redraft the scheme, and took the opportunity to move away from Holden's traditional brick wall plus concrete roof method, adopting instead the more expedient approach of making a full reinforced concrete frame, columns and roof, around which the brick walls were added afterwards. The whole project took only six months. Free of any neighbouring building, and subject to the practical view that a circular plan enabled the freest flow of travellers, a high cylindrical ticket hall was central to the design.[167] The scale of the tower is interesting: at 30 feet (9.1m), it is just 3 feet (0.9m) higher than Sudbury Town, and the drum at 57 feet (17.4m) is only 3 feet (0.9m) wider that the Sudbury Town tower. The drum sits on a broader base, which itself continues effortlessly out to the side to form a bridge parapet. Laid in a mixture of bonds, Buckinghamshire multi-coloured facing brickwork gives the impression of an old English 'diaper' diagonal pattern. For the lower buildings, the architects chose a mottled (or 'brindled') hard blue-brown brick from Staffordshire which corresponded to those used in the adjacent bridge over the railway. Behind the bridge, the walkway from the ticket hall down to the platforms was a bright white, being made entirely from reinforced concrete.

Arnos Grove was listed as being of special architectural interest on 19 February 1971. A member of the station staff here has written on the architecture and design of the Piccadilly line.[169] By the end of the 1980s the station was showing signs of wear and vandalism. It was subsequently restored with meticulous care. A decade since the work, there has been a marked increase in the array of applied equipment throughout the station including numerous security cameras, and the colour scheme of the painted areas has been altered. Closed in 1988 and restored in 1990 the passimeter, which seems cramped and awkward as a place of work, now contains an exhibition of the work undertaken by Charles Holden for the Underground. Recently it has had the original linoleum cladding replaced by new material. On the platforms, lighting ducts have been installed with some sympathy for the original design, but the addition of an ungainly metal footbridge and crude cabins for staff at either end of the platforms is disappointing. Nevertheless this building remains one of the iconic small projects of Adams, Holden and Pearson for the Underground, an exemplar of how architecture, design and commercial needs can combine to make a building which positively adds to the public environment.

Above Arnos Grove was described as 'a dramatic climax to the completed portion of the extension. The booking hall ... rises out of the group of little flat-roofed buildings which surround it'.[168]

Opposite The architects wished to make the construction of the hall clearly evident inside the building: the tower appears solid yet light, carried up around sixteen concrete pilasters and a central column which together support the roof. There are eight of the two window units seen in this view, spaced equally around the walls. Standing in the hall, careful inspection will reveal the rainwater downpipes which drain the roof running down the side edge, or reveal, of certain windows. One writer noted the simple elegance of the tower as a circle rising from a square.[170] The lower range of spaces had the corners notched inwards, and the shops, toilets, and staff rooms were neatly planned into the area between the circle of the ticket hall and the perimeter walls. At the entrances, this in-between space contained sheltered waiting areas and a passage for telephone booths. Interior decoration was the most minimal combination of hard blue-brown bricks and polished teak doors, with bronze in the shop fronts and ticket windows. The cylindrical design appears to have been too revolutionary for Frank Pick who, outnumbered on the New Works Committee, signed approval for it on 14 August 1931 with the words 'under protest'.

Above The exposed concrete interior of the Arnos Grove footbridge.

Left and Bottom Like the footbridge, platform buildings, canopies and lamp standards were fabricated entirely from reinforced concrete to a design supervised by Stanley Heaps. Raised portions of the canopies were glazed to introduce further light, and to 'counteract the sense of depression so often experienced in railway stations'.[171] To minimise marking, lower parts of the walls were painted in the style of the time with a dark colour bordered by a contrasting stripe. Three platforms were provided, enabling terminating trains to occupy the central track without disrupting through services.

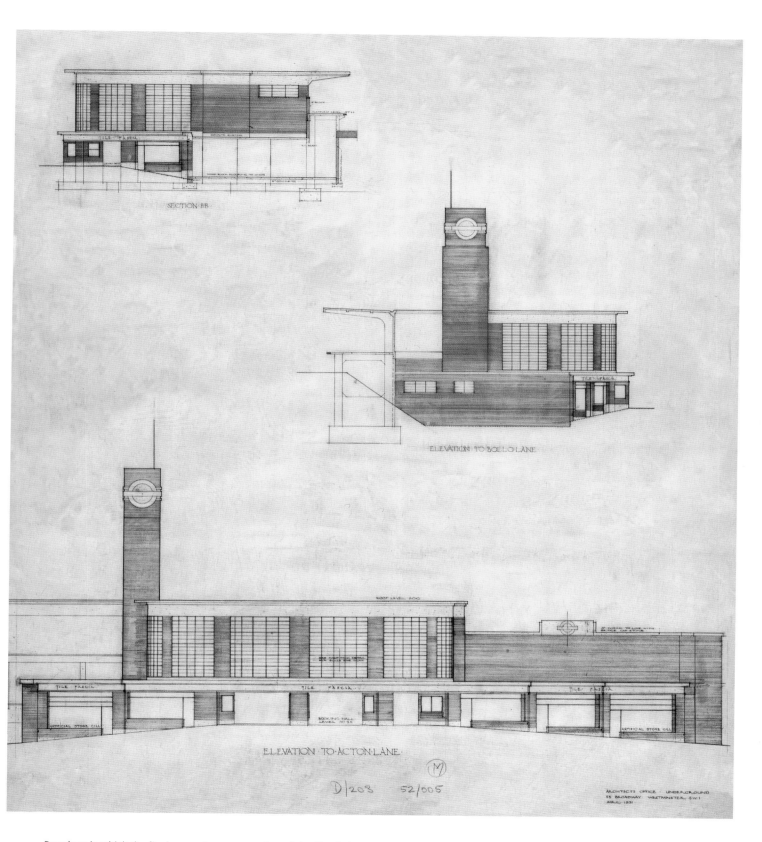

Drawings in which the final general arrangements and details of Chiswick Park station are presented. The encircled 'M' indicates that the drawings have been recorded on microfilm.

Chiswick Park

Ultimately the product of Stanley Heaps, the design for Chiswick Park originated in the Adams, Holden and Pearson office. Chiswick Park suggests a partially successful experiment to marry the Arnos Grove design with a restricted street corner site below a viaduct – exactly the opposite situation to Arnos Grove. By creating a semi-circular hall the windswept yard of the old station was superseded by sheltered accommodation.

The outcome was imposing enough, but lacked the delicacy and clarity of Arnos Grove due to Chiswick Park's exterior design and internal features. The tower had originated in a sketch scheme by Holden's office that showed a tall, slender design terminating with an abstracted bar and circle sky sign in blue and red neon tubes.[172]

In built form, the station retained the vestiges of the tower as a shallow block on the right of the ticket hall, whilst the vertical feature was moved to the left and made shorter. In the grouping of tower and semi-circular drum, through to the positioning of entrances below the wrap-around canopy,

this design was very similar to Brest station, French State Railways by Urbain Cassan.[173]

Forming the piers between the windows, bricks included a handmade variety of mixed red hues. A series of shops took up the triangular space between road, building and viaduct. Here the deep roof cornice was interrupted by application of the station and company names in bronze lettering, and the central column supporting the ticket hall roof inside the building was left as a simple square form without the subtle faceting of Arnos Grove. Planning of the hall in its awkward setting against the viaduct created an unbalanced use of space: all passenger movements were concentrated on the right side, with the ticket sales and collection point placed midway between the three entrances and a narrow subway to the platform stairs. The left side of the hall had two shops, a staff office and telephone booths. A ring of coffered and fluted panels decorated the ceiling. In the late 1980s the hall interior was rebuilt with a booking office and automatic machine unit offering secure operating conditions. This has detracted from the space and balance of the hall.

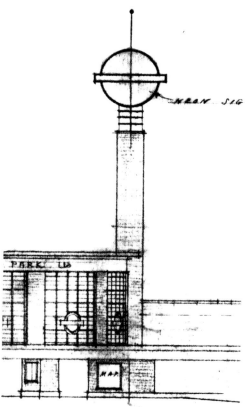

Above Ticket hall at Chiswick Park, with the original passimeter booking booth and an array of ticket issuing machines.

Above right Original proposal for Chiswick Park, showing a tower on the opposite side of the ticket hall and a massive neon tube bar and circle Underground 'sky sign'.

Right The platforms located on the viaduct over the station were distinguished by bracketed concrete canopies, left with the marks of the wooden boards in which they had been cast[174]. Tiled panels gave prominence to the station name.

Manor House[175] occupied space beneath the intersection of two main roads on the eastern perimeter of Finsbury Park, and was mostly below ground. The ticket hall assumed a curious shape in plan, derived from the alignment of the several stairways and subways between street, station and tram loading islands: 'the [passenger] movement graph produced a very definite pattern … Any space not enclosed by this pattern was either dead space or might be used for additional accommodation such as staff room, shops, bookstall or for hesitant passengers or public'.[176] To give interest in this confined space, skilled plasterers made a ceiling patterned with interlocking concentric circles which fitted the difficult plan without appearing fragmented. A terrazzo-like material with the trade name 'Biancola' gave a smooth cream-white finish to the walls, and there were kiosks in the hall, one with a cylindrical display case attracting the traveller's eye yet fitting the flow of movement. Surface buildings comprised a small bus passenger shelter and stairwell entrance on Green Lanes and the tram passenger canopies placed directly over subway entrances, all designed by Adams, Holden and Pearson as part of this integrated transport hub. Trams

serving these shelters ceased in 1939, and the canopies were demolished in 1951. When the Victoria line was planned in the 1950s it was proposed that the line would serve Manor House. This did not occur. Unlike most other Holden stations, Manor House is not protected by statutory listing. It underwent extensive refurbishment works in 2004–05, which encompassed the replacement of all original tiling in the lower station levels with replica finishes. Platforms have extensive cable ductwork over the tiles. Escalators have been replaced and the uplighter columns removed. The ticket hall ceiling remains with some original lamps, but has been damaged by the fitting of fluorescent lights. One shopfront has been crudely rebuilt as a staff room.

Above The tram station at Manor House, with stairs connecting to the railway ticket hall.

Opposite upper The modest surface building, doubling as a bus and tram passenger shelter.

Opposite lower The asymmetrical ticket hall with its distinctive ceiling decoration.

Turnpike Lane too was below ground, set to one side of an intersection of five roads so that the basement level ticket hall, enclosed by a box type tower for natural light and ventilation, was aligned with pedestrian tunnels. Positioning of windows in the tower marked a change from foregoing designs as the main wall had one large central panel of glass bounded by two narrower windows.[177] A similar arrangement was placed between the stairwell and the ticket hall interior. Other windows punctuated the side walls. The gallery in front of the tower enclosed stairways from the east and west, and a low-level kiosk projected from its west end. Beside the ticket hall a ventilation tower formed an additional landmark. Behind this tower, directly over the escalator shaft, a canteen for staff was provided. To preserve the clean lines of the tower other necessary facilities were placed on the perimeter of the ticket hall without any presence at ground level: these included a large lobby for telephone booths, a cloakroom, staff rooms, an auxiliary booking office, confectionery shop, newspaper stall, tobacco stall and other rooms.

In the late 1980s the ticket hall was rebuilt with a booking office in place of the tram island subway. The station was statutorily listed on 17 May 1994. By this time however, all original uplighters had been removed from the ticket hall, though they remain in the lower concourse. New escalators were installed with specially designed lighting units in the spirit of Holden's work. The platforms retain their original tiles and ventilator grilles.

To improve facilities for interchange passengers, the bus station at Turnpike Lane was redeveloped in the late 1990s by architects The Rogers Partnership. The cinema was demolished to create a new route for buses, and a new building provided behind the retained façade of the shopping parade.

Above Turnpike Lane was developed as a civic hub. A bus station behind the railway building, and tram waiting shelters in a nearby road (connected to the ticket hall by subways) were linked by a single storey block on Langham Road, treated with neatly rounded ends and a matching clerestory roof, to provide extensive lavatory accommodation for the public, railway staff and kiosk tenants. Further buildings were added later by other architects.

Previous spread Platform tunnels on the extension followed the German practice of being lined almost entirely in cream tiles, a product of the Poole Pottery. There were limited bands of colour to outline poster panels, seat recesses and other punctuations in the walls; these colours were chrome yellow, flame red, mid-chrome green and cobalt blue. As an aid to ventilation, air was passed through ducts in the platform walls, and these openings were covered by grilles designed by silversmith Harold Stabler to represent an idealised allusion to the localities served (even at the time more myth than reality). Much like the work of Edgar Brandt, who had provided metal panels for the lift interiors at London's Selfridges department store, Stabler's grilles followed stylised art deco imagery with a hint too of Japanese design and a nostalgic longing for rural life. One of these 'Arts and Crafts' grilles can be seen by the arch.

The Turnpike Lane building plan produced a near symmetrical arrangement of ticket booth, four blocks of ticket machines and two lighting standards. The eye was naturally led towards the separate escalator hall by two close-set rows of large opal glass lamp units. Further experimentation in hardwearing materials saw the spaces lined with dark brown quarry tiles of the type more commonly used for floors in hospitals and kitchens. These have proved extremely durable. In line with ground level a deep concrete ring beam supported the tower and formed a frieze polished to reveal the Portland stone aggregate. Above the beam, the brown theme was continued with Welsh bricks. This bright, functional celebration of efficient travel is impressive.

Lower escalator concourse at Turnpike Lane. The large curved grilles were to reduce the discomfort of air moving quickly through the escalator shaft as trains moved through the station.

Wood Green is an interesting example of how the brick box could be adapted to a fully enclosed location. Bowing outwards, the front implies the presence of a three-dimensional building and distracts the eye from the steeply inclined ground level. There is more brickwork than window here, with the glazing a narrow slit in three parts bounded at each end by a ventilation tower, and below by a deep canopy with a gently stepped soffit. At the north end of the station a small block contained a shop and office. Safe entry and exit on this busy corner was assisted by short lengths of iron balustrading projecting out from the building. The railing posts carry a disc and diamond motif by Holden on other projects including his Senate House for the University of London in Bloomsbury.

The ticket hall was elliptical in plan, lit from above by clerestory windows set high in a trapezoid roof light braced by four deep reinforced concrete beams. More concrete formed a band around the upper walls, with a further band at first floor level decorated by a shallow stepped pattern. Above the ground floor walls lined with brown quarry tiles, brickwork here varied subtly from other stations on the line, being carried out in brown-grey bricks except for the sides of the window openings and the recess in the back wall, all of which were highlighted using orange-red bricks. Hard wearing granite lined lower parts of the exterior walls. The hall had the usual passimeter booking booth, with the escalators beyond. In the rear of the building, a special exhibition area two thirds as big as the ticket hall was incorporated for the Underground or approved organizations to provide displays. It was operated in this way only for a short time, and then converted to a staff club room. Other public and staff rooms were squeezed into available space in the basement, ground and first floors around the hall.

Above the façade, the north tower has been raised beyond its original height. Shopfronts are much altered. A new booking office was built against the back and side wall in 1988, in front of the exhibition hall. This has been decorated with a rough approximation of the motifs present in the platform ventilation grilles. Interior concrete surfaces have been painted over. Escalators have been replaced, and now operate beneath heavy lighting ducts which have supplanted the uplighters removed from both the escalator balustrades and the lower concourse. An enclosure was built into the concourse some years ago, breaking the symmetry. Platforms feature original tiling, name board signs, and headwall units with clocks.

Left Original drawing for Wood Green in which the façade of a rectangular ticket hall tower is seen superimposed on the curved frontage.

Below Plan of the station with ticket hall fitted neatly into the site and the surplus space above it used to develop an exhibition area. Note how the group of six telephone kiosks is positioned centrally but out of the main traffic routes.

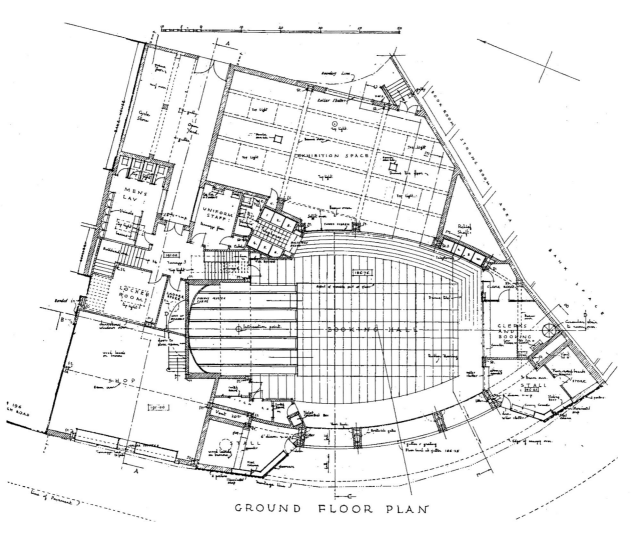

GROUND FLOOR PLAN

Bounds Green

Adams, Holden and Pearson worked with Charles James to produced the fully detailed designs for Bounds Green and Oakwood. James made certain departures from the standard Holden pattern. The Bounds Green ticket hall was unique on the system in having eight sides. The octagon suited the restricted site, and allowed greater expanses of window to be inserted into the splayed corners; it also correlated with the modernist taste for windows which demonstrated the marvel of roofs staying in place apparently without support.[178] A ventilation tower set slightly back from the octagon provided an interesting contrast in forms. The uncompromising rigour of the louvres set right around the tower suggested that the concrete slab roof floated effortlessly above. A thin canopy ran the length of the two public sides of the station, with the deep frieze below it identified by faience tiles of a green hue rather than the blue found elsewhere. James had specified the green and used it again for the station at Oakwood, also choosing it for the window frames at Bounds Green and signs at Oakwood. Enclosing the escalator hall a lower building extended along Bounds Green Road, with a single shop unit. On both street frontages a small kiosk curved out from the recessed entrances. The walls here were stepped in profile, another feature which James repeated at Oakwood. These are small details, but exactly the subtle variations which were permitted to distinguish individual projects within the apparently straightforward template of modernity established with Sudbury Town. James also varied

Holden's interior design schemes by lining the hall up to first floor level with mid-grey tiles between a black dado and frieze inset with flame red, and below a cream frieze. Above, the tower walls were plastered and painted, with the ceiling divided into six segments by the roof beams.

A ticket office was installed in place of the passimeter in the late 1980s. Restoration of the building has meant that replica signs have been fitted on the exterior, although the concrete has been painted over. The name fascia has been altered. Safety and security have brought their own problems: the canopy now features a clumsy railing along its outer edges, and the anti-graffiti paint has become cloudy, discolouring the brickwork. Shop fronts have been disfigured by tenants. The lighting standard in the ticket hall has been added since 1990. Platforms are in near-original condition, with uplighter columns in the lower concourse.

Above Bounds Green station at the time of opening in 1932.

Opposite page First scheme by Adams, Holden and Pearson for Southgate station, showing an elliptical entrance building at street level which would have carried a residential development on the storey above and across the short section of curved roadway.

Southgate

A casual wanderer into the now busy suburb of Southgate might take a bus further into the suburbs, or join the Underground into central London without really noticing the station precincts. Pause however to look around, and Southgate is still recognizable as the most complete transport interchange achieved by Adams, Holden and Pearson. A whole quadrant of land was cleared to realize this work, a road (Crown Lane) diverted, and a new road (Ashfield Parade) provided. With the ticket hall set on an island, the prospect arose of forming a bus station alongside the railway building, populated additionally by a number of shops to increase revenue to the Underground. At first, Adams, Holden and Pearson drafted a building covering the entire island with a lozenge-like outline resembling a circle compressed on two sides. Over the station offices would be two further floors with some twenty residential flats, bridging the bus pull-in at each end. With a semi-circular booking hall and three large shops, this bulky, indeterminate structure would have been little more than a typical inner urban block of the 1930s, with poor external circulation space. Further development generated the solution: a perfectly circular railway station with public areas on two sides, in front of a two storey arcaded building forming the shopping parade.[179] In the best possible way, this design was suburban in scale, and urban in character.

Opened 13 March 1933, Southgate used the round plan of Arnos Grove, adapted for a station with escalators which needed a relatively low roofline. There is no ticket hall tower as such, but instead a continuous strip of windows below the roof. This lightness was achieved by extending the frame construction technique to use slim steel columns as vertical supports, around the outside of the clerestory windows. Architectural details and decoration here suggest a different designer, and a different design approach that set Southgate apart from other stations on the extension. With all the framing of the roof carried on its upper side, the hall ceiling presented a smooth surface with the slightest ripples around a central column. Emerging from the centre of the passimeter booking booth, this column rises through the station as a supporting element, and is then transformed into a decorative object unique on the Underground: a modernistic lighting beacon of pre-cast concrete blocks, bronze, white glass and a copper ball resembling equipment from a power station.[180] Exterior walls comprised mainly glass and bronze shopfronts with panels of Buckinghamshire multi-coloured brick, all above a Cornish grey granite plinth. The full circumference of the station had a projecting concrete canopy, lit from below by a continuous trough which ingeniously combined lamps and the station name on blue glass. The entrance portals are graduated in height from hall to street with two steps, each featuring four inset lamp units.

Southgate lies on high ground, and its platforms are in short lengths of tunnel lined with cream and chrome yellow tiles. This station was restored circa 1991 and retains the Holden-designed lighting columns in the lower concourse. These interesting fitments, installed throughout the extension, combine classical detail with contemporary ingenuity in the use of lamps both around the perimeter dish and in the flared and stepped plaster reflectors; by this means an even light was obtained in the arched space. Escalator shaft column lights of a type once common on the Underground may still be seen at this station.[181]

As a reprise of the cylindrical forms, a small round florist's kiosk was projected to occupy the south-east lawn, which would be converted to a plant nursery and seating area complete with sculpture figure. Added to plans after the main station was completed, this charming enhancement never occurred.[182] Total development of station sites as transport-shopping-interchanges was planned also for Oakwood and Cockfosters on the line north of Southgate: neither project came to fruition.[183] Success of the project can be gauged by the press comment that this was 'yet another example of the enterprise of the London Passenger Transport Board in setting a sterling example to local authorities in general and to town-planning authorities in particular. For it could well serve as a model for the first elements in suburban development'.[184] Southgate formed a model for Hanger Lane station on the Central line, designed by Brian Lewis and Frederick Curtis for the Great Western Railway and opened 30 June 1947.

There is much to be reported about the subsequent history of the station and its environs. One of the entrances was closed to make space for a ticket office in the late 1980s. Restoration of the building's escalators in 1989 was heralded on posters as 'Going up at Southgate: 1930s style'. Walls, windows and roof underwent renewal too, with paintwork reproducing the finishes applied when the building was new, and replica signs fitted. Station staff use the preserved passimeter booking booth. Shop fascias have been controlled to ensure that their names are displayed in a version of the Underground's Johnston typeface. On the platforms, the strip lighting installed during the 1960s continues to give service. Wall tiles are original, and are in places damaged by damp penetrating the tunnels. Excellent as the renewal programme was, its achievements have faded over the last decade. Concrete in the station roof is deteriorating superficially. The station has been subject to a number of restoration projects to maintain its appearance in the face of present-day vandalism and graffiti.

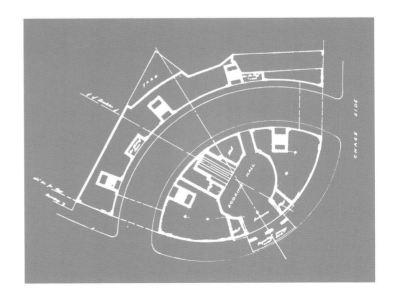

Photographs of Southgate taken soon after opening show the wider urban planning of the station site. As we have seen, the circular station was located on an elliptical island. Each end of the ellipse, in line with the entrance and exit of the bus lay-by, included combined waiting shelter/timetable stand/floodlighting mast, and Underground bar and circle symbol at high level. There were also triangular beds of grass.

Cream and black tiles lined the interior, with an applied bronze strip at head height, bronze fittings for the kiosk fronts, and panels below kiosk windows which were the same patterned panels as those on the exterior, but here made in bronze.

Below With a part round bus inspector's room, passengers' waiting room, staff and public lavatories, the parade of shops was completed by a large rotunda at the south end. Built in same brick as the station, and with details in artificial stone and black Belgian marble mosaic tiles, the parade had as its central feature a large clock, confirming the civic ambitions of the development. In the centre of the arcade a passage led through to the rear service road with its second set of shop windows. Above the shops were spaces for stores, workrooms or residential flats, and the building was designed to take a third floor if future needs made it viable.

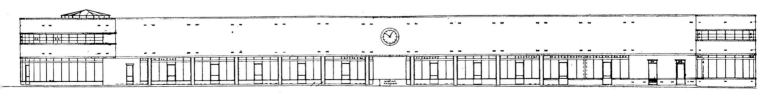

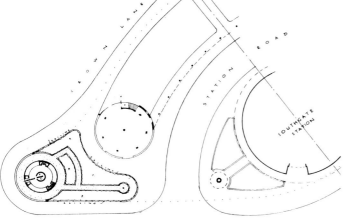

Above By night an eerie glow emanated from the station, as though it were a giant electrical device. The beacon above the roof resembles closely a form of power cell, and is reminiscent of the film *Metropolis*.

Left Adams, Holden and Pearson proposed that a small florist's shop and plant nursery be built adjacent to the shopping centre. This was not developed.

Oakwood

On 13 March 1933 the Piccadilly line extended a further stage to Oakwood. Building in open space gave rise to the primary issue of what to call the station: it would be the first landmark and therefore would serve to give a name to the locality. A number of proposals included the sylvan Merryhills and Oakwood, and the more literal East Barnet, a title recorded on some of the design drawings.[185] Midway between Barnet and Enfield, the station could as easily be called Enfield West, and this was the name adopted for the opening. Soon the suffix Oakwood was added, and finally Oakwood retained as the sole name.

This was the second and final station designed in detail by Charles James under Holden's supervision. With an entirely open rural site, the only constraint on the scale of the station was the width of the railway cutting beneath it, determined by the span of girders, the depth of those girders, and the corresponding height of the trains and ultimate cost of removing earth for the cutting. The station was noted for being 'a definite advance on the rectangular type [of station] … the principal difference being in the large marquise (or canopy) over the main entrance and the extensive double approach to the booking hall'.[186] The bulk of the tower was dissolved into light by the five windows to road and railway, and two in each end wall. Proportions of the plan were as follows: the width of the tower was divided into three central bays of equal width, with two slightly wider outer bays, and three equal bays in its depth. The front elevation was symmetrical, with two large shops in the wings. All the details, including the unusually elaborate moulding to the concrete

fascia and cornice, contributed to a feeling of great solidity. Oakwood shared design features with James's other station at Bounds Green: the lower walls were stepped inwards, and green tiles appeared in the name frieze instead of blue, contrasting with the grey and red bricks.

Making use of cantilever principles to create a dynamic form, a canopy designed by the Underground office of Stanley Heaps sheltered half the single island platform's length and was paralleled on the outside of the tracks by high concrete screens and advertisement hoardings. The 'ingenuity and care lavished upon the truly logical and functional architecture'[187] of the concrete structure encompassed spaces for seats, signs, clocks, lamps, posters and vending machines. Heaps selected an elephant grey dado rising from a black skirting to be topped by a green band for the platform level colour scheme, with yellow and pale primrose panels.[188] One journal stated that this canopy design had been 'standardized for open stations': this was not the case.[189]

Oakwood would later be cited as being too large for traffic requirements; neither it nor the terminus at Cockfosters achieved their full capacity due to the slow development of housing in the area. It was listed Grade II on 19 February 1971. Installation of the ticket office was well integrated with the design. The passimeter has been retained out of use. In the vestibule, the kiosk is a minicab office. Under the front canopy the station name panel is not original. Shop fascias have been altered. Original cylindrical lamp units, signal lamps and clocks are present on the platforms; there are traces too of the bright green tiles used to frame poster panels.

Top View from the entrance vestibule, past the double-sided kiosk and into the ticket hall with the passimeter in the centre and ticket machines to its right. Beyond are the draught-proofing double doors to the gallery and platform stairs. The green colour scheme of the exterior was continued in the ticket hall, where shop fronts and some enamelled signs were coloured green against the background of blue-black glazed bricks, and down onto the platforms as tile borders to posters. An indication of the scale of traffic expected, and old customs of service, was the provision of rooms for both male and female lavatory attendants.[190] The hall had a coffered ceiling and extensive natural lighting, features which

can be compared directly to P. C. Hardwick's Great Hall of 1849 at London's Euston station (demolished).

Above left Oakwood platforms, seen here when the station was still called Enfield West, were sheltered by a canopy which demonstrated the potential of reinforced concrete to produce soaring, expressively functional forms. Three freestanding lighting standards combined with name boards and poster panels made more use of cantilevering on a smaller scale.

Above right The coat of arms of Southgate Urban District Council, then recently awarded and proudly displayed at the new station.

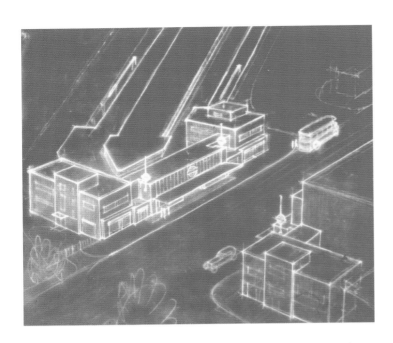

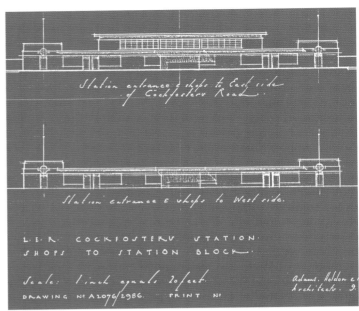

Above Cockfosters was subject to several preliminary proposals, aimed at stimulating development in the area. The architects had first wanted a ticket hall on the south side of Cockfosters Road with low wings terminated by towers reminiscent of Charles Holden's war memorial works. The design evolved into a two storey building bounded at either end by blocks of shops, and with a cinema built over a second station entrance on the north side of the road.

Below Just beyond the station roof's apex is the small surface building, a combined waiting shelter and double stairwell enclosure, with low pylon towers at either end. The simplicity of this building is emphasized by the slender concrete canopy and the friezes of blue tiles outside and inside. Window frames were green. To one side a subsidiary entrance served the car park. The proposed shops were never built.

Cockfosters

Opened on the last day of July 1933, Cockfosters departed from other Holden stations up to this date in not having a box type station building. Set partly in cutting, the station was intended to be submerged below commercial and residential developments, which resulted in the bulk of the design work being invested in the overall roof beneath which 230 feet (70m) of the two island platforms and three tracks were located. At the London end of the platforms an extension of the train shed would incorporate an additional entrance area and footbridge connecting with, alongside the station, a bus stand with inspectors' control tower, a staff institute and a canteen, all enclosed by two parades of shops and a garage for motor cars. None of this was built because further investment was based on increased traffic figures and the Cockfosters area did not develop to produce sufficient traffic. One contemporary account highlighted the rural nature of the area by noting the entrance with its 'liberal area of rubber mat … this provision is one which should be appreciated by travellers from the muddy lanes beyond!'.[191]

The ticket hall was planned symmetrically. At the terminal end the raised roof was completed by an angled junction of the two clerestory windows, creating the sense of a church apse. Indeed out of peak hours this space is quiet enough to suggest the atmosphere of a church. A reviewer praised this station and others on the line for the many elements 'shaped into harmony … the various automata which dispense tickets, chocolates, matches, and the like; all now incorporated in the general design, and not merely adventitious objects'.[192] Concrete featured throughout, so that the roof structure appeared exactly as it had been made: moulded between hundreds of timber boards that formed the shuttering. The portal frames, those arched elements forming the columns and roof

trusses, were placed in pairs at a spacing determined by the position of station name boards (to be seen from inside all tube cars) fixed directly onto panels cast with the structure. Inclined inwards above head height, the portals supported bands of glazing over the centre line of the platforms, intersecting directly with glass blocks inset in the flat lower roofs. This arrangement continued over the ticket hall concourse so that even the deepest recesses received good daylight. Large opal glass spheres lit the interior at night.

It seems the Underground did not give up on expansion plans for Cockfosters. In 1934 Holden's office illustrated how the street level building could be augmented by creating a second floor to form a glazed screen between the pylons, and office blocks added at either end. As with previous ideas, the north entrance was to have been similarly treated and subsumed below a large cinema. The arrangement of sub-surface terminus with triangular apex and subways under adjoining roads was reprised by London Transport architect Stanley Heaps for an early plan (1937) of the proposed last station on the northwards extension of the Northern line to Aldenham.[193]

Cockfosters is an exemplary restoration project. The structure has been carefully conserved and pavement lights replaced. The many original features include the passimeter, train indicator, lamps, signs, seats, floor and wall tiles. On the north side of Cockfosters Road the temporary bus shelter is still in use, now itself also renovated. Replica UNDERGROUND sign graphics have been fitted. Lighting and cabling has been installed sensitively. The colour scheme used on the painted concrete varies from the original and from that applied when the station was refurbished. Sign panels have been painted grey with white borders – this is not authentic.

Left and overleaf The Cockfosters station concourse was lined with shops and railway offices, with a special recess set aside as a waiting area, although how much this was used is debatable given the frequency of trains and the isolation of this spot from the bus stop and car park. Walls in the concourse, and the platform columns, were finished with a grey-green painted dado up to a thin band of yellow, and an olive green band above. Some station name boards here were distinctive for their being without white semicircles inside the red rings, the natural colour of the concrete being used instead.[194]

Acton Town

Opened as Mill Hill Park on 1 July 1879, this station was rebuilt in 1910, and again in 1932–33 by Stanley Heaps with Charles Holden as consultant. Spanning a wide bridge, the ticket hall box was extended laterally with a single storey extension. Within this extension a gallery ran behind the shops to terminate in a recessed entrance. A unique feature in the hall was the frieze band of black and flame red tiles above walls protected from marking by dark brown quarry tiles. As a means of segregating passenger flows, two inter-connected galleries at the rear of the tower linked with four staircases to the two island platforms. (There was formerly a third single-sided platform for trains on the short branch to South Acton.) Partial prefabrication of the structure is evident in the many small concrete slabs which form gallery and walkway roofs. Platform canopies and waiting areas have been made from reinforced concrete cast in-situ. To the south of the railway a staff institute was proposed; in 1934 the Underground's Railway Operating Manager J. P. Thomas urged that this be built as soon as funds permitted.[195] Drawings for this indicate a substantial structure on the same scale as the ticket hall tower, but it was eventually built to a much reduced design. Many original features remain under the layers of electrical equipment, pigeon deterrents and modern information graphics. On the platforms, clocks, enamel signs and train indicator equipment can be seen. Lighting has been replaced. Cable ducts and a footbridge for staff have been added.

Previous page Acton Town under re-construction in 1931.

Top Acton Town as approached from Bollo Lane through the extended lower building, which incorporated a passage behind the shops.

Above The platforms were lit by a profusion of lamp standards designed by Charles Holden.

Alperton

Alperton presented Adams, Holden and Pearson and Stanley Heaps with the problem of designing a building alongside platforms elevated on a viaduct. This situation pertained also at Chiswick Park, and would arise later in the 1930s at South Harrow and Ruislip Manor. The problem lay in the visual relationship of ticket hall to platform structures, which necessarily were close to the hall. It had not been an issue on the Edgware branch of the Northern line (built 1922–24) because the station buildings were single storey, and at stations on the Central line built in the 1940s the matter was addressed by moving the buildings a small distance from the embankment and providing them with low set buildings.[196] Resembling a compressed version of Sudbury Town to which side windows have been added, the grouping of buildings constructed in 1932–33 included a slender arm extending towards the road against the viaduct, to house a kiosk and subway for passengers and a bow-fronted shop. The platform canopies were designed in the same idiom as the station building, but appear to hover above it so that the flat roofline is broken. Given the adjacent viaduct, platforms

here were some distance above ground, necessitating a steep stair climb. To improve passenger access, London Transport obtained a complete escalator from the 'Dome of Discovery' at the 1951 Festival of Britain, and brought it into use at Alperton on 27 November 1955 to carry passengers up to the London-bound platform. Travellers were informed of this fact by a small plaque fixed near the escalator. The unit was taken out of use from 23 September 1988 and the upper and lower lobbies boarded over. Part of the ticket hall has now been given up for a booking office enclosure. A cabling system has been added prominently to platform canopies. The shops which remain in use here have been affected by uncontrolled fascia design and additional graphics applied to their windows. Safety railings now disturb the line of the canopy and the view of the tower.

Above Alperton in 1933. Here the ticket hall tower, based on Sudbury Town, has been creatively adapted to the awkward site against the viaduct, and the platform level structures harmonised with those below.

Northfields

To run a Piccadilly line service over the former District line branch to Hounslow West, a new depot was required for the extra railway vehicles, and this required demolition of the old Northfields station.[197] The official opening date of the Holden and Heaps-designed facility is given as 18 December 1932. Set behind a generous pedestrian forecourt, the rectangular box form was here rotated ninety degrees to present one narrow window to the street and three large windows in each side wall above a long ticket hall running back towards to the footbridge and platforms. Shop units occupied the lower front of the building. The entrance openings were as wide as the tower, so that travellers could traverse the interior without obstruction and the view from the street was clear to the back of the ticket hall. Set forward slightly in the centre, the ground floor roof created the impression of a frontage set between two screen walls behind which were the various station offices. Wing walls flanked the forecourt, providing advertising at the street edge with their two mast-mounted signs. One drawback of this scheme is that the forecourt was devoid of any interesting elements besides the façade itself.

As another experiment in making walls damage resistant, blue-black glazed bricks faced the central section of the street elevation and continued as a lining to the ticket hall, with red bricks on either side and in the tower, all laid in Flemish bond which gave an even overall pattern. The concrete mix used for Northfields incorporated two different aggregates for variety: Portland stone and Kentish rag stone.

In common with Oakwood, the ticket hall ceiling at Northfields featured deep beams creating ninety coffered recesses. An interesting variation in planning occurred here: around the ticket hall the weight of the tower walls was carried down not through solid walls but in two rows of columns

forming vestibules at front and rear of the building, and loggias to either side lit from above by glass blocks in the roof. The side spaces included toilets, an auxiliary booking office, and telephone booths. To improve the convenience of passengers and staff, a cycle store could be found deep inside, and beyond this a covered footway to the signal cabin.

Design of the structures on the two island platforms has much in common with Acton Town, utilising pairs of supporting panels to enclose seat areas and carry station name boards set at regular intervals. The canopies are of the frame and slab construction inaugurated for similar works at Arnos Grove. The loggia around the ticket hall remains on three sides, one having been utilised for the booking office installed in the late 1980s. Specially commissioned combined seating and uplighter units were installed here and at Gants Hill in 1993. Platform canopies have been restored and the concrete painted. Original train describer units are present together with renovated platform clocks. Lamp standards are recent facsimiles.

Opposite page above The perfectly symmetrical road frontage at Northfields, 1933. Note that the central portion of the ground level building is finished with black glazed bricks to reduce marking by passengers.

Opposite page below The narrow front of the ticket hall tower was deceptive, it having been elongated at ninety degrees to the roadway. Beyond the tower concrete covered ways gave access to the platforms and the signal cabin seen set into the cutting on middle left.

Above On either side of the Northfields ticket hall a loggia, or recessed walkway, facilitated free passage past the activities of the ticket issuing and collecting functions. The black glazed brick walls have been continued in from the street frontage.

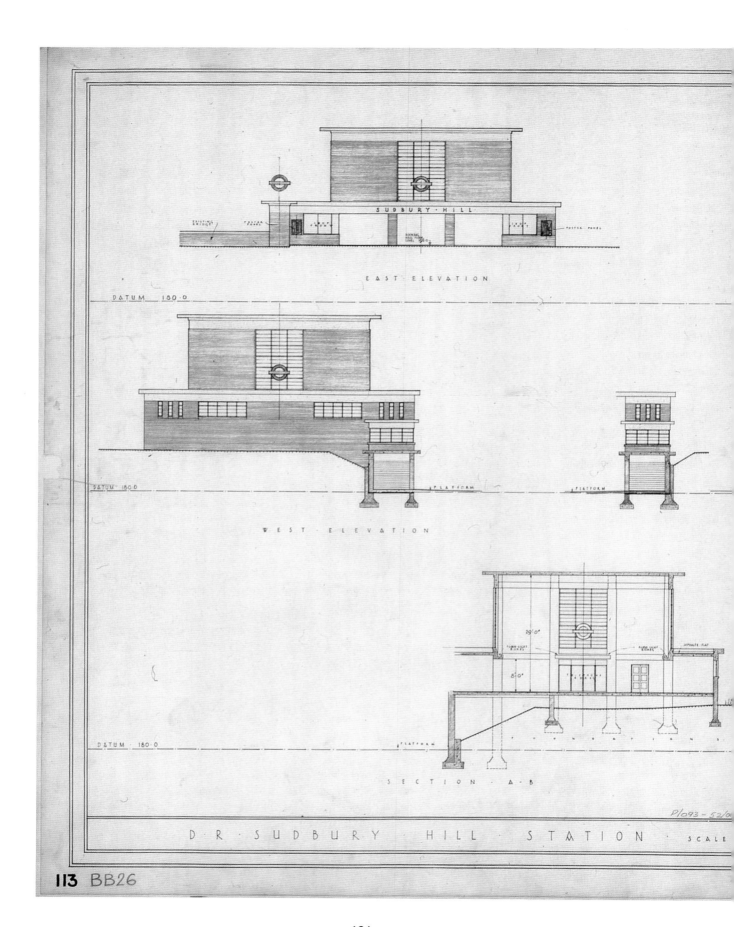

EAST·ELEVATION

DATUM 180·0

SUDBURY·HILL

WEST·ELEVATION

DATUM 180·0

SECTION·A·B

DATUM 180·0

D·R·SUDBURY·HILL·STATION·SCALE

P/093-52/0

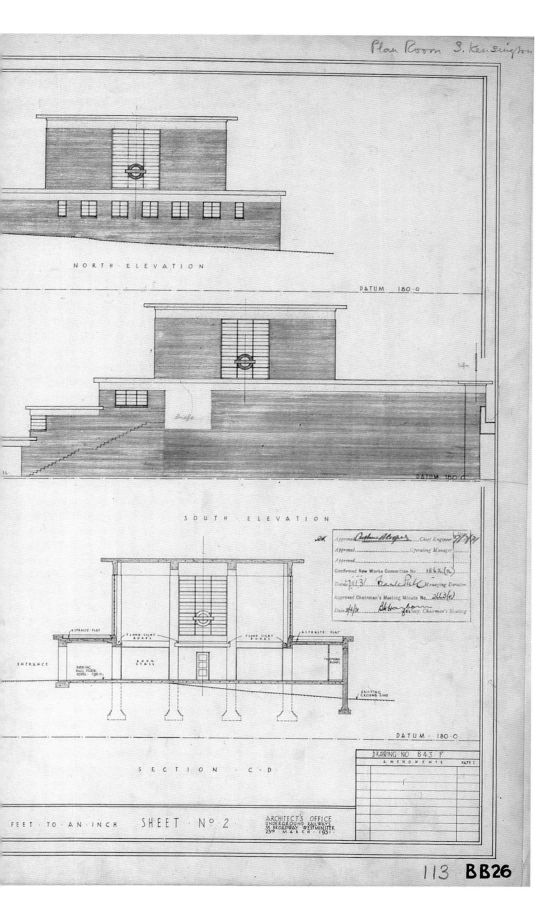

Plan Room S. Kensington

NORTH ELEVATION

DATUM 180·0

SOUTH ELEVATION

DATUM 180·0

SECTION · C·D

DATUM · 180·0

DRAWING NO 843·F

FEET·TO·AN·INCH SHEET·N° 2

ARCHITECT'S OFFICE
UNDERGROUND RAILWAYS
55 BROADWAY WESTMINSTER
25TH MARCH 1931

113 **BB26**

General arrangement drawing for Sudbury Hill, bringing together all the key elements of the design on a single sheet as a summary of the proposal. As Adams, Holden and Pearson were consultants for this design, the final presentation and working drawings were prepared by the Underground Architect's Office under Stanley Heaps. On the right hand side of the drawing is seen the rubber stamp indicating approval of the design by the Underground's management, including Frank Pick.

Sudbury Hill

A short walk south along Greenford Road from the main line station of Sudbury Hill and Harrow, this Underground facility was rebuilt during 1932–33. With platforms in cutting, the architects were able to design Sudbury Hill as a version of the Northfields frontage, made more square in plan to give wide expanses of brick wall either side of a single window, and so that the sides each contained a single window. Orange-red bricks were used here in place of the Buckingham multi-coloured variety. In front of the ticket hall tower the lower buildings provided a vestibule area and sheltered a kiosk to left and right. From the front of the station the left side wall extended to the road and terminated in a cylindrical column carrying the Underground symbol on a mast. For the ground floor fascia the station name appeared in individual bronze letters in place of the usual coloured tiles and illuminated signs. A niche for telephone booths was to be found at the rear of the ticket hall, and passengers had lavatories and a seating niche provided. Platform access is through an all-concrete footbridge. Like certain contemporary stations in Berlin, and in common with the stairways at Ealing Common, these structures had roofs divided into three stepped sections, each one having glazing and a projecting concrete cornice to the roof as though it were a miniature version of the ticket hall. Sheer sided, the stairways functioned also as platform walls carrying poster panels and station name boards. The lowest roofs projected beyond the stairs to form waiting shelters. The large electrical substation on the London-bound platform is also by Adams, Holden and Pearson.

A booking office occupies part of the ticket hall. The station has been well restored with conservation of the concrete and paint selected to match the colour scheme when opened. Reproductions of the original sign graphics were fitted in the early 1990s. Lighting systems both within the building and to the exterior have been changed in the last decade. In contrast to the care of the building, the kiosks now present a poor and untidy appearance.

Boston Manor

By the 1920s the area west of Northfields began to be populated with privately developed semi-detached villas as speculative building spread westward. The rapid increase in passenger numbers fuelled the Underground's desire to reconstruct the station. The station master's house and booking office obstructed track work which would give access to the new Northfields car sheds. In phases the original building was demolished, sharing the site for a time with a temporary structure which presented the public with a hybrid of modern design and parts of the old facilities. A new station opened on 25 March 1934.[198] This, and the re-sited Osterley were designed in detail by Charles Hutton, one of Holden's assistants and the architect who had worked on Arnos Grove.[199] Both stations are remarkable for their departure from the standard box-with-lid ticket hall format. With no space to spare, the new building occupied a deck spanning the railway lines, set directly onto the basement structures of the old station, which can be seen today with the equally antique steel and timber platform canopies, whose valanced awnings appear quaint in contrast with the austere brick and glass of the reconstruction.

Boston Manor and Osterley were inspired by Dutch architecture of the period: the casement is near-identical to a feature on the *de Volharding* department store in the Hague of 1928.[200] Rising from the south-east end of the building a raised brick box gave way to the tower (originally to have been of squat cuboid form but subsequently slimmed down and elevated to a height of 18½ feet (5.6m), which in turn carried a steel and glass casement terminating just above a cream tile-clad block inset with back-lit bar and circle symbols.[201] By night the casement presented a vertical bar of white light. As built it had contained reeded clear glass; this was not felt to provide a sufficiently diffuse light and it was changed to white glass soon after opening. Viewed from the side or front, the tower appears as an arrangement of rectangular forms and grids, rising with ever more slender proportions. An experimental frieze displayed the station name in grey against a white background, giving a pronounced horizontal bar of light to balance the tower casement: this is a clear vestige of constructivist design principles. The more usual white lettering on dark blue replaced the feature within a few years to give better legibility. Behind the front wall, slender columns serving also as partitions divided the ticket hall into five bays. This design worked better in plan than in the fussy elevation: the outer two bays were glazed, the inner two bays contained the entrances-exits, and the central bay had a solid concrete panel incorporating a back-lit diagram of the Underground system. Behind this wall a bench seat neatly occupied the niche formed by two columns. Two blocks containing passenger lavatories and a booking clerks' office bounded the ticket hall on two sides, with a cylindrical shop unit and a small kiosk completing the front elevation. At the rear of the hall a large picture window afforded a panoramic view of the platforms. Until the booking office was built in the late 1980s, a passimeter booth occupied the central back part of the hall between staircases down to the trains. The station remains largely original, except for the replacement of signs and lamps. It is now a grade II listed building.

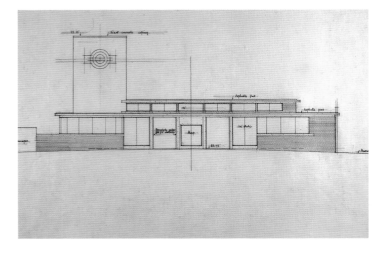

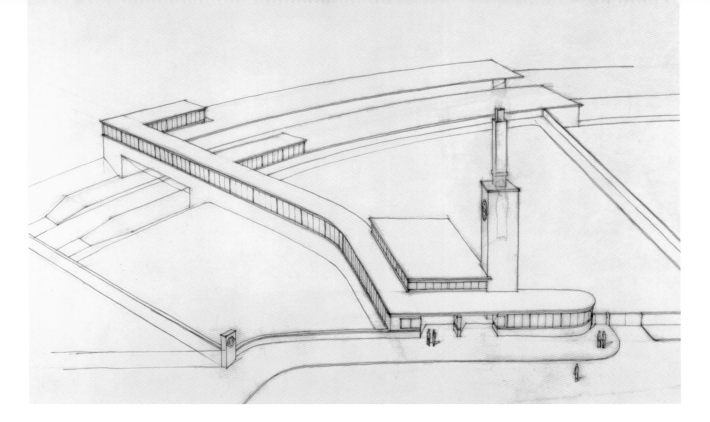

Osterley

This interesting essay in railway architecture shows a departure from its predecessors in the external treatment, the dominant features of which – the tower and the beacon – are particularly appropriate to the rather remote and open situation.[202]

Plans to move this station from its original site emerged in 1931, in recognition of the new source of traffic emerging as speculative suburban house building drifted westward along the concrete ribbon of the Great West Road, one of London's major arterial roads and opened in 1925. A new station was ready to open on 25 March 1934, on the road's margin.[203] The office of Stanley Heaps drafted a box type ticket hall but this was set aside, perhaps because it was too bulky for the open site. Heaps's team also supervised the construction, but the planning and major design features were conceived by the two Charleses: Holden and Hutton. The result is a combination of exuberance and timidity. The structure of railway offices, bay with shop, and footbridge consisted of only one level, the ticket hall box collapsed into a low clerestory roof over the central space. To capitalize on the advertising potential of the position beside a busy highway, a startling contrast came in the 70ft (21.3m) high tower topped by an abstract sculpture showing four vertical lines of light and described by Christian Barman as a 'romantic totem pole finial'.[204] Walls were of dark grey and multi-coloured Buckinghamshire bricks. Just inside the entrance, and decorated with a frieze of the customary bright blue faience tiles, a small vestibule provided waiting space.

The footbridge windows were single panes of plate glass forming a continuous strip of glazing with the roof carried on slim steel columns. Bright, and with a fabulously panoramic view of the two platforms in cutting below, the footbridge was continued as short stubs over the stairwells, creating generously proportioned full-height spaces. The effect of using so much glass was to give an arriving passenger the impression of a building in which the roofs seemed to hover over the walls, and carry the eye upward to the tower beacon.

The geometry of this station is elegant in its simplicity: a near-square ticket hall divided through its depth into four equal bays, with one side projecting beyond the square and curving gently round at an angle of forty degrees to become a passenger footbridge. Below the bridge, the rigorously horizontal reinforced concrete canopies cantilevered out from pairs of columns, aligned with the position of three neat clerestory rooflights. Here there is a wonderful small example of the intricacy of these apparently straightforward designs: the canopy was set at a height to protect passengers from the weather right up to the point they entered the train; as this created insufficient space for the poster panels, the clerestories were introduced to give the required height and adequate light levels. Small waiting areas were provided.

The building was listed on 26 May 1987. In line with the Underground's new ticketing system, the passimeter was removed in 1989 when part of the ticket hall was taken for a secure office and ticket machine enclosure. One waiting space is now an enclosed room. A refurbishment programme was instituted in the mid-1990s to address deterioration which had occurred to the building over a number of years. Restoration work has included replacement of missing lamp lenses and signs in the tower, and the installation of replica poster panels and lamp standards on the platforms.

Above This architect's sketch shows the extensive areas of windows above and around the ticket hall, along the footbridge and over the stairwells, making this station beautifully light and linking the interior directly with the surrounding area.

Above The Great West Road, seen here when new and somewhat unencumbered by traffic, would enable London Transport bus services to deliver passengers straight to the Underground from the outlying suburbs of west London.

Left Platform canopies were supported on pairs of columns, with the zone towards the back of the waiting areas brightened by clerestory windows.

South Harrow

Replacing the station opened as the first terminus of the Ealing and South Harrow on 28 June 1903, this scheme to bring facilities up to a modern standard for passengers who had been using Piccadilly line trains since 4 July 1932, had to include a bus yard on one side of the railway. South Harrow's new station was operational from 5 July 1935. Early sketches show a transformation of the box type ticket hall by lateral extension to wholly enclose stairways and platform shelters. The resulting austere monumentality was out of scale for the setting, and lacked any subtlety. By breaking down the necessary spaces into separate volumes, the architects arrived at a series of forms stepped both vertically and horizontally, all clearly related together as the building ascended to the upper levels. The plan was related to Boston Manor, being a rectangle divided into a series of bays with a kiosk projecting forward on the left side. Space saving, and therefore rationalization of the building, was achieved by placing the ticket hall within the bridge abutment and the offices on either side adjoining the stairs. Bus passengers had their own waiting area and lavatories. Another change is evident in the dark brown-red pressed bricks of the ground floor walls, and the cornices to ticket hall and stairs which were deeper than previous Holden stations and punctuated with windows, creating wide pilasters like those of Alfred Grenander's Krumme Lanke station in Berlin. The cornice overhangs were trimmed back, so that

the group of blocks seemed less fussy. For building above ground level, orange-red sand faced bricks in the walls had the additional detail of header bricks coloured dark blue-grey, like a Tudor building.

Across Northolt Road a public market occupied the arches of the railway viaduct. To enhance the consistency of the streetscape here the market entrances were rebuilt by the Underground to match the station opposite, and fitted with canopies having blue and white illuminated frieze panels. Had further plans been realized three small shops and a two level café would have occupied an island beside the station.[205] Hinting at the future form of Redbridge, the building looked like an awkward combination of signal cabin and kiosk and did not match the design quality of the station itself.

Direct access to the bus yard was removed when the lobby was closed to accommodate a booking office. In recent years the Holden-Heaps building has been subject to much additional equipment. Safety measures have included the increase in provision of television cameras from fourteen to fifty-two. There are safety fences, ladders, gates, guard rails, cabling, trunking, and alarm systems. Bricks in the shopfront wall are now painted over and the concrete of the canopy is painted also. The ticket hall has been retiled up to frieze height and retains its original clock. Piers supporting the platform canopies have been poorly repaired with mismatched quarry tiles and stainless steel trim. All concrete has been painted; some original signs are missing.

Above At South Harrow, finishes for busy public areas were taken from Holden's subterranean station designs, consisting mainly of large cream ceramic slabs up to a concrete beam decorated with fluted cream tiles between blue bands. For passenger guidance special electrically operated signs linked to the train signalling equipment indicated the platform and destination of arriving services. Beneath stepped and glazed roofs, the stairs flooded with light even on a gloomy day. The foot of one of the two staircases can be seen on the right of the picture. Half way up, recesses included seats.

Right The neatly designed newspaper stall at South Harrow.

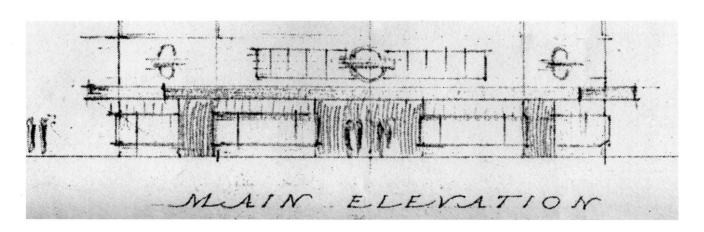

MAIN ELEVATION

IN-TOWN STATIONS

Whilst development was proceeding in the suburbs, Holden also redesigned some stations in central London.[206] Being in established areas, the architecture of these projects varied from the brick and glass idiom that had come to be associated with Holden's work for the Underground. Work included adaptation of existing buildings, additions and alterations including subsurface ticket halls and escalators where previously lifts had operated, and new façades. The chief materials were, on the exteriors, Portland stone or render over brick to simulate stone, and for the interiors large cream-coloured ceramic slabs.

Warren Street

This station demonstrates a solution to a narrow corner site that can be compared to Leicester Square (page 151). Here a Charing Cross, Euston & Hampstead Railway station[207] with lifts by Leslie Green was replaced with a new ticket hall and escalators. Charles Holden drafted the initial designs, and detail development took place in the Underground architect's office. Holden had sketched a heptagonal ticket hall placed close to Euston Road, within a half-octagonal block characterized by a double entrance on the corner of Tottenham Court Road and a prominent strip of clerestory windows. Another proposal followed closely the style of high-ceilinged tower used on the Morden branch of the Northern line and the Piccadilly line extension. The built design is a half drum

of Portland stone with clerestory windows to the ticket hall and a floor of offices above, over a half octagon clad entirely in granite. A brick storey was added when an office building took the place of the old station.

Constrained by the superstructure, and with a heavy emphasis on the ground floor form, Warren Street lacks the elegance of other Underground stations of this period. The many small windows make the building appear fussy. Works for the new Victoria line (this section opened on 1 December 1968) included additional escalators, a lower concourse and two platform tunnels. It had been suggested that additional interchange could be facilitated by linking Warren Street with a new station on the Circle-Metropolitan lines, which pass close by. This was not done. The near-symmetrical ticket hall plan has been altered by blocking of the north entrance to build a booking office.

Two substantial columns followed the line of the ceiling, making the interior space somewhat cramped. Space between the street walls and the hall was given over entirely to four kiosks. Walls were lined with large cream faience slabs and black borders. From the centre of the back wall of the hall a bank of escalators commissioned on 27 June 1933 linked with an intermediate concourse and further escalators for the Northern line platforms (curiously the escalators replaced a set of semi-automatic lifts which had been installed some four years previously).

Opposite page Sketch for Warren Street by Adams, Holden and Pearson proposing a half-octagonal ticket hall tower. Vestiges of this remained in the built design seen **left**.

Above The Warren Street ticket hall interior with ticket issuing and collecting booth, or passimeter, faced in linoleum to imitate marble.

Left An unbuilt proposal for the Green Park entrance to the Underground station of the same name.

Green Park

Leslie Green's Dover Street station of 15 December 1906 was conveniently hidden in a side road off Piccadilly, so that its gaudy redness did not intrude upon either the succession of stone edifices lining that street, or add an odd margin to the park so close to a royal palace. When the Piccadilly line was extended, the station west of Dover Street at Down Street was closed to improve train running, creating the need for further capacity at the remaining station. A fascinating design for the replacement entrance emerged. A small square of the park adjacent to the Ritz Hotel would be raised as a plaza. Ramps gave access to two sides of the plaza, with stairs to the ticket hall beneath a circular rooflight. In the north-east corner of the plaza a small stone tower of hexagonal plan was to take the faceted form of a Morden line type station, but with a significant difference: the stone block would carry a 'luminous turret'. Whilst this design was not built, the turret is a precursor of the beacon at Southgate.

Subterranean ticket hall at Hyde Park Corner.

Ultimately Holden produced a simple pavilion to shelter the station stairwells at Green Park, brought into use on 18 September 1933. This combined stairwell and shelter closely resembled his work for the Imperial War Graves Commission, being a structure of the plainest granite blocks, decorated only with a fluted band and bronze nameplates and patterned strip (the patterned bronze detail was to recur in modified form at Holden's University of London Senate House). The large mast-mounted Underground signs seem an incongruous afterthought. There was a ticket hall excavated beneath the road, accessed also by stairwells from the north side of Piccadilly at the corner with Stratton Street, and escalators provided to the tube platforms. The pavilion was demolished during substantial alterations to prepare for Victoria line services which commenced here on 7th March 1969. The station was altered again below ground for the first phase of the Jubilee line, operating from 1st May 1979. The Piccadilly line platforms, which had until this point retained their pale blue and cream tiling of 1906, were redecorated circa 1985.

Hyde Park Corner

Down Street station, between Green Park and Hyde Park Corner, was closed in 1932 to enable higher train running speeds on the extended Piccadilly line.[208] To improve facilities and meet the needs of increase traffic levels at adjacent stations, reconstruction of the ticket hall provided for the Great Northern, Piccadilly and Brompton Railway station of 1906 at Hyde Park Corner was necessary. This was Holden's local station, the architects having offices at 9 Knightsbridge for a time. In the new scheme, stairwells were provided at a number of points around the road intersection. The Hyde Park Corner ticket hall was carved out under the roadway and lined throughout in biscuit cream coloured glazed tiles and display cases, impressively lit by bands of pressed glass lamps on the ceiling. Leslie Green's surface building was abandoned and then adapted to be let for commercial use, but his platform tunnels, with their patterned tile designs, remained unaltered at the foot of escalators installed to replace the lifts.

Knightsbridge

The Piccadilly line station at Knightsbridge of 1906 was the only Leslie Green Underground station to feature rich Art Nouveau details.[209] Too small for the increase in traffic expected when the Piccadilly extensions were complete, re-development became a necessity.[210] A new entrance, little more than an enclosed stairwell, was provided at the corner of Knightsbridge and Sloane Street. As at Hyde Park Corner, a new ticket hall was excavated under the road. Work began in 1930, with the ticket hall operational from 18 February 1934. To facilitate access from Brompton Road and the Harrods department store, a second entrance and ticket hall was built at Hans Crescent, linked with the platforms by a subterranean shopping arcade and escalators all coming into use on 30 July 1934. For increased passenger capacity the Brompton Road entrance has been closed and converted to a clothes shop, with a new and widened stairwell opened in the now-closed end of the road called Hans Crescent. Work to refurbish the ticket hall and arcade here was undertaken in 2005. The below-ground works include wall linings of an artificial stone resembling a poor imitation of travertine marble, and a false ceiling in the ticket hall resembling a domed canopy. All shop units had been demolished in the arcade. Platform tunnels have been redecorated using contemporary fittings and glazed tiles which approximate to the Underground style of the 1930s.

Marble Arch

Like Knightsbridge, a similar use of granite, tile, and patterned bronze ventilation grille was used by Holden for Marble Arch, where the simplest of entrances was produced within an existing building at the west end, north side, of Oxford Street. Below ground this station ticket hall had rectangular columns subtly fluted in the same style as those at Sudbury Town, but here fashioned with a veneer of travertine marble and with fluted bronze capitals. Certain of those features remain today.

Above The Hans Crescent entrance to Knightsbridge displayed an array of Underground corporate symbols, set over and around a metal grille very much in the Holden idiom – see also the exterior of Marble Arch, **opposite page upper**. This entrance has been closed, replaced by a stairwell and extended subway.

Opposite page lower The north ticket hall ceiling of Knightsbridge booking hall was carried on elaborate octagonal columns with equally complex capitals carrying lamp units. Interiors throughout the passenger areas were devoid of colour beyond the yellow-cream and black wall tiles.

Leicester Square

First tabled in 1923, enlargement of Leicester Square had to wait until the success of Piccadilly Circus spawned a number of subterranean reconstructions on the Piccadilly line in the early 1930s. Commenced in May 1932 and reopened fully on 4 May 1935,[211] the 1906 station was significantly enlarged to serve the western edge of the theatre district, and new cinemas around the Square itself. Street level alterations were confined to revised and new entrances on the corner of Little Newport Street between Cranbourn Street and St Martin's Court set in front of a public house called the *Scotch Stores* designed by Adams, Holden and Pearson, and beneath the Hippodrome Theatre. Two further stairways opened in the old surface building on 8 June 1936 completed the means of access to the new ticket hall. There was additionally a large electric substation not immediately obvious as a railway building, located at the intersection of Upper St Martin's Lane and Long Acre, with a further public house designed by Adams, Holden and Pearson (*The Sussex*) at its foot. Polished granite, slabs of cream faience and ultramarine blue tiles identified the new entrances and stairwells. The Little Newport Street entrance presented a fussy array of pilasters, bronze ventilation grilles, and a canopy wrapping around the corner. A passage under Charing Cross Road linking with the Little Newport Street stairwell included a lobby of telephone booths.

Large ceramic slabs lined the circular ticket hall, interspersed by shop kiosks for a chemist, fruiterer, two tobacconists, a confectioner, and product showcases.[212] The colour of the faience was described as 'new biscuit cream', in fact more like a custard yellow. Similar square tiles were produced for platforms, used with bands of black or bright blue. In the centre of the hall the designers planned 'as the dominant feature … a large glazed circular ticket office'; this was not built.[213] Platforms were interconnected by a second low-level passageway from 5 July 1948. Platforms had a simple decorative scheme of cream, ultramarine blue and black.[214] Subsurface spaces at the station were used during the second world war for the central control of gates in platform tunnels provided to prevent river water flooding the tube system should the Thames be bombed.

As part of a substantial modernization of central London stations, Leicester Square platforms were redecorated in 1985. The Little Newport Street entrance closed so that its connecting subway could be used for installation of a booking office in the late 1980s. Haverstock Associates were architects for the circular control room built in the ticket hall in 2002, and in 2004 were responsible for the refurbishment programme in the lower levels of the station including replacement of the original cream and blue tiles in the lower station areas with new materials matched to the 1980s' work rather than the Holden finishes.

Opposite page The *Scotch Stores* public house was a severe block of building with an equally rigorous arrangement of windows. The front corners of the lower block were to have carried statuary.[215] Architects William Petch and Auguste Fermaud were responsible for the interior design. The front of the building stepped forward, carried on columns cased with grey granite slabs and cream tile fillets.

Above Recognising the changed regime, strips of blue and orange tiles in the converted stairwell of the original station entrance were decorated with the letters 'L' and 'T'. The exterior of this entrance is interesting for the way new white tiles were inserted into the oxblood coloured faience façade.

Below Architects' sketch for the combined public house and electricity substation at Leicester Square, on the corner of Monmouth Street and Long Acre. The building as first constructed is seen overleaf.

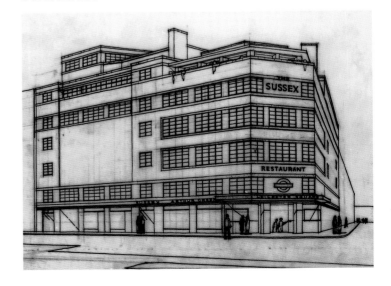

For the corner of St Martin's Lane, Charles Holden designed a second pub, *The Sussex*, dwarfed by the bulk of the railway electricity substation. On the corner of Little Newport Street at Charing Cross Road a further variation in the architectural style produced a neat, modest, granite and Portland stone frontage.

MORE UNDERGROUND SUBURBS

In the second half of the 1930s, the work done by Adams, Holden and Pearson for London Transport was dominated by the extension of the Underground railway system further into the home counties. The effect would be to transform Victorian and Edwardian branch lines, with their attendant ramshackle platforms and nondescript station houses, into busy commuter conduits to the city. There were three main groups of stations, all designed in the period 1936–38, and some were shared with other architects to relieve the work-load in Holden's office. A further shift in design practice was evidenced in work on Ruislip Manor and neighbouring stations, this being an attempt to make the buildings of more lightweight and temporary construction in order to economize in the short term and permit easy alteration when traffic increased.[216]

For the Northern line extensions from Archway and Finsbury Park to Mill Hill, High Barnet, Alexandra Palace and Aldenham/Bushey Heath, the LNER stations at Highgate, East Finchley and Finchley Central would be reconstructed by Holden. Adams, Holden and Pearson also produced a design for the ultimate terminus of the projected Northern line at Aldenham/Bushey Heath. This, and the line which it served, were not built. In the third group for the Central line were Wanstead,[217] Redbridge[218] and Gants Hill. Works for the Northern and Central lines were affected by the onset of the second world war, with the result that there are two sets of designs, those proposed in the pre-war anticipation of extensive investment, and those accomplished to provide facilities for getting London back to work in peacetime.

The ticket hall tower at Rayners Lane saved on space, and made for efficient passenger circulation, by straddling the railway lines. The curved ends of the platform buildings enclose waiting rooms.

Rayners Lane

When planning to supersede a basic timber halt so that the new population of 'Harrow Garden Village' and other speculative developments might be served adequately, the Underground and the Metropolitan Railway had been at loggerheads over building costs, the Metropolitan perhaps unhappy that its younger and more progressive competitor was setting the pace. Piccadilly train services were projected through Rayners Lane to Uxbridge from 23 October 1933, adding to the need for a fully equipped station. Sketch proposals began to emerge in late 1935, Stanley Heaps's office adapting the brick box idea by the insertion of a large semi-circular window.[219] A further interesting variation of the box was tried, with the entire central portion recessed for a great window.[220] From this design Reginald Uren, working with Holden as consultant, returned to more conventional ground, taking the general form of Turnpike Lane – a symmetrical box behind a low building with curved ends – compressing it widthways and increasing the depth to span entrances between shops and railway offices. Set at the highest point in the district and adjacent to a busy road junction, this is the only station built for the Underground which had the ticket hall set forward so as to straddle the pavement and be directly in the flow of pedestrians along the street.

In case anyone failed to notice the building, tall masts with bull's-eye signs projected from the top of the two kiosks, a feature which again can be traced back to earlier Holden stations, and which would recur at Eastcote, the next station on the line. A detail change from foregoing stations evident here and at Eastcote is the treatment of the roof overhang soffit with several square projections instead of the longitudinal steps. The station was conceived as the focus of a shopping parade to be built by London Transport. Once again, the budget did not extend to this ambition, and the short sections of wall started either side of the building were left for others to complete.

From the street, swing doors provided draught free access below windows the same width as the entrances. Like Chiswick Park and Oakwood, blue-black glazed bricks lined the ticket hall, with dark red 'Old English' and Buckinghamshire multi-coloured bricks elsewhere above a plinth of finely finished concrete. In a move towards ever-

Above Rayners Lane, 1938.

154

greater areas of glazing in the ticket hall towers (a trend which would find its ultimate resolution in the first design for Redbridge station, described on page 168), the rear window filled almost the entire back wall. Over all of this, a reinforced concrete ceiling with one hundred and ten coffered recesses, suggesting a modern version of the Pantheon in Rome. Beyond the hall a wide gallery and staircases linked with the two side platforms in cutting. Platform details were similar to South Harrow, and the waiting rooms had narrow bowed ends; bright orange-red bricks make up the walls.

To provide a secure ticket office enclosure, the north station entrance was closed in 1987: the external brick-lined recess created by this work is a dusty and unattractive wind trap. Inside the hall this same work was much more success-ful, carried out in materials making a good match with the original features. In the south entrance the original opal glass lamp units can be seen above the doors. The concrete ticket hall ceiling has been painted white. In the rear gallery there is a train indicator unit (out of use) and the lighting includes small glass cube shades, both items contemporary with the station.

Platforms have some original signs, clocks, concrete fencing and lamp standards. One platform level kiosk is out of use.

Platform level finishes at Rayners Lane: brick walls, exposed concrete, heather brown quarry tiles, and every piece of information graphics embellished with the Underground's bar and circle symbol.

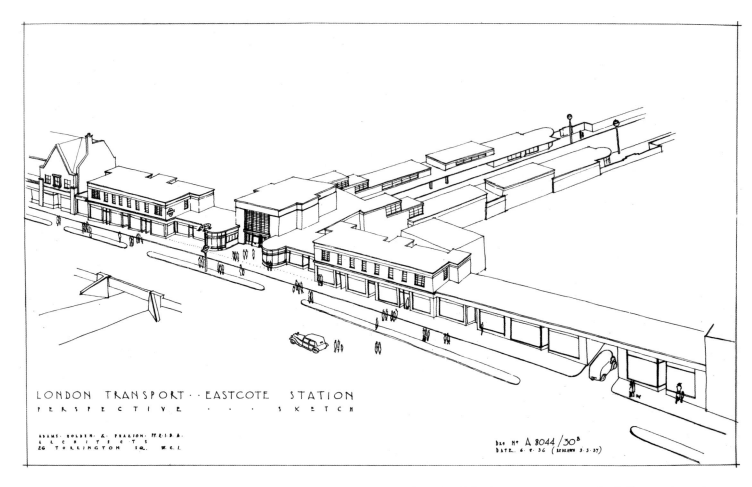

LONDON TRANSPORT · · EASTCOTE STATION
PERSPECTIVE · · · SKETCH

ADAMS · HOLDEN · & · PEARSON · FF.R.I.B.A.
ARCHITECTS
26 TOLLINGTON SQ. W.C.I.

DRG N° A 8044/30ᴮ
DATE. 6·7·36 (REDRAWN 3·3·37)

Eastcote

Like Rayners Lane, Eastcote was for three decades a pair of
rudimentary platforms with few passenger amenities. After
consideration of replacement facilities based on a generic kit
of parts, the first permanent prototype for Eastcote explored
the use of a narrow, deep ticket hall with rounded front and
continuous clerestory. This developed into a building almost
wholly of glass, with a parade of shops set at an angle to it
on one side and the railway in cutting on the other. A flush of
conservatism seems to have overtaken London Transport
and Charles Holden, so that the form of the station approved
and built between late 1937 and 1939, was a near-square
ticket hall box with central side walls set out and a shallow
roof cornice. In the wide windows to front and rear, the glazing bar arrangement was varied to give two narrow strips
as a decoration. Either side of the street elevation, kiosks
sheltered the twin entrances, and from these units rose
masts carrying the bull's-eye signs.

The interior walls followed the Rayners Lane scheme of
black glazed bricks to head height, and red bricks above.
From the rear of the ticket hall a small gallery of trapezoid
plan beneath a large domed rooflight, and stairways under
stepped roofs were integrated with the platform canopies.
Substantial round-ended waiting rooms, with doors from
both the recessed sheltered areas and the platforms, terminated the canopies: an arrangement which would be used
again at East Finchley. In place of the opal glass rectangle

used to give light down onto entrances in Holden stations of
the early 1930s, Eastcote had five round lamps set into the
soffits above the doors. In the two side walls the central portions were set out, a feature marking corresponding recesses
in the ticket hall whose lower portions housed kiosks.

The exterior of the station at ground level is not improved
by current shop fascias or signs. All concrete at platform
level is now painted. Platform lamp standards and poster
panels have been replaced. There are traces of the former
station garden, cultivated in a series of beds along the
platforms.

London Transport · Ruislip Manor Station · Perspective Sketch · Drawing Nº A 8049/33a amendments to station name etc. added 15th September, 1936.

Adams, Holden and Pearson, FF.R.I.B.A. Architects, 9, Knightsbridge, London S.W. 1. 7th August 1936.

Ruislip Manor

This site ushered in a new theme in London Underground station design. Moving on from the large window framed between brick walls or piers, the practice began of incorporating entire walls of glass as enclosures to stairwells, towers and ticket halls. A feature of European buildings for some years, for London Transport it was entirely new. The design of the station here provides an interesting comparison with South Harrow which had preceded it. From 1936 to 1938 Adams, Holden and Pearson made many plans. Whilst the Underground had envisaged a new type of economical and short-life station building for Ruislip Manor and elsewhere on the Uxbridge extension of the Piccadilly line (see pages 56 to 59), temporary structures seem not to have suited the needs of the operator, and a brick, concrete and glass scheme was drafted. The central form of a low street-level building with tall stairwell towers was developed through five stages before the final design was approved. The new station officially opened on 26 June 1938. A ticket hall within the bridge abutment had entrance doors recessed in low pavilions on either side of the bridge, and towering above them stark blocks enclosed the stairs and platform waiting areas. The cornices of the entrances were virtually flush with the walls, and reduced to a thin line of concrete dominated by the rich blue bands of back-lit name friezes. Bow-fronted kiosks, which had been a signature of Holden stations, were set aside in favour of buildings flush with the street line, the shops being placed in arcades. Halfway up the stairways seat recesses were embellished with neat concrete cornices over the wood seats. Platform finishes are the same as those for Rayners Lane and Eastcote, but without the enclosed waiting areas. The shelters were arranged as two raised clerestory units flanked by smaller spaces, each section supported on paired piers.

Small waiting rooms were made within the platform shelters in the late 1960s or early 1970s. A booking office enclosure has been built on the north side of the ticket hall breaking the symmetry and sense of space in the interior. It also partly obscured the station clock. The upper stair handrails have had their natural bronze finish covered by a high visibility lime green coating. One portion of glazing in the prominent position at the road end of the westbound platform has been replaced by louvres, making the building appear brutish and ugly. Anti-pigeon devices encrust many surfaces. Lamp fittings have been altered. One waiting shelter from the 1912 halt is still in use on the westbound platform.

Opposite Eastcote was to have incorporated a shopping parade designed by Adams, Holden and Pearson. This was postponed, and added piecemeal subsequently to the designs of others.

Above Presentation sketch for Ruislip Manor, which like Eastcote was to have been accompanied by a number of retail units.

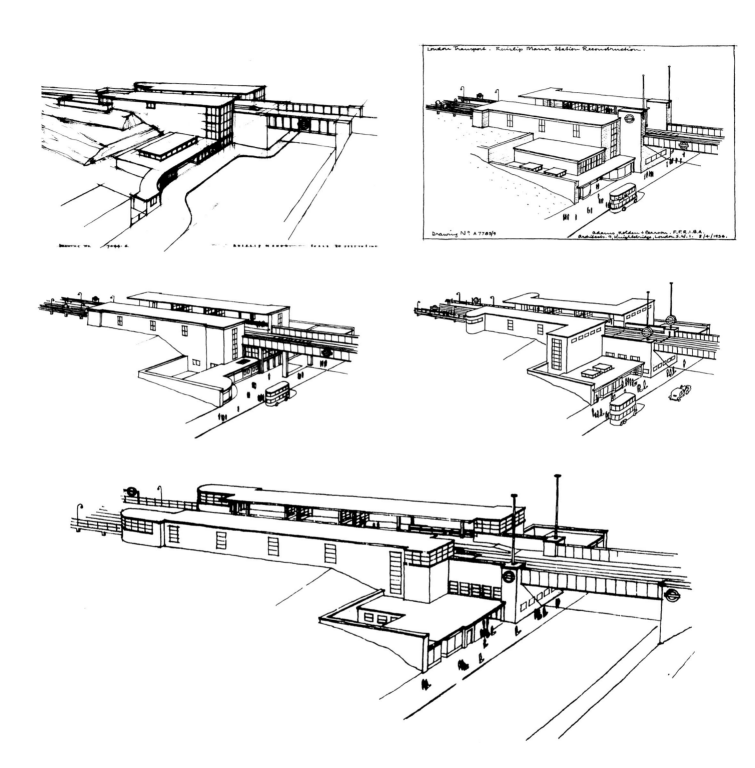

The five design stages of Ruislip Manor from top, left to right, (i) a ticket hall alongside the railway with a small clerestory roof and all-glass stair enclosures; (ii) a box-type ticket hall and brick stair enclosures amalgamated with platform-level shelters and slender brick pylons as bridge abutments; (iii) a ticket hall set entirely under the railway bridge flanked by shop units, with the stair enclosures set back behind the shops; (iv) the under-bridge ticket hall placed against stairs turned parallel to the street to form elongated wings to the platform buildings; (v) the same arrangement as the preceding example, but with the stairs cut back to short projections, and large expanses of wall between ground and platform levels where strips of windows suggested that the concrete roofs were light enough to float away with a passing train. The consistent use of brick throughout (a multi-red wire-cut type having hard, crisp edges), and the careful contrast of ground level and platform structures made for a successful combination of bridge and building.

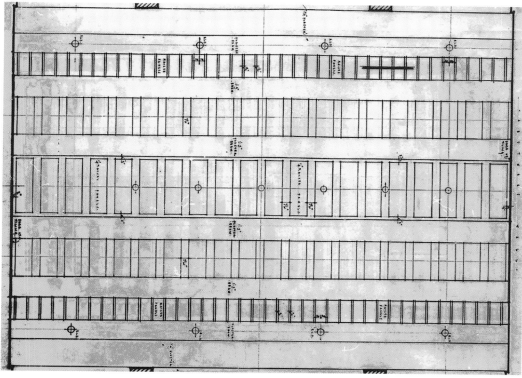

Top The careful contrast of ground level and platform structures, made for a harmonised and satisfyingly proportioned design. This was particularly notable since Charles Holden had struggled with the problem of uniting a strong horizontal engineering element – the bridge – with the more complex horizontal/vertical assemblage of buildings. The ticket hall with cream and taupe ceramic tiles, received daylight through strip windows above the entrances.

Above The plaster ceiling of the ticket hall, where the production of actual recesses was not possible as it had been at other stations due to the thinner concrete roof, was instead decorated with raised rectangular panels, another motif employed by Holden.

Uxbridge

When the Metropolitan Railway arrived at Uxbridge in 1904, it built the terminus of the line on the edge of the town. After assuming control of the route extending Piccadilly services alongside the Metropolitan line, London Transport planned changes which would bring their operations right into the centre of the community. Proposals for Uxbridge span the years 1934–38. The architects took up an idea of modern town-planning then prevalent (but by no means new): cut through the old buildings of the settlement to create a wide, straight boulevard lined with shops and punctuated by traffic roundabouts, giving a grand approach (here called 'Station Avenue') from the High Street to the transport hub ('Station Circus') situated on York Road. Latterly, plans were changed so that it was the railway which made a direct approach into the central area, as a half-mile (0.8km) extension from the existing track. A portion of old Uxbridge was laid waste in the process. Dispensing with the urban boulevard did not deter the designers from producing a massive building. In January 1937 Leonard Bucknell and Ruth Ellis proposed a gargantuan structure, a curious hybrid of brick, concrete and glass for the station offices, and laminated timber trusses for the train shed. Innovative and exciting indeed, but beyond the orbit of anything the Underground or London Transport had yet tried, and too costly. The design was scaled back, and Holden adapted the Cockfosters type of reinforced concrete train shed as a proven solution. This was set into a cutting and made proportionally higher than the Cockfosters example to suit the profile of the railway cars operating on the Metropolitan line. Begun in late 1937, construction work proceeded through to mid-1940 after an official opening on 4 December 1938. London Transport's staff magazine claimed that the station would 'combine old and new materials with due regard to their use and beauty, and to the pleasant brick tradition prevailing in the town of Uxbridge'.[221]

Demonstrating an ambition towards progress through new architecture, the council official responding to London Transport's official invitation to see the new work was proud to state: 'Uxbridge is passing from the status of a coaching town into that of a great suburb, which all hope will become as modern and efficient as any other within fifteen miles of London'. He drew on ideas as current now as they were innovative then: 'I visualize that road traffic in the future will be prevented from going into the Metropolis, because of the enormous growth of traffic, and that a co-ordination of road and rail services will be effected, whereby the bus and coach service will empty their passengers into the railway stations, such as that at Uxbridge'.[222]

The station has been subject to a restoration project, and many original features can be observed both outside and on the platforms, including signs, a weighing machine and lamps. The road in front of the station has been converted to a pedestrian area dominated by large shopping malls and host to temporary stalls. It has not been possible to determine the reason for the lighter coloured brickwork in the upper walls of the façade, but this difference has been evident for many years. Shop fronts now compete visually with the architecture. Around the rear of the station, guard rails, security fences and cameras are present.

The façade to High Street formed a gentle curve behind a pull-in for vehicles, with shops below and offices above. Pale handmade pink-grey brick was the predominant material above black quartzite skirtings, with windows set into concrete and artificial stone frames. Where the first floor broke to admit light into the ticket hall, slender brick piers carried the eye up to two sculptures by Joseph Armitage based on abstractions of railway vehicle wheels and leaf springs 'symbolical of transport services'.[223]

Travellers passed through the low entrance into a double height arcade lined entirely with shuttering board-marked concrete above grey granite ground floor walls: this was a building designed to last. The structure from the arcade forward was characterized by pairs of portal frames, side-lit with clerestory windows. The roof height stepped upwards twice, incorporating five large dome skylights, and the space widened progressively through the arcade and ticket hall. Here a booking booth, kiosks, and a buffet were available. Substantial staff areas lay behind a number of doors.

One further feature distinguishes Uxbridge as an exemplar modern railway station. In pursuit of the plan to identify London Transport buildings with their neighbourhoods, windows in the front of the ticket hall, shaped to match the profile of the train shed, were to be filled with stained glass. Charles Holden persuaded Frank Pick to award the commission to Hungarian refugee Ervin Bossanyi, who was then completing windows for Holden's University of London project. Melding abstract and figurative imagery, Bossanyi submitted a design featuring circular motifs, sunbursts, mechanical-looking elements and human forms. This was too much for Pick, who preferred a more literal illustration of life in Uxbridge. Bossanyi met Pick's request with an illustration of a man driving oxen over a bridge. Unfortunately the association of ox and bridge was found to be a faulty attribution for the town name, and this second of the artist's maquettes had to be abandoned.[224] Building work progressed; a decision was needed. Holden showed Pick Bossanyi's work on his University of London project, with the consequence that the same style was adopted to make windows representing the coats of arms of Uxbridge Urban District Council Buckinghamshire and Middlesex county councils. Arriving at Uxbridge by train, the fusion of colours in these windows is an intriguing and welcoming scene.[225]

161

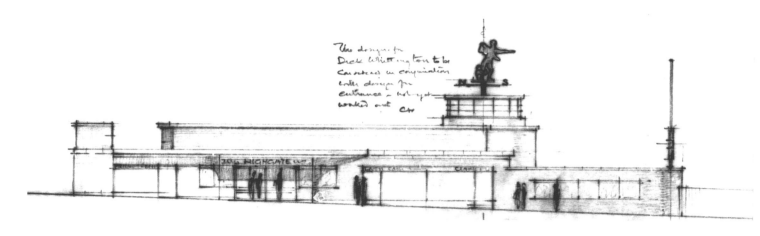

Highgate

There is much to report about the intentions for this station, yet little to view now. Had plans to make Highgate an interchange point between new branches of the Northern line connecting Finsbury Park, Alexandra Palace, Barnet, Edgware, Elstree South and Highgate (Archway) been fulfilled, this station would have been an extensive development. The site was challenging, and the brief required a combination of passenger entrances at three different levels, staff rooms above ground and below, platforms in cutting and in tube tunnels, a subsurface ticket hall, and banks of stairs and escalators to link all together. Stanley Heaps's team suggested a hexagonal ticket hall (drawn 1935) below the existing station, and subsequently a ticket hall on a bridge in the cutting over the surface tracks, with lifts down to the tube platforms (drawn June 1936).[226] Holden's own office produced a striking design for an extensive array of station buildings.

The new tube platforms (termed Highgate Low-Level) were situated 59 feet (18m) below the existing station (Highgate High-Level), which was itself to be entirely rebuilt to Holden's designs. Between tube and surface station, an underground ticket hall and subway spanned between Priory Gardens and escalators from Archway Road. The Priory Gardens entrance was to have had a staff institute with an adjoining cylindrical brick tower as advertising feature and ventilation shaft. This last feature is interesting in itself as a departure from the regular square or rectangular towers of previous stations. On the Archway Road side the scale of the proposal became evident, with the architects drafting a substantial escalator enclosure formed from six tiers of stepped roofs, like an extended version of Holden's platform staircase design or a stairway for giants, next to a small entrance hall with squat brick tower.

At this time Frank Pick's scheme for the decoration of stations with art making reference to their localities was being introduced to station designs. Highgate Hill is known as the place in English folklore where Dick Whittington, with his cat, turned back to London and gained success and wealth. The cat is commemorated by a small statue at the foot of the Hill, and it was planned that both the cat and its master would be present at Highgate. To achieve this, Holden proposed a sculptural group some 12 feet (3.65m) high, carried up on a brick pier 23 feet (7m) high so that it might be seen at once from the main road approaches and by passengers on the open platform below. It is likely that the figures would have been fabricated in the same way as the Archer figure at East Finchley station.

Revisions were subsequently made to the design. The great stepped escalator hall was set aside in favour of a simplified form, to which access was gained by an enlarged building on Archway Road. This had a cylindrical skylight carrying Whittington and his cat pointing towards London styled as an oversize weathervane, very much in the spirit of traditional British sign design. This version featured in an advertisement promoting the new station in 1941. Building began in the first month of 1939, the line opened through the station to East Finchley on 3 July 1939 and the new Highgate subsurface ticket hall and tube platforms came into use on 19 February 1941. Then construction stopped in March 1942 when the last consignment of bricks was cancelled as a wartime economy. Internal decorations comprised cream tiles with bright green bands.

Further works were drastically reduced to meet wartime needs. Staff rooms and the ventilation tower on the Priory Gardens side were deleted, and a simple building opened on 26 August 1957 to enclose the top of the escalators at Archway Road. A further stairwell in the station car park connected via stairs with the subsurface ticket hall. Extension of the Northern line to Alexandra Palace was abandoned, and the island platform with its sharply detailed reinforced concrete canopy remains as a curious ruin in the wooded cutting below Archway Road. During February to August 2004 extensive ground works were undertaken to stabilize the sides of the cutting above the Underground station at the side of Archway Road.

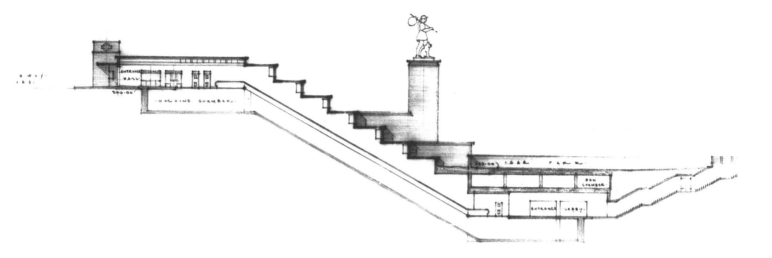

Above Elaborate prototype design for the escalators linking the subterranean ticket hall at Highgate with a street entrance on Archway Road. The mythical Dick Whittington and his cat, placed on top of an air shaft, would have made a significant landmark.

Right Highgate's abandoned surface station, built to serve Northern line trains to Alexandra Palace which never ran.

Below The total organisation of tube platform walls. The tiles were cream, edged by pale green bands. A ventilation grille of similar design to those in the façade at Marble Arch can be seen in the left hand panel of this drawing.

Opposite page Early design for the Archway Road station entrance at Highgate, with a low round tower bearing a weathervane fashioned in the form of Dick Whittington. The stubby rectangular tower to the left of the elevation recalls the building at Cockfosters.

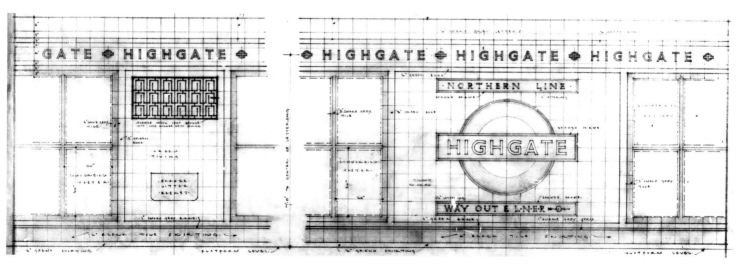

East Finchley

As proof that Charles Holden's work, and the Underground's expansion projects were not wholly abandoned at the start of the second world war, the reconstruction of East Finchley which had begun in March 1939 was completed in 1942, much of the work having taken place around operating tube train and main-line services. Holden worked on the design with Leonard Bucknell and Ruth Ellis.[227] The difficulties arising from this scheme, after Frank Pick objected to Holden's having passed it on to another architect, have already been discussed in the first part of this book, so here we focus on the architectural details. It is possible that as this was Pick's local station, he may have taken greater than usual interest in its appearance.[228] In common with concept schemes produced for London Transport at this time by Holden, East Finchley was to have extensive areas of glass curtain walling, enclosing the entire ticket hall, the half-round towers of the staircases and the four sides of the bridge level. When the design was rejected much of the glass was deleted, in favour of brick margins to the ticket hall and bridge windows. The railway was carried on viaducts across a main road, and the scale of the street buildings rising up to platform level suggested a further storey to provide visual balance. The need to house offices for railway staff resulted in a further block being added to bridge the tracks, accessed by two staircases from the platforms. The north entrance was based on a square plan, the bulk of it being set into the railway embankment to leave a narrow triple-height vestibule between the entrance openings. The south hall was a compressed octagon. Each had passimeter ticket booths and bookstalls. Opening for use on 3 July 1939, and with the first Underground services operating from 14 April 1940, the building diverged from its approved design: in the north side one large opening replaced three vertical windows, and an ungainly tower attached to one corner of the bridge block was deleted. A subway took care of passenger circulation between the two halls.

As a remnant of Bucknell and Ellis's first design, the platform structures on the two island platforms did retain large windows, so that the stair enclosures were smaller versions of those designed by Walter Gropius for his model factory at the Werkbund Exhibition in Cologne of 1914. The exposed position of the platforms on an embankment resulted in brick screen walls being provided, so that the outer two of the four railway tracks were enclosed for part of the station's length by concrete roof slabs. The station was built mainly from Buckinghamshire multi-coloured bricks, with the distinguishing feature of having the south side made from mixed red wire-cut bricks. The assemblage of blocks which made up the station gave the visual impression of a structure rising ever upwards. To complement this effect, and to give interest to the severe line of the bridge, viaduct and station roofline on the north side of the site, Holden proposed a sculpture as part of Frank Pick's programme of endowing stations with local references. The loose association of hunters once roaming the Highgate woods, and the choice of a metaphor for speedy travel culminated in the sculpture being the kneeling figure of an archer poised to loose an arrow towards the city.[229] The archer makes for an interesting decoration in what is otherwise an awkward and uninspiring design. Excepting the glazed stairways, the bridge appears clumsy and ordinary in its details. Any emphasis in the north frontage is lost with the grouping of ticket hall and offices, and the south side building presents a number of blank walls. The quality of the interior spaces is compromised by the lack of depth in the double height ticket hall vestibule and the low headroom of the subway.

With installation of the Underground Ticketing System in 1989 the south side became unstaffed and the north ticket hall was rebuilt with a booking office and extensively retiled. The oval panel in the north ticket hall window formerly held the London and North Eastern Railway's company logotype. Anti-graffiti paint has discoloured and appears as a grey sheen on the brick façade.

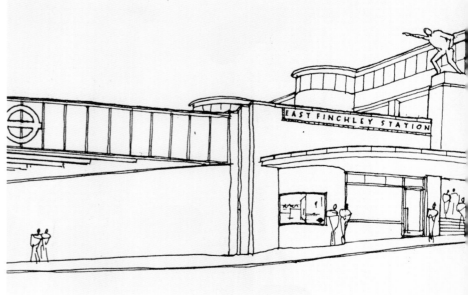

Opposite page, left Office building by Walter Gropius with Adolf Meyer for the Deutscher Werkbund exhibition in Cologne, Germany, 1914. Its glazed stairwells were a model for East Finchley.

Left Here the main, north, ticket hall is contained within the first part of the double height block, with offices beyond.

The two island platforms at East Finchley. The waiting shelters show the influence of German Underground stations built in the late 1920s in their arrangement of high level glazing to admit light below the canopies. The brick walls on the extreme margins of the station were to protect passengers in this elevated location from winds. Beyond the platform buildings is the bridge of offices spanning the tracks.

Left Sketch by Adams, Holden and Pearson for East Finchley after the project was brought back into the practice from Bucknell and Ellis. The design is composed of conflicting elements and distinct forms which would be amalgamated into the more streamlined final version seen at top of page.

Below The south entrance at East Finchley with half-octagonal ticket hall below the overbridge carrying staff rooms above the railway tracks and station platforms on the embankment.

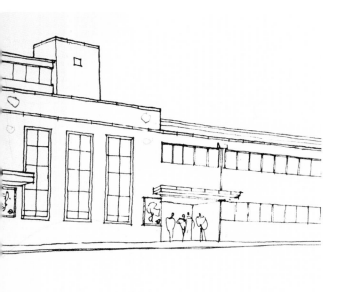

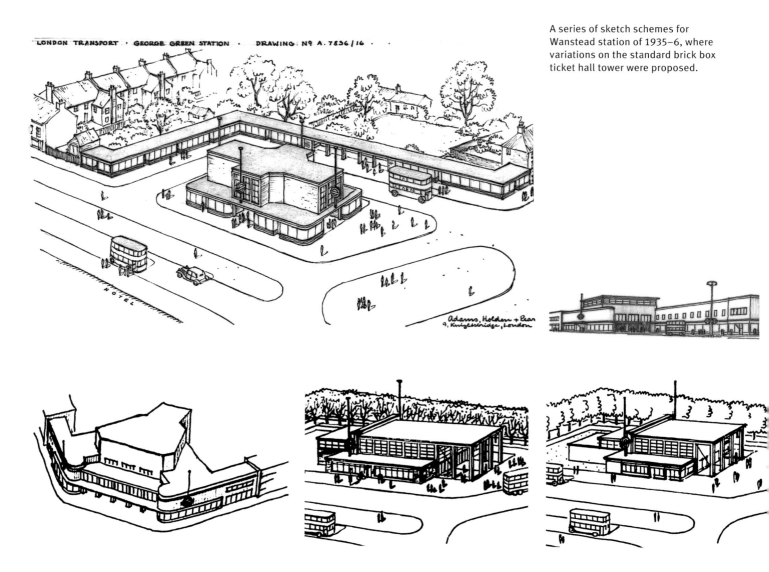

LONDON TRANSPORT · GEORGE GREEN STATION · DRAWING Nº A.7836/16 ·

Adams, Holden + Pearson
9, Knightsbridge, London

A series of sketch schemes for Wanstead station of 1935–6, where variations on the standard brick box ticket hall tower were proposed.

Wanstead

Several of the early Adams, Holden and Pearson Underground stations were built with few major modifications to the original design concept. But by 1935, the office was moving away from the routine brick box and Wanstead,[230] on which planning started in that year, is an example of a project where many different schemes were drafted. As we shall see the final, rudimentary building was unremarkable: it is the evolution of the project which is interesting. In April 1936 Adams Holden and Pearson produced two quite distinct alternative schemes. One, for the north-west corner of the road crossing, showed a three-storey brick box set behind a paved plaza between parades of shops. The ticket hall would have the innovation of a continuous clerestory window just below the roof cornice. The second design, occupied the south-east corner of the intersection, and here the ticket hall entrance was set forward to the street line on a splayed corner, the railway facilities sharing space with a concourse, shops and a café, whilst the dominating feature of the block

was a cinema. A third idea mooted by Holden had the station as part of a two-storey block with tall tower on the north-west corner opposite George Green. With revisions to the design in May 1936, the south-east position was fixed, and the additional commercial activities removed, leaving a roughly rectangular ticket hall. Here various forms of surface building appeared in the sketch designs. The most curious is a ticket hall box elongated on its four sides into a cruciform shape aligned with the entrances and escalators, and placed on a rectangular ground floor filled with shops. This is an interesting solution to the need for a building to make a feature of the island site, visible on the main road and edged on two sides by small retail units. Next, in June of the same year, an extensively glazed and double height rectangular hall was tried, with low side wings and rear extension over the platform access. At first, this design had a high entrance portico two bays deep, resembling the design of the Crematorium (1935–40) in Stockholm's South Cemetery by Holden's near contemporary, the influential

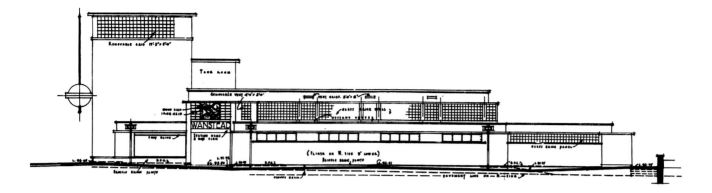

Above Adams, Holden and Pearson's revision of the building for Wanstead, and a design which went through successive stages of development before being halted by world war 2. Its final realisation is seen **left**, a development of much reduced ambition and expense.

Swedish architect Gunnar Asplund (1885–1940). The perimeter shops were deleted. In December 1936 the portico design was altered to become one bay deep. Nothing was built.

In 1939 four successive proposals, based on the foregoing rectangular plan but with a drastically altered building profile, incorporated low rectangular blocks enclosing the ticket and escalator halls, with adjoining low wings housing staff a public rooms, and tall ventilation towers at the western end. The first version of these four designs was entirely of brick with thin bands of concrete, and a clerestory of glass blocks to light the ticket hall.[231] Joseph Armitage, artist for the sculptures at Uxbridge, was to provide a carving of St George and the dragon, making reference to the Green. In the second and third versions the clerestory was replaced by plain windows. Work on the station started February 1940, but was abandoned in May 1940 so that little had been accomplished on the ground. The tunnels were converted for wartime use in November 1940 and five miles of their length used as a factory making aircraft parts.

Trains ran through the station from 14 December 1947. In the final pattern of building, started in May 1947 and completed January 1950, severe economies were made. As designed, Wanstead demonstrated that Adams, Holden and Pearson, with Holden himself now in his seventh decade, was still a practice adventurous in its innovation for tube station designs. As built, Wanstead is the result of post-war economies.

The finished station comprised prefabricated panels coated in a grey and cream grit finish. Entrances built into the corners between tower and ticket hall created a through-vestibule. Their decoration was minimal: black tiles outside and cream faience slabs within. High up in the tower the 'Underground' symbols were illuminated at night.

Wanstead was restored during the 1990s and the immediate area to the west of the station including George Green has been substantially reconstructed to enclose a road tunnel as part of major works relating to the A12 Eastern Avenue arterial road.

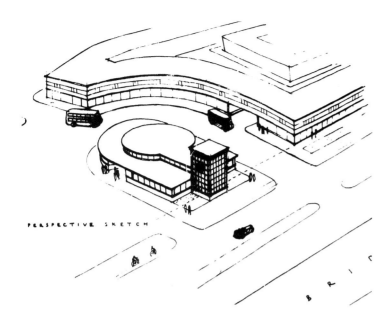

PERSPECTIVE SKETCH

Redbridge

On the drawing board in 1935, the early design for Redbridge[232] incorporated extensive areas of glass, so extensive in fact that the entire tower would be a translucent manifestation of the relationship between subterranean activity and suburban sky, proclaiming the presence of Underground for some distance along the A12 road.[233] This station would occupy an island site so that buses might circulate around it for the easy transfer of passengers. To evoke this movement vector, the ticket hall adjoining the tower was of a drum form like Southgate, but merged with a small rectangular block at the tower base. Beyond the station a parade of shops curved around into Redbridge Lane and into Eastern Avenue. No surface works had been completed when the war began, and the railway tunnels were used for other purposes. In the post-war economic situation various economies came into force. The glass tower, and a footbridge which was to have been integrated with the station building, were shelved. The drum and tower forms were retained, the vertical element resembling other Holden projects in its stepped profile. Illuminated Underground symbols served as an advertising feature in the two sides not fitted with ventilation grilles.

Restricted budgets ensured that the decoration was minimal, with Buckinghamshire bricks and a band of blue tiles for the exterior (a reprise of proven pre-war Holden style), and the round ticket hall being distinguished by walls of blue-brown Staffordshire bricks and light brown cement bricks below a coffered concrete roof.

At the side of the building facing Eastern Avenue the pavement lights over the stairway are enclosed by a low brick wall and a metal balustrade incorporating the letters 'L' and 'T' and the Underground bar and circle symbol. From the stairwell one can look upwards into the tower.

Redbridge opened for service on 14 December 1947. Installation of an enclosed ticket office has resulted in the closure of one entrance. Platforms have been refurbished and the original finishes replaced.

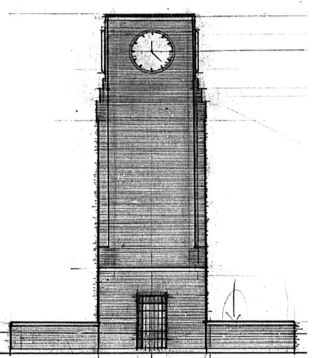

Gants Hill

Started in 1937, abandoned in November 1938, with a train service from 14 December 1947 and other facilities in operation from 4 April 1948, Gants Hill is a station mostly under a road roundabout, the first such intersection on the A12 east of Redbridge station. A large clock tower was planned, a squared column all in brick doubling as a disguise for the air ventilation duct. The form of the tower, with its projecting wings at ground level, had echoes of the tower at 55 Broadway, and of the rather smaller tower at Redbridge. Cost reductions removed the tower, so that the lozenge-shaped ticket hall has only a few clerestory grilles apparent at the surface. Built within a network of pedestrian subways beneath the busy road roundabout, the ticket hall funnels passengers between subways and escalators. There is one marvel here: the inspiration of the Moscow Metro. After a visit to the Russian city, the idea had been advanced by the Underground's management in August 1936, when Charles Holden presented drawings 'showing the proposed treatment

of the "Moscow" type of platform construction at Acacia Road and Gants Hill stations'.[234] During 1963–64 the platforms were fitted with experimental lighting and a suspended ceiling. In 1994 the lower concourse and associated areas were renovated with a new suspended ceiling and combined seat/lighting units. Original tiles were removed and replaced by replicas.

Achieved by boring five tunnels together and interconnecting them, the concourse had a ceiling 20 feet (6.1m) high lined with a system of suspended panelling, and extended for 150 feet (45.7m) between the platforms. Under the many fluorescent lighting units of this super-modern public space, the traveller could sit here until a train arrived bound for London or the fields of Essex. Platform tunnels continued as separate tubes, lined like the concourse in the late Holden style of cream tiles with horizontal coloured bands, in this case of chrome yellow with a frieze of red and blue bull's-eye symbols. Unlike Redbridge, no other decorated tiles were used here.

Opposite page left the design for a clock tower to act as civic focus on the traffic roundabout at Gants Hill (compare with photograph on page 63).

Above and opposite page right The Moscow Metro style concourse excavated between the platforms at Gants Hill. The decorative bands around the pier tops are extensions of the station name friezes along the platform tunnels (compare this with the advertisement on page 65).

UNREALIZED SCHEMES

Adams, Holden and Pearson designed a number of stations which were not built, largely due to financial restraints, but also because of difficulties obtaining planning consent or other strategic problems. These projects are interesting because, by filling in the gaps between built projects, they give further evidence of the way in which the architects sought to evolve and adapt their Underground buildings. Through these projects, as well as the preliminary designs for built stations, we see many permutations in design theory and ideas, changes in attitudes to materials and longevity of buildings, variation in forms, and different responses to particular situations.

Notting Hill Gate

This station would have stood at the corner of Pembridge Gardens and Notting Hill Gate on the north side of the main A40 road, serving the Central line. Designed in December 1928 soon after Bond Street was built, it showed the intention of using brick and stone in a simplified version of the Morden line station. The work was not carried out.[235]

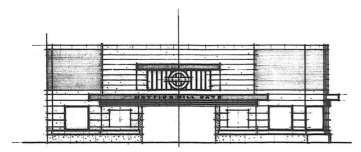

Hounslow East

One other box type tower was proposed on the Hounslow branch of the Piccadilly, for the station immediately west of Osterley. Designed in detail by the office of the Underground Architect, it was modelled on Alperton with a box type tower immediately abutting the railway embankment. On the south side of the platforms a subsidiary entrance was to be identified by a slender brick column. It was approved by Frank Pick for construction in June 1931 but curiously never started. The station retained its Edwardian ticket office, with additions and alterations over the years, until the whole site was redeveloped to a design by Acanthus Lawrence & Wrightson during 2002–04.

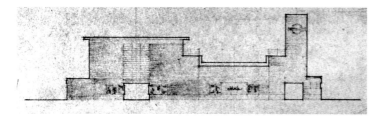

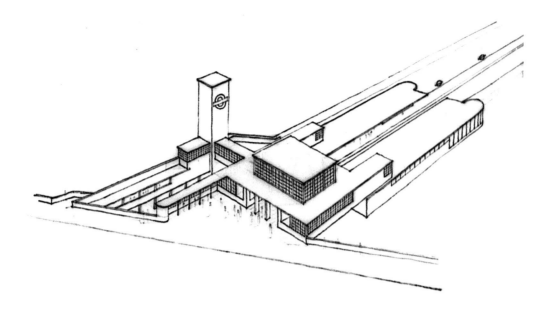

Hillingdon

As discussed in section one, a lightweight station building of modular construction was developed for use along the Uxbridge line, and various versions were drawn for Hillingdon. More substantial brick station buildings are also recorded. One had a squat ticket hall box in the typical Holden style, with an adjoining low tower and a footbridge emanating from the rear of the ticket hall to bridge the railway tracks and provide a second entrance. Another scheme placed the box ticket hall directly over the platforms, with fully glazed upper walls in the box and a glazed footbridge leading off to a similarly glazed tower at one side down to track level; this design was shown with, and without, a narrow brick extension to the glazed tower. Also supported over the tracks was a brick tower like that at Oakwood, accessible only by footbridges from either side of the railway cutting. None of these works was realized, and the mainly timber station survived until its removal was required for the reconstruction of the A40. Architects Cassidy Taggart designed a new steel and glass station, opened in 1993.

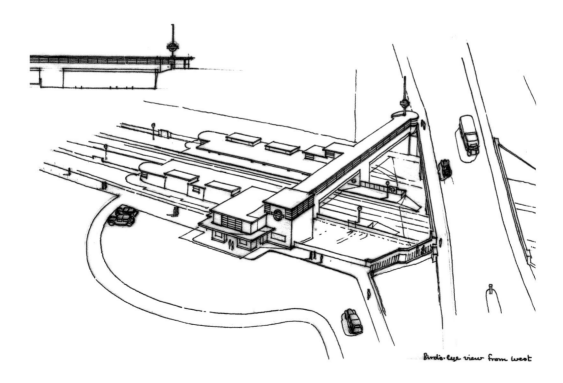

Bird's-eye view from west

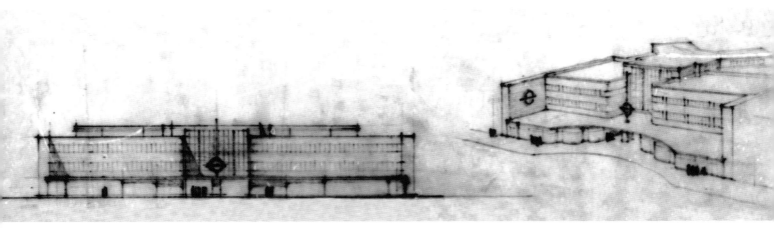

Uxbridge

Before handing the work on to Leonard Bucknell and Ruth Ellis, Holden's office issued designs for a building based on blocks joined together to form a three-pointed star, with the platforms meeting the ticket hall in the apex between of the blocks. To the High Street the building presented a massive wall of glass set back between three floors of offices and shops. As with each revision that followed, the ground level façade was stepped back into the central entrance area.

Finchley Central

Many plans were made between 1937 and 1947 to rebuild the station previously known as Finchley (Church End),[236] and it is unclear why work was given up: perhaps because there were insufficient funds, or because traffic figures did not justify the expenditure. Charles Holden worked on the design with Reginald Uren while they designed Rayners Lane. The station site is in cutting with a high overbridge carrying Regents Park Road and Ballards Lane, immediately west of

the junction with Nether Street. This suggested buildings at road level on either side of Ballards Lane, with stairways down to the platforms to replace the small Victorian station building in the cutting. The street aspect was planned asymmetrically, with a low clerestoried building and associated tower arranged like Boston Manor or Osterley. Tall narrow brick towers, fully glazed to the street side, were set back from the main building edge and accompanied by shorter solid brick towers. In another version, the structure on the road overbridge had its upper walls fully glazed, and the arrangement of taller and shorter towers (this time entirely in brick) was reversed. One other scheme included only a single tower on each side of the road, placed next to a double height colonnaded loggia aligned to the curve of the street corner. After the second world war, retrenchment of extension projects included abandonment of the Finchley Central works and the Victorian station located at one side of the railway is still in use.

Elstree South

North of the Watford By-Pass and on the Elstree Hill portion of what was then major trunk road A5 (following the London Transport development pattern used on the Central line of siting stations near major road intersections), Elstree South would serve a sparsely populated area where future development was expected. The site comprised a pond and ditches, skirted by Elstree Hill and a private road. Evidence of design work is limited. Platforms were to be situated in the railway cutting immediately north of tube tunnels. A Holden sketch indicates a small booking hall with stub tower and projecting kiosk, similar in form to Boston Manor, but with three interesting features which diverged from conventional Underground and London Transport style of architecture: the station name would be formed from cut-out metal letters raised over the entrance canopy; the footbridge would be designed as a loggia but open to the weather; a second stub tower at the far end of the footbridge would serve as a plinth for a statue in Roman dress, as an identifying symbol making reference to the site of the ancient settlement of Sullonicae just north of Stanmore. The last drawing for Elstree South is a perspective drawing of December 1944 by the London Transport architects, showing a building spanning the road overbridge, with a tower to one side and a projecting kiosk with rounded front in typical Holden style. Work on the extension had been largely abandoned by early 1942. Design

of stations and other constructions continued sporadically, with a view to restarting the project after the cessation of hostilities in 1945. Despite post-war endeavours to revive the scheme this did not occur, and the Bushey Heath extension was formally abandoned in late 1953.

Bushey Heath

Situated at the intersection of the Watford By-Pass and Elstree Road, Bushey Heath was initially referred to as Aldenham, being near the reservoir of the same name, and had other names proposed including Bushey Heath. It would serve as a major terminus of the Northern line. The station would be the centre of a large-scale town planning exercise, with, at various stages in the development, a sizeable public house (roadhouse was then the popular term, as the venue catered especially to motorized traffic), cinema, and two parades of shops arranged about a large roundabout, accompanied by bus lay-bys and shelters, subways, service roads and cycle tracks. Frank Pick requested Charles Holden to prepare plans for the site in early 1938.[237] The office of the London Transport Architect, in the charge of Thomas Bilbow[238] after Stanley Heaps's retirement in September 1943, worked on the design of Bushey Heath during 1943–44, by which time the proposed station had moved north and east of the road intersection, and was now to accommodate provision for through services.

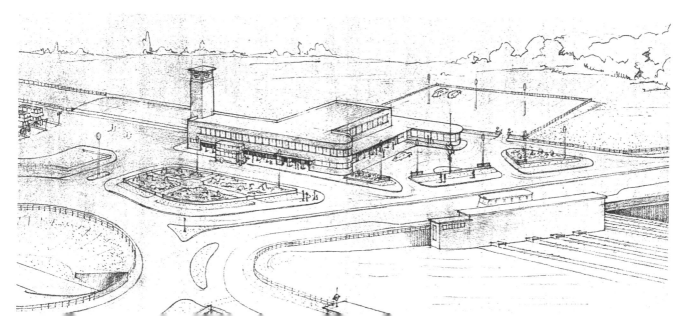

A typical prefabricated steel, enamelled steel and glass bus passenger waiting shelter designed by Charles Holden.

BUS STOPS AND SHELTERS

London Transport operated buses in town and country, trams on rails in the street, and rubber tyred trolleybuses drawing their electrical power from wires suspended over the streets, usually between traction poles. Extensive acclaim has been attached to Holden's railway work, but the architect and his team also developed a series of prototypes for passenger waiting shelters, bus stop posts and the small signs or 'flags' carried on the posts. These forays into product design are less well-known and also less successful. They are, however, useful to include as an illustration of the extent to which Charles Holden and Frank Pick worked to shape the physical presence of the transport system in the city. The bus shelters were manufactured; the posts and the majority of the flags were not. Industrial designer Norbert Dutton called the shelters 'a miniature essay in contemporary architecture, the appearance of which proclaims both their purpose and their method of construction. Essentially simple and unassertive, they blend comfortably with any kind of architectural surroundings, whether urban or rural'.[239]

To indicate the type of service available from a particular stopping point, Holden proposed a series of signs and symbols to be fixed to posts as part of the country bus, trolleybus and bus infrastructures. Remaining as samples only, they had been superseded within a few years by a much simpler,

cheaper and more effective design produced by the artist Hans Schleger, working with the London Transport publicity officer, architect and industrial designer Christian Barman. This was an area where modernity in design had advanced beyond Holden's own vision.

Two patterns of bus shelter are recorded as being designed by Holden between 1933 and 1934, the first seating six to twelve persons below a rectangular canopy, and the second providing accommodation for a (slender) eight persons under a circular canopy. These objects were made using steel tubes as columns (neatly also acting as enclosed rain water pipes), partially enclosed by glazed panels, poster-map panels, and solid enamelled iron sections which sometimes incorporated the London Transport bar and circle symbol. The canopies were like miniature versions of the tube station roofs, made as shallow, hollow metal boxes and enamelled or painted. In the early examples short masts projected from the hoods and carried additional bar and circle signs. Holden's sketches show that these totem poles could also have carried cast sculptures of the London Transport griffin device. Each shelter sat on its own stone plinth. The round shelter was really too small to give much protection from the weather, but this did not prevent it from be deployed across London and into rural districts. Few examples of the bus shelter projects survive.

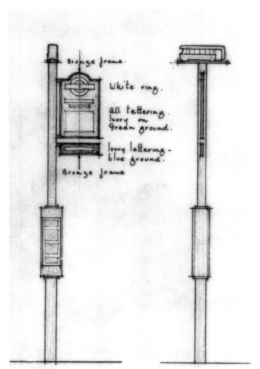

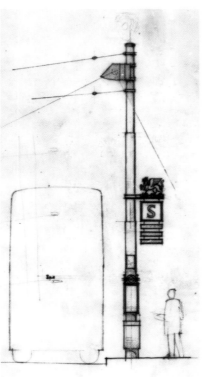

Above Compact circular bus shelter with seats placed in each quadrant of the structure. This design afforded little protection from he elements.

Left Examples of the bus stops designed by Charles Holden for the Green Line coach and the trolleybus services. The materials employed would be enamelled iron signs, in combinations of green, ivory, red and blue, and bronze frames. Green Line coach stops would feature the miniature coach shown here, or a white wheel pierced by an arrow. Trolleybus stop flags were massive constructions supporting a fully modelled griffin (the mythical beast used as a symbol by the London Transport organisation), below which, like an inn sign, hung a large plate bearing the letter 'S' for stop and three or more subsidiary plates carrying route information. There was a further town centre bus stop comprising a number of framed enamelled signs, with a bar and circle finial carrying the fleet name 'General'. Holden's designs were rejected as over elaborate and costly to produce.

THE STATIONS TODAY

Holden's stations are all still operational.[240] The suburban sites have fared reasonably well in adapting to some seventy years of change in transport operation. The statutory listing process, affording legal protection to buildings considered to be of 'special architectural or historic interest' has resulted in the conservation of several Adams, Holden and Pearson Underground stations, the first recommended by architectural historian Nikolaus (later Sir) Pevsner, in 1970 (55 Broadway/St James's Park) and four in the following year (Arnos Grove, Oakwood, Southgate and Sudbury Town). Since that time, London Transport and London Underground have officially been responsible for care of its architectural heritage, whilst the Thirties Society, which has since become the Twentieth Century Society, has been an able proponent in the battle to protect and conserve historic buildings including Underground buildings. In a talk given in 2004, railway writer John Glover noted that certain station capacities, based on platform widths, passageways, circulating areas, entrances and exits, and ticket issue and collection are becoming a problem.[241] Some stations are now worn and overcrowded. Leicester Square, the subject of a major refurbishment programme, has tested the operator's ability to either attempt a match of the original finishes, or select an acceptable replacement treatment. Stations have also become subject to the commercial pressures, with the effect that building exteriors incorporating retail units or other business activities are now subject to altered colours, lettering and fascias, and to a more chaotic arrangement of visual elements. The proliferation of advertising across the Underground recalls the Victorian period where station walls were subsumed beneath masses of posters, and frames the austere total design vision advanced by Frank Pick and Charles Holden, as a distinctly twentieth century phenomenon.

Modern life brings other effects, of which a significant problem for the Underground has been graffiti which is difficult to remove from porous surfaces such as concrete and brick. A number of stations were redecorated in the early 1980s, and many more altered to accommodate secure booking offices and a new system of ticket machines in the latter part of the decade. By this time many sites had been subject to graffiti and vandalism, for example the breaking of glass lamp enclosures and sign panels, removal of tiles, damage to wooden furniture. There has been official harm too, in poor maintenance since the end of the 1960s, the ad-hoc repainting of window frames, application of fluorescent lighting and other features by engineers without consideration for the original design, and the addition of various equipments by contractors. Much of this work has resulted from contemporary safety standards and security of passengers and premises.

Original signs had been removed as a matter of course each time a new graphic style was developed, particularly when the change from the original Edward Johnston-designed UNDERGROUND operating name to one shown in capitals of the same height took place during the 1960s. However, the transition was never applied consistently (it would cost a great deal and enamel signs were designed for longevity). An audit of the thousands of different signs on the system in the late 1980s caused London Underground to institute a new standard sign system. This wholesale replacement process resulted in restoration of what were believed to be original style signs at some of the listed and 'heritage' stations, but it also provided a massive stock of objects to be disposed of to collectors and dealers at auction. Certain items which had been scheduled to be conserved in-situ were removed, and the trade in former Underground station enamel and glass signs continues in auction houses a decade or more after the replacement programme.

During the last decade of the twentieth century there has been significant restoration work undertaken by London Underground, with research and investment to conserve and reinstate important elements of decoration and furnishings, and scientific studies of correct original paint colours. London Underground has from time to time issued guidelines which aimed to describe in detail the history and fabric of their stations, and the means by which they might be maintained, updated, adapted and conserved with respect for the architecture and historical features. A number of London Undergound reports and guidelines have addressed these matters. Graffiti has posed problems for the care of exposed concrete surfaces. In outlying areas the material has weathered badly, with cracking brought about by ageing and chemical changes permitting the ingress of water which causes the steel reinforcing bars to rust. Techniques have been developed to arrest the ageing of the concrete by treating the metal and cement chemically, but repair of concrete is not easy. It is also a solid, monolithic material, and the designers of these stations could not envisage the future need for installation of equipment such as ticket barriers, closed circuit television cameras, radio transmission cables, passenger help points, and updated fire, lighting and public announcement equipment. Consequently, the cabling which connects all these devices has to be placed on the surfaces of the concrete, altering the original appearance.

The London Underground railways had for some eighty years been managed by one overall organization. Through the Public Private Partnership there are now two main consortia responsible for maintenance of the Underground's infrastructure, which assumed control in December 2002 and April 2003.[242] How the at times disparate needs and views of operators and conservation bodies are successfully met remains an open question. Unlike the restoration activities of a decade ago, recent projects have featured utilitarian finishes rather than bespoke materials. This may be argued as appropriate in the climate of economic pragmatism, and indeed how many passengers will notice the difference, but it does not quite equal the quality of the original. As a further change, aged original tiles are now replaced with replica tiles. The stations thus appear new and clean, rather than worn and authentic. Provision of disabled access across the network promises another major challenge to the buildings.

Holden's stations continue to give service, and the influence of this great achievement will be found across the Capital in prestigious central locations and in unassuming suburbs: a very good reason to make a tube journey soon and discover the Underground's architecture.

Notes to the text

1. Frank Pick. 'Design in relation to the London of the future'. Speech given at the Design and Industries Association dinner, 18 November 1926, p. 6.

2. 'Progress in railway architecture – Cockfosters station'. *The Architect and Building News*, 10 November 1933, Vol. 136, p. 165.

3. Successive clients, all related organisations operating the same system, included the London Electric Railway (to 1933), a part of the Underground group of companies; the London Passenger Transport Board (1933–48); and the London Transport Executive (1948–1962).

4. Charles Holden. *Aesthetic aspects of Civil Engineering*. [draft paper], 1944.

5. A brief note of Walter Gott's career is given in *Pennyfare* [the LPTB staff magazine], April 1946, no. 79 [war series], p. 751.

6. Albert Stanley (1874–1948), was appointed first as general manager of the Underground group railways in Spring 1907, then general manager and managing director of the Underground group of companies from the end of 1910, Chairman of the group in 1919, and finally chairman of the London Passenger Transport Board between July 1933 and October 1947. He retired shortly before London Transport became part of a nationally own railway network.

7. 'Uxbridge has a new station'. *Pennyfare*, January 1939, p. 4.

8. 'Pick and Portal'. *Architects' Journal,* 26 March 1942, vol. 95, p. 225.

9. This date was recalled by Charles Holden in: 'Personal'. *Architects' Journal*, 26 March 1942, vol. 95, p. 233. Another anecdotal account of the coming together of Pick and Holden is given by Christian Barman in *The man who built London Transport: a biography of Frank Pick*. Newton Abbot: David & Charles, 1979, pp. 114–115.

10. The Design and Industries Association, which still operates today, was formed after the example of the German Deutscher Werkbund, which had been set up in 1907 to ally the arts and crafts with manufacturing industry.

11. Frank Pick, speaking at the presentation of the Royal Institute of British Architect's royal Gold Medal to Charles Holden. *Journal of the RIBA*, 25 April 1936, vol. 43, no. 12, p. 626.

12. The pictures may be seen in the Frank Pick files of the library at the London Transport Museum; his texts are available from a number of sources.

13. Charles Holden. *Aesthetic Aspects of Civil Engineering Design*, [draft paper], 1944, p. 1.

14. From an undated note by Charles Holden circa 1941.

15. Lord Sempill. 'Pick's legacy: the Underground Style: a preliminary tribute: Pick and the D. I. A.' *Architects' Journal*, 26 March 1942, vol. 95, pp. 228–232.

16. Charles Holden. 'Personal'. *Architects' Journal*, 26 March 1942, vol. 95, p. 233.

17. Charles Hutton (1905–1995) was chief assistant to Charles Holden 1929–36. He taught at the Liverpool School of Architecture 1936–39, and after World War Two ran his own private practice designing buildings for the Danish Bacon Company, Guinness, Murphy Radio, Oxford University, the Wellcome Foundation, and schools for Berkshire County Council. Hutton maintained an archive of Holden papers for many years and assisted researchers with enquiries into Holden's work and life.

18. Charles Hutton, in a letter to Oliver Green of London's Transport Museum, 17 April 1987.

19. *Ibid.*

20. Stanley Arthur Heaps FRIBA (1880–1962) joined the Underground in 1903, and was appointed architect to the company in 1911. He supervised the design of railway, tramway and bus facilities for the Underground and its successor London Transport until 1943.

21. Whilst essentially accurate, this list gave the following inconsistencies when compared with other documentary evidence, stating the following: Bond Street 1924 (actually completed 1926–28); Piccadilly Circus 1931–33 (completed 1928), Ealing Common 1933 (completed 1931), Sudbury Town 1932 (completed 1931).

22. Charles Holloway James RA FRIBA (1893–1953), worked first with Holden on an exhibition stand for the Empire Marketing Board in 1931. He was in practice with surveyor Stuart Frank Bywaters from 1925, and additionally with S. Rowland Pierce 1933–48.

23. From New Zealand, Reginald Harold Uren FRIBA ANZIA (1903–1988) came to the notice of the English architectural community when he won the Royal Institute of British Architects' London Architecture Bronze Medal with a competition design for a New Hornsey Town Hall, built 1933–36.

24. Leonard Holcombe Bucknell FRIBA (1887–1963) was President of the Architectural Association 1936–38, and a founder member of London's Building Centre. He worked in partnership with Ruth Ellis, his former student and later wife. They designed the pavilion in London's Coram Fields, number of buildings for Imperial Chemical Industries, and designed the standard 'British Restaurants' sponsored by government to ensure cheap meals for all during World War Two.

25. *The Morden Extension and the Kennington Loop*. London: Underground Group, 1926.

26. The change was achieved by plastering over the old façade, and not, as stated by others, by using new Portland stone blocks.

27. See David Lawrence. *A logo for London*. Harrow Weald: Capital Transport, 2000.

28. Christian Barman. *The man who built London Transport: a biography of Frank Pick*. Newton Abbot: David & Charles, 1979, p. 113.

29. It was previously stated in David Lawrence's *Underground Architecture* (Harrow Weald: Capital Transport, 1994) that the Westminster station was followed by a design for Bond Street on the Central London Railway. It has since become apparent that Bond Street was in fact designed as a development of the Portland stone Morden line stations.

30. See: David Lawrence, *Underground Architecture*. Harrow Weald Capital Transport, 1994.

31. The blocks are known as faience: glazed ceramic.
32. The original stations on the City & South London Railway had been designed by architect Thomas Phillips Figgis, and opened between 1890 and 1900.
33. F. R. S. Yorke. 'New work on London's Underground stations. *The Architects' Journal*, 28 December 1932, vol. 76, p. 819.
34. Construction of the Morden extension began on 31st December 1923. It was made possible by government grants to relieve unemployment after world war one through the Trade Facilities Act, 1921.
35. London's Transport Museum Photographic Library negative number U3608.
36. The ziggurat pattern resembles a zigzag line, and had its form in common with certain pyramid structures of middle America.
37. It is likely that this model was made by Eric Aumonier and his colleagues at the firm of William Aumonier and Sons, architectural sculptors, furniture and modelmakers. Eric Aumonier was commissioned to sculpt a stone relief for the Underground headquarters building in 1929, and in 1939 designed and made the figure of an archer displayed at East Finchley station.
38. Quarried on the Isle of Portland in Dorset, the stone was shipped by barge around the coast of southern England and up the River Thames to London. There it would be worked into the finished blocks. The stone is characterised in colour and texture by the quantity of fossil shells in it, less generally being found in the deeper layers of stone called the whitbed and basebed. The colour varied from one quarry to another.
39. This had been a stipulation in the brief given to Charles Holden by the Underground group.
40. For a discussion of the typographic work of Edward Johnston CBE (1872–1944) see Justin Howes. *Johnston's Underground type*. Harrow Weald: Capital Transport, 2000.
41. Harold Stabler (1872–1945), designer of silverware, ceramics, graphics and low-relief sculpture. Head of the department of Arts and Crafts at the John Cass Institute, London. Stabler formed the company of Carter, Stabler and Adams in 1921 as a subsidiary of Carter and Company's pottery at Poole, Dorset. The parent organisation had been in the business of making architectural ceramics and tiles for many years, and Stabler, with his wife Phoebe and John and Truda Adams, developed many ceramic designs and a faience range of wares. Carter, Stabler and Adams became Poole Pottery Limited circa 1964, and continues to operate.
42. J. P. Thomas. *Handling London's Underground traffic*. London: Underground group, 1928.
43. F. R. S. Yorke. 'New work on London's Underground stations. *The Architects' Journal*, 28 December 1932, vol. 76, p. 819.
44. P. Morton Shand. *Architectural Review*, November 1929, p. 218.
45. Alan A. Jackson 'Northern to Morden'. *Railways South East*, Winter 1988/89, vol. 1, no. 3, p. 165.
46. London Transport Museum, reference: negative U15567.
47. Steen Eiler Rasmussen. *London: the unique city* [new and revised edition]. London: Jonathan Cape, 1948 [first published in Danish 1934], pp. 349–350.
48. The preliminary schemes are kept in the RIBA British Architectural Library Drawings & Archives Collections at the Victoria and Albert Museum, ref. PA1422.
49. C. H. Reilly. 'Landmarks of the year: a retrospect of 1929', *Architects' Journal*, 8 January 1930, vol. 71, p. 55.
50. Charles Holden, giving his acceptance speech upon being awarded the Gold Medal of the Royal Institute of British Architects. *Journal of the RIBA*, 25 April 1936, vol. 43, no. 12, p. 624.
51. London Transport Museum, ref.: Old Photos Album 3, p. 63, negative U9683.
52. 'Progress in railway architecture: three new stations for London Underground Railways'. *The Architect and Building News*, 21 April 1933, vol. 134, p. 66.
53. W. P. N. 'Bill' Edwards joined the Underground group in 1927, and worked with it and the successor organisations until 1966. Information given in interviews with David Lawrence, November 1990.
54. For further discussion see for example: Elizabeth Darling. *Re-forming Britain: narratives of modernity before reconstruction*. London: Routledge, 2006.
55. The Underground group had sent officials on study visits to the United States of America in 1919, 1929 and 1930, and to Europe in 1928. See file refs. UER4/79, 4/81, 4/82 and 4/80 respectively, at the London Metropolitan Archives.
56. W. P. N. Edwards. A note on contemporary architecture in Northern Europe. Written as the result of a tour of Holland, Germany, Denmark and Sweden, made by Mr. Frank Pick, Mr. Charles Holden and Mr. W. P. N. Edwards, 20th June–7th July, 1930. London: Underground Group, April 1931. Edwards noted that he compiled the report with little intervention from Pick or Holden.
57. 'A modern underground station: Alexanderplatz, Berlin: Professor Alfred Grenander, architect'. *The Architects' Journal*, 6 April 1932, vol. 75, supplement between pages 452 and 453.
58. *Op. Cit.*
59. Charles Holden. *Aesthetic Aspects of Civil Engineering* [draft paper], 1944, p. 2.
60. Brest station was illustrated in Christian Barman's *The things we see-No. 5: Public Transport*. Harmondsworth: Penguin Books, 1949, p. 27, plate 4. Urbain Cassan (1890–1979) was an architect and engineer responsible for several French railway stations.
61. See Alan A. Jackson. 'Northern to Morden'. *Railways Southeast*, Winter 1988/89, vol. 1, no. 3, p. 166.
62. Charles Holden. 'The Designer and his problem: IV. Designing a Passenger station'. *Design for Today*, August 1933, vol. 1, no. 1, p. 135.
63. Stanley Heaps had also employed the concourse principle in his stations on the Edgware extension of the northern line opened 1923–24.
64. Describing the planning of Sudbury Town, Holden wrote 'the first stage was to prepare a graph of the passengers' movements ... The ultimate plan was

produced by enclosing the graph by walls'. Charles Holden. *Aesthetic aspects of Civil Engineering* [draft paper], 1944.

65. Charles Holden. *Aesthetic Aspects of Civil Engineering Design* [draft paper], 1944.

66. F. R. S. Yorke. 'New work on London's Underground stations. *The Architects' Journal*, 28 December 1932, vol. 76, p. 819.

67. The exact dates are: construction commenced 13 December 1930, new station opened 19 July 1931. Successful as this station was in design terms, it cost twenty five percent more than the estimated build price.

68. This window style was extremely common in architecture during the 1918–1939 period, and is sometimes referred to colloquially by the name of one of the major manufacturers: the Crittall Manufacturing Company of Braintree, Essex.

69. Frederick Francis Charles Curtis Dr. Ing. FRIBA (1903–1975). Assistant Architect to England's Southern Railway 1934; worked for Adams, Holden and Pearson 1935–36. Architect to England's Great Western Railway 1947, and afterwards Chief Architect to the British Transport Commission 1948–68.

70. Felix James Lander FRIBA (1897–1960) worked in Holden's office for a time, in practice with N. F. Cachemaille-Day from 1928, and with Herbert Welch from 1930. He designed the Park Royal Underground station, and a number of churches and housing developments.

71. 'Underground Architecture'. *The Builder*, 7 October 1932, vol. 143, no. 4679, p. 607.

72. Chris Hawkins and George Reeve. *Southern Nouveau: 'An essay in concrete', No. 1*. Didcot: Wild Swan Publications, 1987.

73. See especially the work of Eugène Freyssinet, François Hennebique, Robert Maillart and Auguste Perret.

74. Multicoloured bricks came into popularity in the first two decades of the twentieth century. They were so described because the means of their manufacture produced a range of hues from brown and purple to pink and orange within the same batch, which when laid randomly in walls gave a soft, warm appearance.

75. See Ken Garland. *Mr Beck's Underground map*. Harrow Weald: Capital Transport, 1994.

76. During the 1920s and 1930s the Berlin U-Bahn system also used this colour for tiles in ticket halls and passageways. Biscuit cream describes these tiles well because their eggshell finish glaze is a mixture of an off-white, sometimes yellower, sometime greyer, speckled with pinpoints of mid-brown.

77. Charles Holden. 'Personal'. *Architects' Journal*, 26 March 1942, vol. 95, p. 233.

78. For further information on the Bushey Heath scheme see Tony Beard. *By tube beyond Edgware*. Harrow Weald: Capital Transport, 2002, especially pp. 66–67.

79. 'Progress in railway architecture: three new stations for London Underground Railways'. *The Architect and Building News*, 21 April 1933, vol. 134, pp. 65–66.

80. 'A visit to the Underground railway stations on the Cockfosters Line'. *Journal of the Royal Institute of British Architects*, 11 November 1933, vol. 41–3rd series, no. 1, p. 28.

81. Baird Dennison. 'Architecture at the Royal Academy: ii'. *Architects' Journal*, 11 May 1932, vol. 75, p. 626.

82. London Passenger Transport Board: Office of General Manager (Railways) – J. P. Thomas. *Piccadilly line – western extension. Review of the first year's working*. [Report for internal circulation]. 10th March 1934, p. 14. LT Museum Library ref. G52.032 PIC.

83. The figures given were 4 feet 6 inches/1.37m and 6 feet/1.83m.

84. London Passenger Transport Board: Office of General Manager (Railways) – J. P. Thomas, *ibid*.

85. *Ibid*, p. 15.

86. *Ibid*, p. 16.

87. Sir (John) Leslie Martin (1908–2000) was appointed principal assistant architect to the London, Midland and Scottish Railway in 1939. Sir Leslie joined the London County Council in 1948, and served as its Architect from 1953–56. He was afterwards head of the Cambridge University School of Architecture.

88. Richard Llewelyn-Davies (1912–1981). Principal in the practice Llewelyn-Davies Weeks Forestier-Walker and Bor.

89. See The Railway Executive, London Midland Region. *Passenger stations: standards for planning and equipment*. London Euston, August 1948.

90. Confederation of Local Authorities' Schools Programme. CLASP itself was a development of the Hertfordshire Schools programme. See Andrew Saint. *Towards a Social Architecture: The Role of School Building in Post-War England*. New Haven; London: Yale University Press, 1987.

91. London Passenger Transport Board. 1935–1940 New Works Programme. 5 June 1935. Other London Transport activities included in the programme were the replacement of London's tram system by trolleybus services and modernisation of several central London stations.

92. Stations allocated to Adams, Holden and Pearson were South Harrow, Rayners Lane, Eastcote, Ruislip Manor, Ickenham (unbuilt), Hillingdon (unbuilt), and Uxbridge (Metropolitan and Piccadilly lines); Wanstead, Redbridge, Gants Hill and South Woodford (Central line). On the Northern line the stations were Highgate (not completed); East Finchley, Finchley Central (unbuilt), Elstree South (unbuilt) and Aldenham/Bushey Heath (unbuilt). Other stations allocated to the Underground Architect's office were those on the Northern and Central lines not being handled by Adams, Holden and Pearson.

93. For the London and North Eastern Railway, Stanley Hall, Easton and Robertson designed Loughton, and Oliver Hill designed Newbury Park, which was only partially built.

94. The house architect for the Great Western Railway stations at West Acton, North Acton, Hanger Lane, Perivale and Greenford was Brian B. Lewis MA PhD BArch FRIBA LFRAIA (1906–1991), succeeded by F. F. C. Curtis. Northolt, South Ruislip, Ruislip Gardens and

West Ruislip were designed later by Howard Cavanagh, Roy Turner, Peter MacIver and others.

95. David Lawrence. *Underground Architecture*. Harrow Weald: Capital Transport, 1994, p. 131, note 3.

96. 'London Transport: Items of interest: Symbols at new London tube stations'. *Passenger Transport Journal*, 25 February 1938, n. p.

97. Correspondence indicates that in the event of Charles Holden not concurring with Frank Pick's instructions, the architect Raymond McGrath (1903–1977) was to have been commissioned to undertake the design of Elstree South and Aldenham (afterwards Bushey Heath) stations on the extension of the Northern line.

98. Charles Holden agreed with Pick's request to take back direct responsibility for the development of the East Finchley and Uxbridge designs, despite stating that the projects were produced as a result of his own sketches, and that he had always remained aware of the work's progress. See letter Frank Pick to Charles Holden, 13 April 1937. Contrary to the assertions of other writers, correspondence shows that Holden remained involved in the detailed design of Underground stations at this time.

99. Frank Pick to Charles Holden, 9 May 1940.

100. An interesting anecdote is that Thomas Bilbow, Assistant Architect to Stanley Heaps, visited Germany in 1938 to study concrete finishing on behalf of the LPTB, indicating that the exchange of architectural ideas continued under the threat of international conflict.

101. Frank Pick speaking at the presentation of the Royal Institute of Architects' Royal Gold Medal to Charles Holden. *Journal of the RIBA*, 25 April 1936, vol. 43, no. 12, p. 626.

102. In this role conducting a study of British docks, Pick retained an office in 55 Broadway.

103. Frank Pick to Charles Holden, 9 May 1940.

104. Frank Pick in a letter to Anthony Bull, 8 April 1940.

105. Frank Pick, 20 May 1940.

106. In a letter of 10 August 1940 Pick wrote to Anthony Bull stating that he 'seemed to have no other choice'.

107. An account of this period is given in two useful sources: Christian Barman. *The man who built London Transport*. Newton Abbot: David & Charles, 1979, pp. 262–63; and Michael T. Saler. *The Avant-Garde in Interwar England: Medieval Modernism and the London Underground*. New York; Oxford: Oxford University Press, 1999, pp. 148–64.

108. Charles Holden. 'Personal'. *Architects' Journal*, 26 March 1942, vol. 95, p. 233.

109. Charles Holden in a letter to Hope Bagenal, March 1942, quoted by Bagenal in his speech at Holden's memorial service, 2 June 1960 and reproduced on page four of the order of service. Now contained in *Charles Holden manuscripts, papers and personal memorabilia 1928–55* in the RIBA British Architectural Library archive at the Victoria and Albert Museum.

110. 'Socialist realism'. *The Architectural Review*, January 1944, vol. 95, no. 565, p. 24.

111. Nikolaus Pevsner. 'Obituary: C. H. Holden 1874–1960'. *The Architectural Review*, vol. 128, no. 766, December 1960, p. 446.

112. A multi-disciplinary design practice funded by Misha Black and Milner Gray in 1943.

113. Norbert Dutton. 'Living Design: a review of London Transport'. *Art & Industry* [special London Transport issue]. Reprinted from the issue of October 1946, p. 98.

114. Nikolaus Pevsner. 'Obituary: C. H. Holden 1874–1960'. *The Architectural Review*, vol. 128, no. 766, December 1960, p. 446.

115. I make reference in the entry for 55 Broadway in part two of this book, to Holden's desire not to be further distanced from the craftspeople with whom he worked; he also commented later that a Knighthood 'would not go with me or Margaret [his wife]'. Charles Holden to Jean Ward, 18 May 1954.

116. Representatives of the Underground Group/LPTB acted as consultants to the Moscow authorities and Frank Pick was awarded the Honorary Badge of Merit by Josef Stalin.

117. Charles Holden's wife Margaret predeceased him. They had no children but he was survived by relatives including Minnie Frances Green, the daughter of his sister Emma. On his death, his house and its entire contents were sold in auction on 28 July 1960. He was given a memorial service at St Pancras Church, Upper Woburn Place, London on 2 June 1960, after a funeral at Enfield crematorium on 5 May 1960. His ashes were mixed with those of his wife and placed in the garden of the Religious Society of Friends Meeting House, Hertford.

118. The practice for this project was Welch, Cachemaille-Day and Lander. Park Royal is interesting for its associated shopping arcade, former petrol filing station and roadhouse facing the station across the semicircular lay-by. This project included a housing estate of blocks and semi-detached dwellings by the same practice: urban design on a scale not achieved by Holden.

119. Architect for Loughton was John Murray Easton of the practice Stanley Hall, Easton and Robertson. The London and North Eastern Railway architect reconstructed Stratford after the second world war.

120. Stanley Heaps had returned to serve London Transport during the war, directing work at railway facilities turned over to aircraft production. He retired in September 1943 and was succeeded as architect by Thomas Bilbow, his assistant since the Edgware line station work of the early 1922–24. One of their final works together was the reconstruction of Sloane Square station, opened on 27 March 1940 but destroyed by bombing soon afterwards.

121. Hanger Lane is a late interpretation of the drum type ticket hall for a difficult site, and Greenford shows another approach to the task of providing a street-level building against a viaduct.

122. See especially Wimbledon Chase (1929), Kingston (1935), Durrington-on-Sea (1937), Surbiton (1937), Bishopstone (1938), and the Motspur Park–Chessington South line (1938–39). Nigel Wikeley and John Middleton. *Railway stations: Southern Region*. Seaton: Peco Publications, 1971, pp. 125–130.

123. Corin Hughes-Stanton. 'Design Management: planning policies'. *Design*, 1965, no. 197, p. 45.

124. J. M. Richards. *Modern Architecture* [revised edition]. Harmondsworth: Penguin Books, 1962, p. 99.

125. In recent years it has proved to be a model for the relationship between Roland Paoletti, chief architect for the Jubilee Line Extension, and the consultant architectural practices with whom he worked to develop and build the line's stations.

126. True to the tradition of figurative decoration favoured by the Underground in the 1920s, this design is a simple representation of cricketing activities at the nearby Surrey County Cricket Club ground which gives the station its name.

127. The architects, who also restored Holden's surface building, described the new structure as 'a segment of a cone [which] sits within a curved wall which reflects the adjacent rotunda'. See http://www. aukett. com/people/press_releases/pr_2000/2000_01_21. htm. (Accessed 10 May 2005).

128. Also referred to on certain early Adams, Holden and Pearson drawings as 'North Morden'.

129. Alan A. Jackson has previously suggested that plans to extend the portico into an arcade on either side were not carried out. Alan A. Jackson. 'Northern to Morden'. *Railways South East*, Winter 1988/89, vol. 1, no. 3, p. 169.

130. Jackson, Alan A. 'Northern to Morden'. *Railways South East*, Winter 1988/89, vol. 1, no. 3, p. 167.

131. 'A new tube tunnel shelter, London'. *The Builder*, 1942, September 25, vol. 163, no. 5199, pp. 264–265. The tunnels were built under eight stations including Stockwell, Clapham North, Clapham Common and Clapham South on the Northern line. Each shelter had space for eight thousand people, with lavatories and medical services.

132. A visit to Morden provides an interesting example of the contrast between the ordered environment of the Underground, and the somewhat ad-hoc evolution of a typical London suburb.

133. Steen Eiler Rasmussen. *London: the unique city* [new and revised edition]. London: Jonathan Cape, 1948 [first published in Danish 1934], pp. 346–347.

134. Review of the Piccadilly Circus station found in an undated and unidentified press cutting collected from a Bolton (his home town) newspaper by Holden's relatives, and now contained in *Charles Holden manuscripts, papers and personal memorabilia 1928–55* in the RIBA British Architectural Library Drawings & Archives Collections at the Victoria and Albert Museum.

135. The work of making the concourse in this delicate way was very costly as there were a number of pipes and cables which had to be re-routed around the site. In view of the benefit to the public, the Office of Woods and Forests, the government department then responsible for such matters, transferred the subsoil rights to the Underground company for a nominal fee.

136. In 2005 this building was occupied by a large music store.

137. 'Piccadilly Circus Underground Station'. *The Architect &* *Building News*, 14 December 1928, vol. 120, no. 3130, p. 765.

138. Stephen Bone (1904–58) painted the mural; interestingly it had been his soon-to-be wife, the artist Mary Adshead (1904–1995) who had painted the mural at Bank station which immediately preceded the Piccadilly Circus project. The centre panel was installed in November 1928, and the other four in March 1929. Stephen Bone was the son of Sir Muirhead Bone (1976–1953), a friend of Charles Holden and the artist responsible for a fine impression of the 55 Broadway headquarters' building. Mary Adshead painted many murals for public transport, public buildings and private houses.

139. Holden had written to Frank Pick in protest over this change.

140. Sir William Holford, in *The Listener*, 19 May 1960, pp. 879–880. *Charles Holden manuscripts, papers and personal memorabilia 1928–55* in the RIBA British Architectural Library Drawings & Archives Collections at the Victoria and Albert Museum.

141. Press cutting from an unidentified Bolton newspaper circa 1929. *Charles Holden manuscripts, papers and personal memorabilia 1928–55* in the RIBA British Architectural Library Drawings & Archives Collections at the Victoria and Albert Museum.

142. The first station on this site opened on Christmas Eve 1868. It was enlarged in 1896, and two years later architect Henry L. Florence designed an office building for the District Railway company on Petty France, completed in 1899. Further buildings were added in 1905, and yet more alterations undertaken by the District's architect Harry W. Ford in 1909, after which the accretion of blocks became collectively 'Electric Railway House'. In little more than a decade the Underground had again outgrown its home, so that yet another building was added during 1922–24 to the designs of Charles Lovett Gill and Albert E. Richardson. Development of this six storey block followed a practice which was then innovative but has now become a frequently applied solution to space problems: the building was carried on a supporting structure directly over the railway platforms, running from Electric Railway House towards Palmer Street. Due to this position it has come to be known as 'wing over station', and it is still in use.

143. Charles Holden, in notes for a lecture given with photographic transparencies entitled 'Aesthetic Aspects of Civil Engineering Design' (undated).

144. Contemporary accounts note that the granite was quarried in Norway, and polished in Aberdeen, Scotland.

145. Henry Moore OM CH (1898–1986).

146. Samuel Rabinovitch (1903–1991), incorrectly reported as 'F. Rabinovitch' in the contemporary press, presumably due to an error in hearing the name. Later a respected painter and teacher working under the name Sam Rabin.

147. Eric Gill ARA RDI Hon ARIBA (1882–1940).

148. The Reverend Allan Gairdner Wyon FRBS (1882–1962), sculptor and medallist received into Holy Orders 1933,

149. Aubrey Eric Stacey Aumonier ARBS (1899–1974), sculptor, architectural modelmaker and stage and film set designer and maker.

150. Alfred Horace Gerrard (1899–1998) Professor and subsequently Emeritus Professor at the Slade School of Art, University College, London.

151. Sir Jacob Epstein KBE LG, (1880–1959). Epstein first worked for Holden when he produced a frieze of figures for the architect's British Medical Association building in The Strand, London, in 1908. These works were damaged by the action of the weather, and were reported to have been defaced subsequently in the process of rendering them safe. This account is sometimes mentioned in tandem with reference to the problems experienced with other public sculptures by Epstein, including the 'Rima' memorial to naturalist W. H. Hudson in Hyde Park, and the figures on the Underground's headquarters.

152. Former London Transport officer Christian Barman, in a letter to Charles Holden, 17 August 1953.

153. Holden had selected Epstein for the works, but was asked not to use him by Frank Pick. Holden persuaded Pick that Epstein was suitable. When the press furore arose over the expressive and explicit physicality of the boy figure in 'Day', Pick supported Holden's, and ultimately his own decision, in working with Epstein. Rejecting the received understanding of sculpture taught in the classical tradition, Epstein drew on archaeological discoveries of works by peoples from Africa and elsewhere, adopting their 'primitive' representational techniques in his pursuit of more direct forms of expression of human emotions and life forces.

154. Former London Transport officer Christian Barman, in a letter to Charles Holden, 17 August 1953.

155. Charles Holden in a letter to Jean Ward, 19 August 1953.

156. Charles Holden in a letter to Jean Ward, 18 May 1954.

157. During the second world war this was used for the production of tomatoes.

158. The memorial stone was designed by Charles Holden, and shows his hand in its subtly stepped form. Herbert Palliser designed the lettering and the bronze medallion with a relief sculpture of Lord Ashfield. Ever true to the Arts and Crafts tradition, Adams, Holden and Pearson purchased curtains for the official unveiling of the memorial from Heal's department store on Tottenham Court Road, London.

159. Basil Ionides FRIBA (1884–1950) was an architect and interior designer best known for his redecoration of the Savoy Theatre, London during 1926–1929, as a fantasy of Art Deco metalwork. The Theatre was badly damaged by fire in 1990 and has since been restored.

160. F. R. S. Yorke. 'New work on London's Underground stations'. *The Architects' Journal*, 28 December 1932, vol. 76, pp. 819–823.

161. The essence of Heaps' scheme appeared in revised form as John Robb Scott's Bishopstone station for the Southern Railway. Nigel Wikeley and John Middleton. *Railway stations: Southern region*. Seaton: Peco Publications, 1971, p. 128.

162. Born Charles-Edouard Jeanneret (1887–1965). Cited by Moritz Besser in the Thames and Hudson Encyclopaedia of 20th Century Architecture (1986, general editor V. M. Lampugnani) as 'the dominant figure internationally in modern architecture from 1920 to 1960' (p. 193).

163. Baird Dennison. 'Architecture at the Royal Academy: ii'. *Architects' Journal*, 11 May 1932, vol. 75, p. 626.

164. Charles Hutton suggested that this sign represented Holden's efforts to find an appropriate modern idiom for every element.

165. Frank Pick quoted in Christian Barman, *The man who built London Transport: a biography of Frank Pick*. Newton Abbot: David & Charles, 1980, pp. 137–138. Barman gives a fuller account of Pick's comments about the various aspects of equipment installation at Sudbury Town which detracted from the overall sense of total design.

166. The seriffed form of the Underground's Johnston typeface was developed for the purpose of cutting letters in stone at the Underground headquarters 55 Broadway by Percy J. Delf Smith R. D. I. working with Charles Holden circa 1929. It features in signs at a limited number of Holden stations built in the early 1930s including Boston Manor.

167. Stanley Heaps had proposed another polygonal hall like Hounslow West, here an octagon with side wings and a curved colonnade with several shop units.

168. F. R. S. Yorke. 'New work on London's Underground stations. *The Architects' Journal*, 28 December 1932, vol. 76, p. 823.

169. Barry Carpenter. *Piccadilly line extension: the diamond jubilee*. London: London Transport, 1992.

170. Charles Hutton identified the origins of the circle within a square plan at Arnos Grove in Holden's design for a groundsman's lodge at Midhurst Sanatorium, designed by Adams, Holden and Pearson and built circa 1904–06. In a letter, Hutton described it as 'a regular geometrical form into which the component parts can be fitted comfortably. The skill comes in making it look natural and inevitable'.

171. F. R. S. Yorke. 'New work on London's Underground stations. *The Architects' Journal*, 28 December 1932, vol. 76, p. 823.

172. This feature appears in a drawing dated 24 December 1930.

173. Christian Barman. *The things we see-No. 5: Public Transport*. Harmondsworth: Penguin Books, 1949, p. 27.

174. Similar canopies, with additional streamlining, were employed by John Robb Scott for the Southern Railway's line from Motspur Park to Chessington South in Surrey, built 1938–39. See Nigel Wikeley and John Middleton. *Railway stations: Southern region*. Seaton: Peco Publications, 1971, p. 127.

175. Named after the adjacent public house.

176. Charles Holden. *Aesthetic Aspects of Civil Engineering Design* [draft paper], 1944.

177. This pattern is derived from the so-called Palladian window of classical design: a group of main window flanked on either side by smaller windows.

178. The eight sided form was in part a development

of Holden's first sketch scheme for Bounds Green incorporating a half-octagon.

179. 'Shopping centre at Southgate'. *The Architects' Journal*, 14 December 1933, vol. 78, pp. 761–769.

180. Unique to the Underground as it is, this sculptural piece is a direct likeness of a similar finial atop the tower of the Gare de la Ville (city station), Le Havre, France by Henri Paçon (1882–1946) of 1931–32, which appears as plate 203 in: Carroll L. V. Meeks. *The Railroad Station*. [first published 1956]. Secaucus (New Jersey): Castle Books, 1978. The tower was demolished in 1970.

181. This is one of a very few sites where the column lights have been preserved, many having been removed when lighting systems were updated and altered in the post-1945 period. The bronze metal from which the lamps are fabricated has historically had a value on the scrap metal market.

182. Noted in an Adams, Holden and Pearson drawing of 10 October 1933.

183. Reference to these plans is made in 'Shopping centre at Southgate'. *The Architects' Journal*, 14 December 1933, vol. 78, p. 762.

184. 'A station shopping centre at Southgate'. *The Architect & Building News*, 8 December 1933, vol. 136, p. 280.

185. One official drawing, signed and approved by the Underground management, shows 'East Barnet' crossed through and the name Enfield West added by hand.

186. 'Progress in railway architecture: Three new stations for London Underground Railways'. *The Architect and Building News*, 21 April 1933, vol. 134, p. 67.

187. 'The architect portfolio no. 213: a platform canopy and shelter: Enfield West Underground Station'. *The Architect and Building News*, 26 May 1933, vol. 134, supplement between pages 192 and 193; 'The architect portfolio no. 214: a station name and lighting unit; a station sign mast and shelter: Enfield West Underground Station'. *The Architect and Building News*, 26 May 1933, vol. 134, supplement between pages 222 and 223.

188. 'Enfield West underground station'. *The Architects' Journal*, 29 March 1933, vol. 77, supplement between pages 434 and 435.

189. 'Enfield West underground station'. *The Architects' Journal*, 29 March 1933, vol. 77, pp. 435–439.

190. Installed in the hall was a plaque informing passengers that the station was, at 300 feet/ 91 metres above sea level, 'the highest point in Europe in a direct line west of the Ural Mountains of Russia'.

191. 'Progress in railway architecture – Cockfosters station'. *The Architect & Building News*, 10 November 1933, vol. 136, p. 167.

192. 'Progress in railway architecture – Cockfosters station'. *The Architect & Building News*, 10 November 1933, vol. 136, p. 166.

193. It was not unusual for the London Transport architect to prepare a first design, perhaps for comparison with that supplied by Charles Holden, or to fulfil the needs of a submission to Parliament or planning authorities. Stanley Heaps found a suitable approach was to present a scheme based generally on earlier works by the consultant architects which had proved serviceable. For

a reproduction of the 1937 plan see Tony Beard. *By tube beyond Edgware*. Harrow Weald: Capital Transport, 2002, pp. 30–31.

194. A grey, yellow and black colour scheme had been used previously by Holden and his partner H. Percy Adams at the Belgrave Children's Hospital, Kennington, London, circa 1899.

195. J. P. Thomas, General Manager (Railways), London Passenger Transport Board. *Piccadilly line – western extension. Review of the first year's working*. 10th March 1934, p. 19. LT Museum Library ref. G52.032 PIC.

196. Contemporary solutions to this situation can be seen at Southwark [Waterloo East] Jubilee Line, and the recent Acanthus Lawrence and Wrightson reconstruction of Hounslow East.

197. Northfields was opened as a simple halt in the first decade of the twentieth century and provided with permanent buildings designed by Harry W. Ford in 1911. Harry Wharton Ford (1878–1947) was appointed resident architect to the District Railway in 1900, thus preceding Leslie Green and Stanley Heaps's employment in the associated Underground group by a few years. He resigned from the post in 1911, and continued as a consultant to the company until 1916.

198. The District Railway had opened a station named Boston Road after the nearby Boston House on 1st May 1883, on a branch line from Acton Town (then called Mill Hill Park) to Hounslow. On 11 November 1911 the station received its present name. See 'Boston Manor Underground station'. *The Architects' Journal*, 26 April 1934, vol. 79, pp. 597–600.

199. Others have argued that Boston Manor and Osterley were mainly from the hand of Underground architect Stanley Heaps: documentation from the office of Adams, Holden and Pearson demonstrates that Boston Manor was handled entirely by the consultants, and Osterley carried out by Stanley Heaps from a Holden design.

200. The 'de Volharding' store in den Haag, Netherlands, by J. W. E. Buys with J. B. Lursen opened in 1928 and is now an office building.

201. A similar combination of round kiosk, low block building and slender lighting casement was present in the proposal for Eric Richter's tramway waiting hall and café for Berlin Tempelhof Airport, published in *Bauwelt* magazine in 1928.

202. 'A new station at Osterley'. *The Architect & Building News*, 27 April 1934, vol. 138, p. 95.

203. The first station serving the Osterley Park area (like Boston Manor the area takes it name from a large house) opened on 1st May 1883 as Osterley and Spring Grove. The old station remained entirely intact until 1957, and in 2005 its street-level building remains in use as a dwelling and bookshop.

204. Christian Barman. *An introduction to Railway Architecture*. London: Art and Technics, 1950, p. 93. Trained as architect, and working also as an industrial designer, Barman spent a period at London Transport supervising all aspects of its visual identity. He later played an important role in the development of design for the nationalized British Railways system from 1948.

In a 1993 interview with David Lawrence, Charles Hutton described in detail the design of Osterley and the sources for the lighting beacon design. He claimed that the form of the beacon alluded to a natural object, perhaps a cactus. However, it is near-identical to a feature on the former *de Telegraaf* newspaper offices in Voorburgwal, Amsterdam, Netherlands by J. F. Staal and G. J. Langhout of 1927–30. This too is a concrete finial to a brick tower, designed by the sculptor Hildo Krop.

205. The café scheme exists as a few rough sketches only. The broken ground seen in the photograph on page 144 suggests the scheme was considered for development, and no documentation has come to light to explain its suspension.

206. The in-town improvement works were made necessary by increasing traffic levels arising in no small part from the suburban extensions.

207. Opened 22 June 1907 as Euston Road, renamed 7 June 1908.

208. During the second world war Down Street was used as a safe and secret refuge for the British Railway Executive Committee and War Cabinet.

209. The only remaining evidence of Green's station here is to be found in the side passage Hooper's Court, and in Basil Street adjacent to the Court.

210. Brompton Road station still stands near the Brompton Oratory, set back from Brompton Road in South Kensington. During world war two it was used by Anti-Aircraft Control personnel.

211. The old station and lifts had closed on 29 April 1935.

212. It is recorded that the artist Margaret Blunden painted a mural on the roller shutter of the W. H. Smith newsagents stall. See *Shelf Appeal*, October 1946, p. 46.

213. 'The new tube station, Leicester Square'. *The Builder*, vol. 148, no. 4815, 17 May 1935, p. 934.

214. When this work was done, most of the tiling design installed under Leslie Green's direction was removed, posing problems for historians who have attempted to establish the original features at platform level. In more recent years, refurbishment schemes have tended to include the application of new tiles *over* the old as a cost reduction measure, with the unintended benefit that they can in time be rediscovered.

215. Holden had intended that this project should feature sculpted figures on front corners of the lower building.

216. As proposed by J. P. Thomas, General Manager (Railways) of the London Passenger Transport Board. *Piccadilly line – western extension. Review of the first year's working.* [Report for internal circulation]. 10 March 1934, p. 17. LT Museum Library ref. G52.032 PIC.

217. Originally to be called George Green.

218. Originally to be called West Ilford or Red House.

219. London Transport Architects' Department drawing of December 1935.

220. London Transport Architects' Department drawing of April 1936.

221. 'Uxbridge has a new station'. *Pennyfare*, January 1939, pp. 3–4.

222. Councillor H. A. Leno, J. P. (Chairman of Uxbridge Council), speaking at an official visit to Uxbridge in late 1938, and quoted in 'Uxbridge has a new station'. *Pennyfare*, January 1939, p. 4.

223. 'Uxbridge has a new station'. *Pennyfare*, January 1939, p. 3.

224. Noted in a letter from Charles Holden to Ervin Bossanyi, 23 November 1938.

225. Due to the problems over selecting an appropriate design for the stained glass, the station opened without the windows. They were removed for safe-keeping during the second world war, and restored in January 1949.

226. This ticket hall-on-a-bridge form was also put forward for the reconstruction of High Barnet (not built).

227. As his business and life partner and his former student, Ruth Ellis did much of the architectural design and drawing for many projects attributed to Bucknell, and continued the practice after his death.

228. Frank Pick lived at 15 Wildwood Road, Hampstead Garden Suburb, London.

229. The original fee for the sculpture, with its beech wood body and reclaimed lead casing was £245. The workmanship proved to be less than durable (the wood decayed) and it had to be remade fifteen years later, when its reconstruction in 1957 cost over six times the original sum.

230. Known in the early stages of planning as George Green after the nearby fragment of Wanstead Park and Epping Forest.

231. In its materials and details, this unbuilt design can be compared to the Gemeente Museum, The Hague, Netherlands by H. P. Berlage (1856–1934), a late work by one of the fathers of Dutch modern architecture.

232. At first to be called West Ilford or 'Red House' after a local inn.

233. In architect Oliver Hill's papers there is a reference to the possibility of the glass tower at Redbridge having a large decorated glass panel installed. This was made by the artist Gertrude Hermes for Hill's British Pavilion at the 1937 Paris International Exhibition. Pick wanted to reuse the panel after the exhibition, and considered it for both Redbridge and Hill's planned station at Newbury Park. With the intervention of the second world war, the glass was stored, and is presumed lost.

234. London Passenger Transport Board minute 905 of 27 August 1936. Acacia Road was renamed St John's Wood and designed under the supervision of Stanley Heaps.

235. Adams, Holden and Pearson drawing ref. 12928/280, 21 December 1928.

236. For an extended discussion of proposed station names for the Northern line extension see Chapter Six of Tony Beard's *By tube beyond Edgware*. Harrow Weald: Capital Transport, 2002.

237. A letter of acceptance to undertake design work was sent by Charles Holden to Frank Pick on 24 March 1938, and is reproduced in Tony Beard's *By tube beyond Edgware*. Harrow Weald: Capital Transport, 2002, p. 81.

238. Thomas Bilbow had been assistant to Stanley Heaps for many years, and had designed some of the stations on the original Edgware extension of the Northern line in the early 1920s.

239. Norbert Dutton. 'Living Design: a review of London Transport'. *Art & Industry* [special London Transport issue]. Reprinted from the issue of October 1946, p. 111.

240. With the exception of the station building at Highgate (High Level).

241. John Glover, speaking on 'Piccadilly prospects: T5 and other developments', at *Holden in Heathrowland*, an event organised by *Modern Railways* magazine association with Acanthus Lawrence & Wrightson Architects, 24 April 2004.

242. See Charles Gates. 'Design warning to new tube bosses'. *Building Design*, 20 June 2003, p. 4.

Bibliography

Charles Holden manuscripts, papers and personal memorabilia 1928-55 in the Royal Institute of British Architects (RIBA) British Architectural Library Drawings and Archives Collections at the Victoria and Albert Museum. Much of the Adams, Holden and Pearson office archive was presented to the RIBA British Architectural Library Drawings Collection in 1972. Cataloguing of the archive commenced in 1986. An exhibition of the material was held at the former Heinz Gallery of the Drawings Collection in 1988. The material is now held at the RIBA British Architectural Library Drawings and Archives Collections at the Victoria and Albert Museum. Frank Pick's papers, which railway folklore has it were to be destroyed by his staff after his death, have survived in quantity. They were sorted and listed by (Jonathan) Glancey and Johnson in 1976, and their catalogue revised in 1978. The list was updated by others in 1995 and 1999.

Books and journals

Acanthus Lawrence and Wrightson. *Transport Projects*. [Promotional folder.] Chiswick: Acanthus Lawrence and Wrightson, 2004

Adams, Holden and Pearson Contract Register. RIBA British Architectural Library Drawings & Archives Collections ref. AHP\2\1

A guide to repair of listed buildings. Issue 1. London: London Underground Limited, March 1997

Allibone, Finch, and Eitan Karol. 'Charles Holden, Architect'. *RIBA Journal*, April 1988, vol. 95, no. 4, pp. 50-51

All Stations: a journey through 150 years of railway history. [first published in France 1978 as *Le Temps des Gares* by the Centre Georges Pompidou]. London: Thames and Hudson, 1981

'Architecture for London Transport'. *The Builder*, 11 January 1946, vol. 170, no. 5371, pp. 39-43

'The architect portfolio no. 213: a platform canopy and shelter: Enfield West Underground Station'. *The Architect and Building News*, 26 May 1933, vol. 134, supplement between pp. 192 and 193

'The architect portfolio no. 214: a station name and lighting unit; a station sign mast and shelter: Enfield West Underground Station'. *The Architect and Building News*, 26 May 1933, vol. 134, supplement between pp. 222 and 223

'The architect portfolio no. 234: a station entrance and shelter: Cockfosters Station - I'. *The Architect and Building News*, 10 November 1933, vol. 136, supplement between pp. 166 and 167

'The architect portfolio no. 235: station construction: Cockfosters Station - II'. *The Architect and Building News*, 17 November 1933, vol. 136, supplement between pp. 196 and 197

'Arnos Grove station, Underground Railways'. *The Builder*, 1 September 1933, vol. 145, no. 4726, p. 340

A-Z London Street Atlas. Borough Green: Geographers' A-Z Map Company, various editions. [An invaluable and enjoyable work of reference and discovery]

Barker, T. C., and Michael Robbins. *A History of London Transport - Vol. 2*. London: Allen & Unwin, 1974

Barman, Christian. 'Frank Pick'. *The Architectural Review*, January 1942, vol. 91, no. 541, pp. 1-2

-----. *Next Station: a railway plans for the future*. London: George Allen & Unwin, 1947. [A piece of private railway company propaganda produced by the Great Western Railway in the face of impending nationalization.]

-----. *The things we see-No.5: Public Transport*. Harmondsworth: Penguin Books, 1949

-----. *An introduction to Railway Architecture*. London: Art and Technics, 1950

-----. *The man who built London Transport*. Newton Abbott: David and Charles, 1979

Beard, Tony. *By tube beyond Edgware*. Harrow Weald: Capital Transport, 2002

Blake, Jim and Jonathan James. *Northern Wastes: the story of the uncompleted Northern line extensions*. London: Platform Ten Productions, 1987

'Boston Manor Underground station'. *Architects' Journal*, 26 April 1934, vol. 79, pp. 597-600

Carpenter, Barry. *Piccadilly line extension: the diamond jubilee*. London: London Transport, 1992.

'Cockfosters Railway Station'. *Journal of the Royal Institute of British Architects*, 11 November 1933, vol. 41-3rd series, no. 1, pp. 23-27

Conservation of the Underground's Heritage. London: London Underground, 1987

Darling, Elizabeth. *Re-forming Britain: narratives of modernity before reconstruction*. London: Routledge, 2006

Darwent, Charles. 'The right change for the tube?'. *Independent on Sunday Magazine*, 9 November 1997, pp. 24-25

Dawson, Susan. 'All change, please'. *Architects' Journal*, 29 March 2001, vol. 213, no. 12, pp. 27-29

Day, John R. *The story of London's Underground* [first published 1963]. London: London Transport, 1979

Dennison, Baird. 'Architecture at the Royal Academy: ii'. *Architects' Journal*, 11 May 1932, vol. 75, pp. 626-632

Dutton, Norbert. 'Living Design: a review of London Transport'. *Art & Industry* [special London Transport issue]. Reprinted from the issue of October 1946, pp. 98-123

Edwards, W. P. N. *A note on contemporary architecture in Northern Europe. Written as the result of a tour of Holland, Germany, Denmark and Sweden, made by Mr. Frank Pick, Mr. Charles Holden and Mr. W. P. N. Edwards, 20th June-7th July, 1930.* London: Underground Group, April 1931

'Enfield West underground station'. *Architects' Journal*, 29 March 1933, vol. 77, pp. 435-439 and supplement between pp. 434 and 435

Eyres, Patrick. 'The Archer: Eric Aumonier's icon of urban travel and of the pre- and post-war London Underground'. *Sculpture Journal*, 2002, vol. VIII, pp. 36-53.

Follenfant, H. G. *Reconstructing London's Underground.* London: London Transport, 1974.

Garland, Ken. *Mr. Beck's underground map.* Harrow Weald: Capital Transport, 1994

Green, Oliver and John Reed. *London Transport Golden Jubilee Book.* London: The Daily Telegraph, 1983

Harris, Cyril M. *What's in a name?* [First published by Midas Books in association with London Transport, 1977]. Fourth edition 2001, reprinted 2003. Harrow Weald: Capital Transport, in association with London's Transport Museum

Harwood, Elain, and Alan Powers [eds.] *Twentieth Century Architecture 7: The Heroic Period of Conservation.* London: The Twentieth Century Society, 2004.

Hayward, Leslie [ed. Paul Atterbury]. *Poole Pottery: Carter and Company and their successors, 1873-2002* [first published 1995]. Shepton Beauchamp, Somerset: Richard Dennis, 2002

Holden, Charles. '55 Broadway'. *DIA Quarterly Journal*, December 1929, New Series, no. 10, pp. 10-11

–––––. 'The designer and his problem: IV. Designing a passenger station'. *Design for To-day*, August 1933, vol. 1, no. 1, pp. 134-138

–––––. 'Personal'. *Architects' Journal*, 26 March 1942, vol. 95, pp. 233-236

Hughes-Stanton, Corin. 'Design Management: planning policies'. *Design*, November 1965, no. 197, pp. 37-47

–––––. Transport design. London: Studio Vista; Reinhold, 1967.

'Improving London's Transport'. Supplement to the *Railway Gazette*, 1946

Jackson, Alan A. and Desmond F. Croome. *Rails through the Clay.* London: Allen & Unwin, 1962, and second edition published by Capital Transport 1993.

Jackson, Alan A. London's Metropolitan Railway. Newton Abbott: David and Charles, 1986

–––––. 'Northern to Morden'. *Railways South East*, Winter 1988/89, vol. 1, no. 3, pp. 164-169

Karol, Eitan, and Finch Allibone. *Charles Holden architect 1875-1960* [exhibition catalogue]. London: Royal Institute of British Architects, 1988

Karol, Eitan. *Charles Holden: Architect.* Donington (Lincs.): Shaun Tyas, 2008

Kidder Smith, G. E. *The New Architecture of Europe.* Harmondsworth: Penguin/Pelican Books, 1962

Lawrence, David. *Underground Architecture.* Harrow Weald: Capital Transport, 1994

Leboff, David. *London Underground Stations.* Shepperton, Ian Allan Publishing, 1994

Lee, Charles E. *Fifty years of the Hampstead Tube.* London: London Transport, 1957

–––––. *Sixty years of the Bakerloo.* London: London Transport, 1966

–––––. *Sixty years of the Piccadilly.* London: London Transport, 1966

–––––. *Sixty years of the Northern.* London: London Transport, 1967

–––––. *100 years of the District.* London: London Transport, 1968

–––––. *Seventy years of the Central.* London: London Transport, 1970

'London Transport: Items of interest: Symbols at new London tube stations'. *Passenger Transport Journal*, 25 February 1938, no page number

London Passenger Transport Board: Office of General Manager (Railways). *Piccadilly Line-Western Extension: Review of first year's working.* [Report for internal circulation]. 10 March 1934

–––––. *New works- key to buildings and architects.* Annotated line diagram. [undated]

–––––. *Second Annual Report and Accounts.* 1935

–––––. *Fifth Annual Report and Accounts.* June 1938

Lord Sempill. 'Pick's legacy: the Underground Style: a preliminary tribute: Pick and the D. I. A.' *Architects' Journal*, 26 March 1942, vol. 95, pp. 228-232

'LPTB Architect Retires' [Stanley Heaps]. *Architects' Journal*, 7 October 1943, vol. 98, p. 246

Meeks, Carroll L. V. *The Railroad Station.* [first published 1956]. Secaucus (New Jersey): Castle Books, 1978

Middleton, Grahame. 'Charles Holden and his London Underground Stations'. *Architectural Association Quarterly*, 1976, vol. 8, no. 2, pp. 28-39

'A modern underground station: Alexanderplatz, Berlin: Professor Alfred Grenander, architect'. *Architects' Journal*, 6 April 1932, vol. 75, supplement between pp. 452 and 453

'The new London Transport station at Uxbridge'. *The Builder*, 18 February 1938, vol. 154, no. 4959, p. 337

The new Piccadilly Circus Station [official publicity booklet]. London: Underground Group, 1928

'A new station at Osterley'. *The Architect & Building News*, 27 April 1934, vol. 138, pp. 94-96

'The new tube station, Leicester Square'. *The Builder*, 17 May 1935, vol. 148, no. 4815, p. 934

'A new tube tunnel shelter, London'. *The Builder*, 25 September 1942, vol. 163, no. 5199, pp. 264-265

Pevsner, Nikolaus. 'Patient progress: the life and work of Frank Pick'. *The Architectural Review*, August 1942, vol. 92, pp. 31-48

–––––. 'Obituary: C. H. Holden'. *The Architectural Review*, December 1960, vol. 128, no. 766, p. 446-448

'Piccadilly Circus Underground Station'. *The Architect & Building News*, 14 December 1928, vol. 120, no. 3130, pp. 765-766

Pick, Frank. 'The art of the street mainly illustrated from London'. Notes from a lecture given to The London Society, 9 March 1923

–––––. 'Design in relation to the London of the future'. Speech given at the Design and Industries Association dinner, 18 November 1926

Powers, Alan [ed.] End of the Line? The Future of London Underground's Past. London: the Victorian Society and the Thirties Society, 1987

'Progress in railway architecture: three new stations for London Underground Railways'. *The Architect and Building News*, 21 April 1933, vol. 134, pp. 64-69

'Progress in railway architecture - Cockfosters station'. *The Architect & Building News*, 10 November 1933, vol. 136, pp. 165-169

The Railway Executive, London Midland Region. *Passenger stations: standards for planning and equipment.* London Euston, August 1948

Rasmussen, Steen Eiler. *London: the unique city* [new and revised edition]. London: Jonathan Cape, 1948 [first published in Danish 1934]

'Rayners Lane station for London Transport'. *The Builder*, 2 September 1938, vol. 155, no. 4987, p. 430

Reilly, C. H. *Landmarks of the year: a retrospect of 1929'. Architects' Journal*, 8 January 1930, vol. 71, no. 1825, pp. 55-62

Richards, Jeffrey, and John M. Mackenzie. *The Railway Station: a social history.* Oxford: Oxford University Press, 1986, paperback edition reprinted 1988

Richards, J. M. *An introduction to Modern Architecture* [revised edition]. Harmondsworth: Penguin Books, 1962

-----. 'Station architecture'. *Design*, September 1955, no. 81, pp. 32-41

'The Royal Gold Medal: presentation to Mr. Charles Henry Holden [Fellow], vice-president, at the Royal Institute of British Architects on Monday, 6 April 1936'. *Journal of the RIBA*, 25 April 1936, vol. 43, no. 12, p. 626, pp. 621-627

Saler, Michael T. *The Avant-Garde in Interwar England: Medieval Modernism and the London Underground.* New York; Oxford: Oxford University Press, 1999

'Shopping centre at Southgate'. *Architects' Journal*, 14 December 1933, vol. 78, pp. 761-769

'Socialist realism'. *The Architectural Review*, January 1944, vol. 95, no. 565, p. 24

'Southgate Underground station'. *Architects' Journal*, 26 April 1933, vol. 77, pp. 553-554.

'South Harrow station'. *Architects' Journal*, 24 October 1935, vol. 82, pp. 599-601

'A station shopping centre at Southgate'. *The Architect & Building News*, 8 December 1933, vol. 136, pp. 279-282

Taylor, Sheila [ed.], with introductions by Oliver Green. *The Moving Metropolis: a History of London's Transport since 1800.* London: Laurence King in association with London's Transport Museum, 2001

Thomas, J. P. *Handling London's Underground Traffic.* London: Underground group, 1928

-----. London Passenger Transport Board: Office of General Manager (Railways). *Piccadilly line - western extension. Review of the first year's working.* [Report for internal circulation]. 10th March 1934. LT Museum Library ref. G52.032 PIC

Turnpike Lane. Pete Moore's Orchestra and Chorus. Western Forest/Shaftesbury Music Company, 1966.

'Underground Architecture'. *The Builder*, 7 October 1932, vol. 143, no. 4679, pp. 599-607.

'Uxbridge has a new station'. *Pennyfare*, January 1939, pp. 3-4

'A visit to the Underground railway Stations on the Cockfosters Line'. *Journal of the Royal Institute of British Architects*, 11 November 1933, vol. 41-3rd series, no. 1, p. 28

Welsh, John. 'Clean lines'. *Building Design*, 13 October 1989, no. 957, pp. 20-23

Woodward, Christopher. 'Modern Mover'. *Building Design*, 25 March 1988, pp. 18-19

Yorke, F. R. S. 'New work on London's Underground stations. *Architects' Journal*, 28 December 1932, vol. 76, pp. 819-826

Below Architecture on wheels: unbuilt London bus design by Charles Holden, 1931–33.

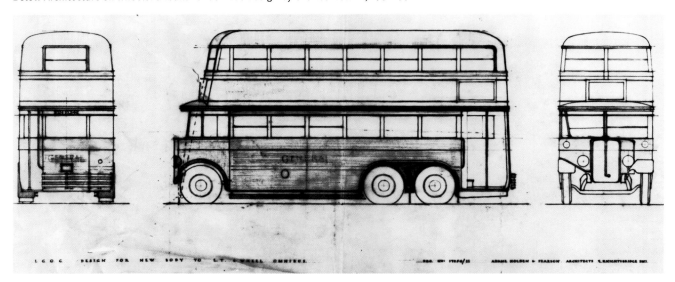

Index